The Complete Idiot's Reference Card

Sari's Sexy Coupons

Being sexy is about being creative and fun. These little coupons can help get you and your partner into a sexy mood. Just fill one out, tear it out, and share it with that sexy someone special.

W9-CCS-226

The bearer of this coupon is entitled to:
Hugging Time
I'll make you feel sexy by holding you
close to me all day long.
Given by: _____ Date: _____
To: _____
To be redeemed:
Date: _____ Time: _____ Place: _____

The bearer of this coupon is entitled to:
Delicious Night
I'll get the chocolate syrup, whipped cream, or anything
you crave to for a fun night of mixing food and sex.
Given by: _____ Date: _____
To: _____
To be redeemed:
Date: _____ Time: _____ Place: _____

The bearer of this coupon is entitled to:
Picnic in the Park
We'll feed each other grapes and have a
sexy romp through the grass together.
Given by: _____ Date: _____
To: _____
To be redeemed:
Date: _____ Time: _____ Place: _____

The bearer of this coupon is entitled to:
Bubble Bath
Scented bubbles, candlelight, soft music, rubber ducky.
Rub-a-dub-dub—I'll even make love to you in the tub.
Given by: _____ Date: _____
To: _____
To be redeemed:
Date: _____ Time: _____ Place: _____

The bearer of this coupon is entitled to:
Dress-Up Night
We can either wear our finest for a night out, or put on
costumes and stay in for a night of fantasy role-playing.
Given by: _____ Date: _____
To: _____
To be redeemed:
Date: _____ Time: _____ Place: _____

The bearer of this coupon is entitled to:
Sex Toy Shopping Spree
Whatever your body desires will be yours if the price is right.
Let's browse, buy, and then play with our new toys.
Given by: _____ Date: _____
To: _____
To be redeemed:
Date: _____ Time: _____ Place: _____

The bearer of this coupon is entitled to:
Candlelight and Romance
Candles, romantic music, flowers, and a sexy night of
love, affection, and romance will be yours.
Given by: _____ Date: _____
To: _____
To be redeemed:
Date: _____ Time: _____ Place: _____

The bearer of this coupon is entitled to:
Seductive Striptease
Sit back and watch me take it all off for you.
You won't even have to put a dollar in my garter.
Given by: _____ Date: _____
To: _____
To be redeemed:
Date: _____ Time: _____ Place: _____

The bearer of this coupon is entitled to:
30-Minute Personal Massage
Given by the one you love.
I'll touch you all over and make you feel sexier than ever.
Given by: _____ Date: _____
To: _____
To be redeemed:
Date: _____ Time: _____ Place: _____

The bearer of this coupon is entitled to:
New Sex Position
I'll think of something wild, and together
we'll make out bodies fit into it.
Given by: _____ Date: _____
To: _____
To be redeemed:
Date: _____ Time: _____ Place: _____

---

alpha books

The Complete Idiot's Guide to Being Sexy Coupon

The Complete Idiot's Guide to Being Sexy Coupon

The Complete Idiot's Guide to Being Sexy Coupon

The Complete Idiot's Guide to Being Sexy Coupon

The Complete Idiot's Guide to Being Sexy Coupon

The Complete Idiot's Guide to Being Sexy Coupon

The Complete Idiot's Guide to Being Sexy Coupon

The Complete Idiot's Guide to Being Sexy Coupon

The Complete Idiot's Guide to Being Sexy Coupon

The Complete Idiot's Guide to Being Sexy Coupon

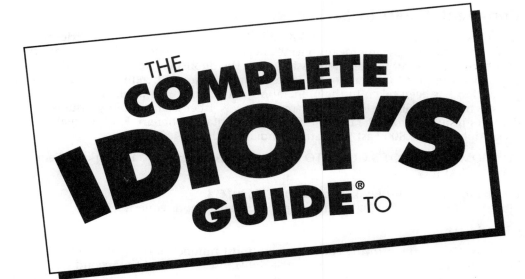

THE COMPLETE IDIOT'S GUIDE® TO

Being Sexy

by Sari Locker

alpha books

A member of Penguin Group (USA) Inc.

THE COMPLETE IDIOT'S GUIDE TO and Design are registered trademarks of Penguin Group (USA) Inc.

International Standard Book Number: 0-02-863916-2
Library of Congress Catalog Card Number: Available upon request.

05   04   03   8   7   6   5   4   3   2

Interpretation of the printing code: The rightmost number of the first series of numbers is the year of the book's printing; the rightmost number of the second series of numbers is the number of the book's printing. For example, a printing code of 01-1 shows that the first printing occurred in 2001.

Printed in the United States of America

Publisher
Marie Butler-Knight

Product Manager
Phil Kitchel

Managing Editor
Cari Luna

Senior Acquisitions Editor
Randy Ladenheim-Gil

Development Editor
Lynn Northrup

Production Editors
JoAnna Kremer
Christy Wagner

Copy Editor
Susan Aufheimer

Cartoonist
Jody Schaeffer

Illustrator
Jessica Wolk-Stanley

Photo Editor
Sari Locker

Cover Designers
Mike Freeland
Kevin Spear

Book Designers
Scott Cook and Amy Adams of DesignLab

Indexer
Angie Bess

Layout/Proofreading
Angela Calvert
Svetlana Dominguez
Natashia Rardin

Contents at a Glance

Contents

Appendixes

Introduction

Mention the word "sexy," and most people have some image of what they think is attractive or sexually charged. The fact is that being sexy means different things to different people. A tall body and muscular build may seem hot to one person, while someone else may find short and plump more appealing. Slinky lingerie may look sexy, but sometimes so does jeans and a T-shirt. Someone who's quiet and pensive may suit one person's taste, while a boisterous comic may seem sexier to someone else. Because there is so much variety in human behavior and appearance, there is a vast array of what is considered sexy. That's good news, because in your quest to be sexy, you'll have a lot to work with.

The Complete Idiot's Guide to Being Sexy is your guide to all things sexy—from looks, to surroundings, even to your sex life—and this book will sex you up. It is for anyone who wants to feel more attractive, or who wants to put a charge in a long-term relationship that has lost its fizz, or who wants to seduce someone new. Also, here you'll learn how being sexy can enhance your day-to-day life, in addition to your sex life. People who feel sexy generally have confidence and are comfortable with their bodies and their sexuality. You really can improve your life by learning some of the tactics in this book.

You'll find lots of exercises in this book that will help you figure out who you are and how you can discover the sexiness inside yourself. You'll even find a quiz at the end of the book that helps you determine what areas you can work on to bring out the sexiest parts of yourself.

The Complete Idiot's Guide to Being Sexy has something for everyone. Dive into the book, and I'm sure you'll find tons of great tips to make your sexy side soar. Everyone has what it takes to be totally hot!

How This Book Is Organized

This book is divided into five parts to direct you through different aspects of how to be sexy:

Part 1, "What Is Sexy?" defines all aspects of being sexy. Sexiness has some biological components and a cultural and historical background, all of which are explored here. Also, this section explains the different attitudes that make someone sexy, and how possessing those attitudes can enhance your life. Finally, you'll learn about different styles that you can use to express your sexiness.

Part 2, "Looking and Feeling Sexy," explains how you can express all things sexy. This section gives you how-to's about everything from using sexy body language, to making your home sexier. It also tells you how to be sexy well into your golden years. Perhaps most important of all, this section helps you get rid of your inhibitions about sex and your body.

Part 3, "Sexiness in Dating and Relationships," helps you sex-up your dates, and create more sexiness in your relationships. With great ideas for ways to flirt, what to do on dates, sexy gifts you can give, and ways to enhance sexiness with a life-long love, you're bound to learn a few new sexy things here.

Part 4, "Sex and Sexiness," explains how having sex can be sexier. From how to initiate sex, to why you don't have to have sex even if you're sexy, this part covers everything in the sexual realm. With erotic illustrations and detailed descriptions of how you can experiment with a wide range of sexual activities, you'll really get you hot.

Part 5, "Sexy Superstars," gives you great advice on being sexy from sexy celebrities. There are famous legends, sexy sirens, handsome hunks, and natural beauties to choose from, and they all have something to teach about sexiness.

At the end of the book, you'll find Appendix A, which contains a very cool quiz that will help you figure out what areas you most need to work on to become sexier. You may even want to check that out before you start reading this book to get some direction on what sections you need to focus on the most. In Appendix B, you'll find a glossary of terms used in this book. Finally, in Appendix C, I've included a helpful list of resources for more information and referrals regarding issues that are discussed in this book.

Sexy Sidebars

For some extra info, this book is peppered with sidebars. They contain a variety of information to spice up the text. There are five types of sidebars:

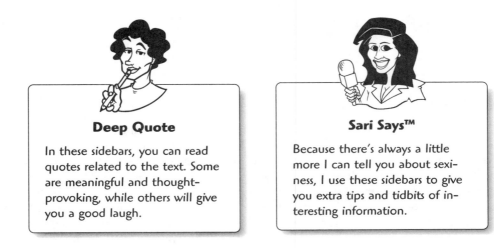

Deep Quote

In these sidebars, you can read quotes related to the text. Some are meaningful and thought-provoking, while others will give you a good laugh.

Sari Says™

Because there's always a little more I can tell you about sexiness, I use these sidebars to give you extra tips and tidbits of interesting information.

Flirt Alert

Being sexy may mean being un-inhibited, but that doesn't mean that you can cross all the boundaries. These sidebars explain some pitfalls to watch out for while you're being sexy.

Sexy Stats

Statistics can give you some idea of where you fit into the world of sexiness. These sidebars contain some stats to give you the scientific side of sexiness.

Lusty Lingo

What does "sexy" really mean, anyway? These sidebars define the terms related to sexiness that are mentioned in the book.

Acknowledgments

Thanks to my supportive friends and family: Molly, Jeffrey, Aliza, Larry, Murray, Gert, Jodi, Jonathan, Edward, Paul, Erica, Marc, Amanda, and Daniel. Thanks to my superb editor, Lynn Northrup; copy editor, Susan Aufheimer; and the entire fabulous team at Alpha Books, especially Randy Ladenheim-Gil, JoAnna Kremer, Christy Wagner, Marie Butler-Knight, and Amy Zavatto. Thanks to those whose artwork appears in the book, cartoonist Jody Schaeffer, illustrator Jessica Wolk-Stanley, Photonica and Archive Photos for the photos inside the book, and Darryl Estrine for taking the sexy cover photo of me. As always, special thanks to my amazing agent at William Morris Agency, Mel Berger.

Trademarks

"Sari Says" is a trademark of Sari Locker. All other terms mentioned in this book that are known to be or are suspected of being trademarks or service marks have been appropriately capitalized. Alpha Books and Penguin Group (USA) Inc. cannot attest to the accuracy of this information. Use of a term in this book should not be regarded as affecting the validity of any trademark or service mark.

Part 1

What Is Sexy?

Seems like a simple question, doesn't it? When you think about what is sexy, maybe you think of a particular model in a really hot pose; maybe you think of a steamy scene in a movie; maybe you think of someone you know who's a magnet for the attentions of others. What all these sexy examples have in common is that there isn't one particular ingredient you point to and say, "Ah-ha! That's what's sexy!"

Sexiness is tenuous and intangible—is it about pouty lips and soft skin, or is it all about attitude and how you carry yourself? The fact is, it could be all these things, or one of them, or a combination of a few, or something else that's totally unexpected. Sexiness is a strange brew, and each chef whips up his or her own fabulous creation from the ingredients he or she holds.

In the chapters in this part, we're going to dive right into that stew. I'm not only going to define what sexy is, I'm going to examine individual sexy qualities and what makes them so appealing. Keep a glass of ice water nearby, though, because things could get hot!

Chapter 1

Defining What Is "Sexy"

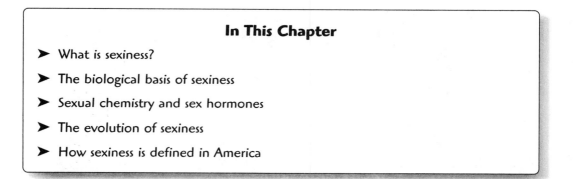

In This Chapter

➤ What is sexiness?

➤ The biological basis of sexiness

➤ Sexual chemistry and sex hormones

➤ The evolution of sexiness

➤ How sexiness is defined in America

When you notice a totally sexy person, what is it about him or her that attracts you? Is that person as gorgeous as a movie star or a model? Does the person have an exotic image, or a look of familiarity, perhaps even reminding you of your past lover? Does the person sparkle with vitality and confidence? Or is "sexiness" a quality that you can't quite put your finger on?

The fact is that sexiness can be defined if we explore the basis of it by examining biology, sexual chemistry, culture, history, and the media. In this chapter I'll help you understand sexiness as more than just something that you'll know when you see it.

What Do You Think Is Sexy?

The male peacock struts proudly and sports brilliant tail feathers. The lion roars and shakes its luxurious mane. The *Playboy* Playmate tantalizingly reveals a ravishing pair of breasts. Sexy characteristics—the way a person looks or acts—attract someone else, and can lead to sexual desire. Sexiness is, therefore, a component of sexual desire, which is transmitted through behavior, look, gesture, or innuendo. Being sexy is

Sari Says

You are sexy! That's right. There's something about everyone that is sexy—no matter what the person's age. You are sexy even if your look or style is different from other people's. Being sexy is all about being yourself.

Lusty Lingo

Sexiness is a component of sexual desire, which is transmitted through behavior, look, gesture, or innuendo, meaning that the way a person looks or acts can make someone desire that person sexually.

about being noticed for your look, the things you say, or your style. And being sexy is about having the confidence to show off your attributes.

Sexiness is highly qualitative. What's sexy to one person may not be sexy to someone else. This individuality is what makes life interesting, whether it is beauty or brazenness, sparring or seduction, assertiveness or aloofness.

Sexiness can be ...

➤ Passion.

➤ Romance.

➤ Flirtation.

➤ Devotion.

➤ Humor.

➤ Tenderness.

➤ Raciness.

➤ Warmth.

➤ Suggestiveness.

➤ Mysterious.

➤ Lustiness.

➤ Sensuality.

➤ Wanton desire.

Sexy can be subtle—the purposeful stride of a woman as she enters a room or the engaging grin of a man who spies you across the bar. Other times it's as blatant as Marilyn Monroe cooing "boop-boop-be-do" while singing "I Wanna Be Loved by You."

Biology 101

At the biological level, the primary function of sex is reproduction, and the primary function of sexiness is to attract people to each other, thus triggering their instinct to reproduce. Simply put, it is imperative that every living creature reproduce in order to perpetuate life for its species. In order for humans to have the desire to reproduce, they must be biologically programmed to want to have sex with each other. In addition, a species strives to reproduce with those who seem to continue the best features of that species. In other words, when they want to have sex, people generally look for those who are the most attractive to them.

Of course, most of the sexual activity between people is not solely for the purpose of reproduction, and few people say that they want to have sex with someone *only* because they want that person to have children with them. However, sexual attraction still has its biological roots there.

Researchers of evolutionary biology have found that females may be more selective than males when it comes to choosing a mate. From an evolutionary perspective, since a female produces only one egg each month, she looks carefully for a male to fertilize the egg. Males, who manufacture millions of sperm, want to spread their seed as much as possible. Of course, these factors do not necessarily hold true today, but they could account for why, for example, some women may find it sexy if a man is powerful or has money, because they feel he'd be a good provider.

Deep Quote

"It is better to be looked over than overlooked."

—Mae West

Love Stinks: The Power of Scent

When you think someone is sexy, it could be because of overt factors, such as the person's body or style is the type that you find most attractive. But many times, it is something completely intangible: a glint in someone's eye, the sound of his or her voice, or even the way the person smells.

Sari Says

Sometimes it is not so easy to determine why someone is sexy, and if you try to figure it out, you might not always choose the right reason, because chemical factors in your body can cloud your mind. For example, if a man and a woman meet immediately after they get off of a roller coaster, they might feel a spark of sexual attraction for each other. However, that spark may actually be excitement from the roller coaster—an adrenaline rush—misconstrued as physical attraction.

These traits may be chemical attraction. For example, the sense of smell can have an impact on what is considered sexy. Everyone has a distinct personal odor. Some of this is related to the soap, shampoo, or fragrance a person uses. Yet most of it is biological, based on emission from glands near a person's armpits, nipples, and groin. These natural smells can seem almost undetectable, but in fact they are often what draw people together. If you like someone, but you can't quite put your finger on why, it could be because you unconsciously like how that person smells. These smells are called *pheromones*.

The debate has raged for years on whether or not pheromones truly have scientific merit in humans and other mammals. The first pheromone was identified in 1956 after 20 years of research, when German scientists pinpointed a powerful sexual attractant in silkworm moths. They found that a particular compound in the glands of female moths made the male moths beat their wings so wildly that the researchers nicknamed the movement "the flutter dance." Afterward, when they identified the compound as a pheromone, they calculated that one spray of it from a female moth could attract up to a *trillion* male moths!

Lusty Lingo

Pheromones are chemical sex attractants that are detected by smell, but usually have such a mild odor that they are not consciously noticeable.

Since then, scientists have found evidence of pheromones on other creatures as well. For example, queen bees give forth pheromones that actually stunt other female bees from fully maturing, thus keeping the queen's reign—and devotion of the male bees—securely intact. (And you thought the dating scene in your neck of the woods was competitive!) It's also been found that female fish release "scent markers" that cause male fish sperm counts to actually increase by five times overnight.

As far as mammals and reptiles go, scientists have found that they detect pheromones via a small nasal cavity called the *vomeronasal organ,* or *VNO.* Although the jury is still out on whether or not humans have this VNO, research by psychologist Dr. Martha McClintock of the University of Chicago shows that science may be closer to proving the existence of pheromone detectors in humans then they knew. "Once you establish that pheromones exist," she said in an interview with *Time* in 1998, "the question becomes how far-ranging they can be."

Lusty Lingo

The **vomeronasal organ,** or **VNO,** is a small nasal cavity found in mammals and reptiles that detects the scent of pheromones.

How far-ranging, indeed. If the perfume industry has any say in the matter, it's extensive. Think about it—how many times have you wanted to get closer to someone because of some great perfume or cologne, or, conversely, been repelled by one that smells too strong or unattractive to you? Clearly, odors can arouse or repel us. But because the information on pheromones is inconclusive, don't rush out to buy any perfume that claims to contain pheromones.

Sex on the Brain

As unromantic as it sounds, your brain is biologically designed to respond to stimuli as either sexually compelling, sexually repulsive, or sexually neutral. Scientists believe that the pea-sized structure in the brain called the hypothalamus is where sexual attraction begins. When you feel sexual attraction, the nerve endings in your hypothalamus notify the pituitary gland to rush *hormones* into your sex glands. The sex glands react by producing more hormones: estrogen, progesterone, and testosterone. As a result you feel aroused, your heart beats faster, your muscles tense, and you get that sexy tingly feeling.

How Do You Make a Hormone?

When someone is going through puberty, that person is said to have raging hormones, but in fact, hormones can rage at any time in a person's life. As I mentioned earlier, when you feel attracted to someone, your hormones come in to play and your body shows its arousal.

Major fluctuations in hormones can also influence how sexy someone behaves or seems to you. A man who has an excessive amount of testosterone—what we traditionally think of as a male hormone—may have a very high sex drive. A woman with an excessive amount of testosterone may act more aggressively than other women, which could be an attractive quality to some men. However, an excess of testosterone could also give her much more body hair and facial hair than most women, which could look unattractive to many.

American Graffiti: Mixed Messages of Sexiness in Our Culture

To a large extent, the culture and time in which we live define what is sexy. In fact, if you go back through history, you'll find very different ideas

Lusty Lingo

Hormones are chemical substances that are secreted into the bloodstream by glands in the body. Many hormones including estrogen, progesterone, and testosterone have a bearing on sex.

Flirt Alert

Some symptoms of a hormone imbalance include an increase in hair growth around the nipples, on the face, or in the pubic area in women; and mood swings and lack of sex drive in both men and women. If you think that you have a hormone imbalance, consult a doctor right away.

about what was sexy in different decades and centuries. The Rubenesque women portrayed so lovingly in seventeenth-century European art had no place in the Twiggy-inspired influences of 1960s America, and vice versa.

In the modern-day United States, images of sexiness often focus on thin, sensual young women being swept off their feet by strong, virile men. Just take a look at the cover of any romance novel! However, there are some so-called cultural ideals evident in our society that aren't always easy to digest. Many of them are notions beyond our control, like age, body type, skin color, and height. Are we doomed to long for what we don't have, or is there hope?

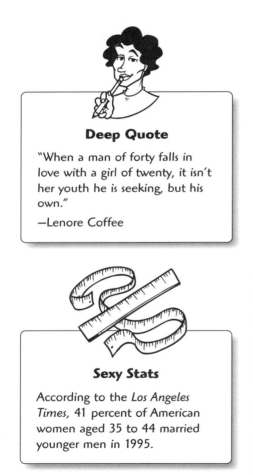

Deep Quote

"When a man of forty falls in love with a girl of twenty, it isn't her youth he *is* seeking, but his own."

—Lenore Coffee

Sexy Stats

According to the *Los Angeles Times*, 41 percent of American women aged 35 to 44 married younger men in 1995.

The Young and the (Sexually) Restless

Unfortunately, one of the staples that defines sexiness in our culture is youth. While people of any age can (and should) certainly be sexy (see Chapter 9, "Sexy at Any Age!"), the media and our society dictate that youth is sexier in women, while men seem to have much more leeway.

For example, let's take a look at all the famous May-December romances: There was the mature Humphrey Bogart and the very young Lauren Bacall, Marilyn Monroe and Arthur Miller, Katherine Hepburn and Spencer Tracy, Elvis and Priscilla Presley, and, more recently, Angelina Jolie and Billy Bob Thornton, or Michael Douglas and Catherine Zeta-Jones. And then look at the fantasy portrayals idealizing such couplings, in movies such as *Indecent Proposal, Autumn in New York, Great Balls of Fire* (based on the real-life romance of Jerry Lee Lewis and his child-bride cousin), and any James Bond movie. The message being sent here is men just get better as they get older (lucky for you guys!), while women must stay eternally young to be considered attractive.

But take heart, there is good news. There are hints that this trend is finally beginning to turn around, albeit slowly. Look at Goldie Hawn, Madonna, Raquel Welch, Susan Sarandon, and Cher—each of these women is far from her dewey youth, and each is also involved with a younger man. This isn't just a trend to the stars, either. It's becoming more and more accepted for an older woman to get involved with a younger man.

In addition to this switching of the traditional May-December setup, there's another thing these famous women have in common—they aren't trying to hide their age and they are *still* considered very sexy. Look at other celebrities, like Tina Turner, Michele Pfieffer, Jessica Lange, Sophia Loren, Lauren Hutton, and Angela Bassett. All are well past middle age, but can you picture any one of them sitting in a rocking chair knitting an afghan? I didn't think so.

Sex and the Media

In the United States, the media is a huge factor in determining what is sexy. Every minute we are bombarded with images of what is sexy from TV, literature, film, music, and advertising. Every time some hot new model is splashed onto magazine covers, TV commercials, and in movie roles, our idea of what is sexy is reshaped ever so slightly.

The most prevalent image in the media that defines sexiness is an overt display of sexuality. A woman is considered conventionally sexy when she fits some model ideal: 5'7", 115 pounds, 34-24-32, a thin waist, large breasts, long silky hair, tan skin, a beautiful face, large eyes, small nose, and high cheekbones. In addition, the so-called ideal has seemed to overtly favor those with white skin, so the media's image of what is sexy is not only unrealistic, it also seems racist. The media thrusts at us these images in the form of Victoria's Secret models, fashion ads, and television and movie actresses. For men, the most prevalent image is of a muscular and handsome man, like the men in the Calvin Klein underwear ads.

All these media images can be damaging to real people who do not look like models—which is most of the population! But never fear, there is hope. There have been a few noteworthy trends in our society that appear to be showing the emergence of a more realistic—and healthy—attitude. One such trend is the de-boobing of Hollywood. Thanks to silicon-shedding Pamela Anderson, many Hollywood actresses are getting rid of, or foregoing altogether, breast implants. Hopefully, this will help women to see that the Barbie 38DD isn't any sexier than a natural, unaugmented 32B.

Sari Says

Traditions of sexiness in other cultures are sometimes quite different from American culture; for example, in Latin culture. For Latin men, sexiness is defined as "machismo," meaning that the man shows his maleness by being dominant. For Latin women, sexiness is *etiqueta*, which requires women to be both feminine and virginal.

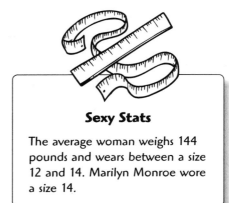

Sexy Stats

The average woman weighs 144 pounds and wears between a size 12 and 14. Marilyn Monroe wore a size 14.

And then there are magazines like *Mode,* which is devoted to plus-sized women; and role models like actress Camryn Manheim of *The Practice* and plus-size model Emme, who flaunt their full-figures with style and pride, showing that you don't have to be stick-thin to be beautiful, successful, and confident. There is also the ever-evolving fitness trend. In the early twenty-first century, fitness finally seems to be less about how hard your body is than about how healthy you are and how fitness can enhance your whole life, not just your ability to wear Lycra. Instead of reaching for unattainable goals, men and women are focusing more on what makes them feel good to be in their own skin, what enhances their lives, what makes them *healthy*.

To the issue of race, this is an area of sexiness that has been long overdue for a radical change. Images of sexy, attractive people in the twentieth century were predominantly white, frequently blue-eyed, and, more often than not, blond, leaving anyone not of that palette feeling like the left-out ugly duckling. Fortunately, this is another trend that seems to be turning to reflect the people who actually make up our country. Open the pages of your favorite fashion magazine and you'll see more African-American models than ever before, as well as more people of color in movies and on television. In addition, Latinos have all but exploded onto the music and modeling scenes, as well as Asians, showing that beauty, style, and sexiness have many faces.

You'll notice in this book that I emphasize finding your own, personal sexy qualities. That's because I'm a firm believer that *everyone* is sexy, no matter what your age, body type, skin color, height, or weight. Don't let the media distort your image of your own sexiness—break the mold and define sexiness for yourself!

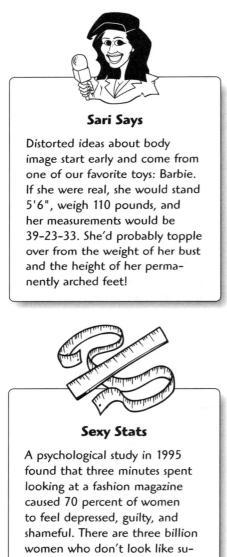

Sari Says

Distorted ideas about body image start early and come from one of our favorite toys: Barbie. If she were real, she would stand 5'6", weigh 110 pounds, and her measurements would be 39-23-33. She'd probably topple over from the weight of her bust and the height of her permanently arched feet!

Sexy Stats

A psychological study in 1995 found that three minutes spent looking at a fashion magazine caused 70 percent of women to feel depressed, guilty, and shameful. There are three billion women who don't look like supermodels and only a handful who do.

Changing Concepts of Sexiness over Generations

As we've seen in this chapter, the concept of sexiness changes over each decade—for better and for worse.

Sometimes we tend to think of history as dates of battles and presidents, country formations, and glacial movements. But history is more than this. History is also about our culture. When you look back at it, it becomes a map of our attitudes and, hopefully more often than not, progress. Let's take a quick tour through history, and see how far we've come by focusing on what has been considered sexy for women's style over time:

➤ In ancient times, women's bodies were revered as sexy if they were round or fat because this was considered an obvious sign that a woman would be fertile.

➤ In Greek and Roman times, the most ideal images of women were those of Greek goddesses, who had strong muscular forms.

➤ During the Middle Ages, women were supposed to hide their bodies because of the oppressive religious climate.

➤ During the Renaissance, women were considered sexually attractive if they had rolls of soft flesh, as exemplified in the art of Peter Paul Rubens, thus the term Rubenesque, meaning a voluptuous, full-figured woman.

➤ In the late 1800s having an exaggerated hourglass figure was considered sexy, something that was achieved by corsets. Women wearing corsets signaled the beginning of suffering for the sake of beauty. Remember that scene from *Gone with the Wind,* in which Scarlett was laced into her corset? Corsets really hurt, and they often caused breathing problems and sometimes even heart or lung damage.

➤ In the 1920s women's style was not so formfitting, but thin was still in. In fact, the flapper look put an emphasis on women looking flat, so much so that they looked almost androgynous.

➤ In the 1930s and 1940s it was considered sexy for a woman to be fit and muscular. This image was influenced by wartime, with its images of "Rosie the Riveter."

➤ In the late 1940s women's styles put more emphasis on curvaceous shapes and more feminine fashion. A famous pin-up shot was that of Betty Grable wearing a swimsuit and looking coyly over her shoulder.

➤ By the 1950s curvy was in style, with Marilyn Monroe as the role model of sexiness. She also popularized the overtly sexy look of low-cut dresses that revealed cleavage.

➤ The 1960s reverted to sexiness equaling skinniness, such as the British model Twiggy who was popular at that time.

➤ Into the 1970s bouncing and busty was back: Farrah Fawcett and Suzanne Somers had "the look."

Photo by Voller Ernst.   *Photo by Voller Ernst.*

➤ By the 1980s and 1990s, fit and muscular were again sexy. Singer Madonna had a rock-hard body plus tons of sex appeal.

➤ As we enter the new millennium, the fit image is still in, but there's a renewed emphasis on being slim, with many models who are very tall and thin.

Sexiness today can take on many forms. In the next chapter, we'll look at some specifics about what is sexy about the human body. Then we'll examine the attitudes that define sexiness. But no matter what biology, chemistry, and history tell us, if you are self-confident and have a positive outlook, you can be sexy!

The Least You Need to Know

➤ Sexiness—the way a person looks or acts—can make someone desire that person sexually.

➤ Sexiness is partially determined by biology and sexual chemistry.

➤ In the United States, the media plays a large role in determining what we think is sexy.

➤ Over time, different images have defined what is sexy.

➤ You should not let cultural or media images affect how you feel about yourself, since everyone can be sexy!

Chapter 2

Your Sexy Body

In This Chapter

➤ What facial features are the sexiest

➤ Which body types and body parts are considered sexy

➤ Which hair styles look sexiest

➤ What feels good: learning about your erogenous zones

➤ How all five senses play important roles in sexiness

Do you love looking at a great butt? Are hot legs more your thing? Or are you intrigued most by someone's eyes? Whatever body part attracts you at first, chances are it's more about the whole physical package (and, more important, what's inside) in the end. But because physical appearance is what makes the first impression, let's take this chapter to reflect on the human body in all its glory.

If you flip open to the centerfold of a *Playboy* magazine, you'll see an image of a woman's body that our society deems as sexy. Or if you look at the latest underwear billboard in Times Square, you'll see what that ideal is for a man. There are some elements of the face or body that are considered sexy from a social or anthropological perspective. But how can sexiness be quantified? Let's take a look to see what is sexy about the human body, and what makes yours sexy!

Face It!

Those lips, those eyes, that symmetry. According to research, human attractiveness is defined by *facial symmetry,* meaning that the right and left sides of the face match. In many research studies to determine what makes a face attractive, time and again, subjects pointed to the most symmetrical faces. One study, which was reported in *Newsweek* magazine in 1996, contrasted the famous faces of musician Lyle Lovett and actor Denzel Washington. Denzel is said to have a very symmetrical face, while Lyle's features are not as even. Due to his more symmetrical features, more positive appraisal was given to Denzel. (For more about what makes Denzel sexy, check out Chapter 22, "Sexy Men We Can Learn From.") Of course, Lyle might fit some women's taste in men—maybe Julia Roberts's, since she was married to him—but his look does not fit that of ideal attractiveness.

Lusty Lingo

Facial symmetry defines a person's face when their features appear even, equal, balanced, and virtually identical on both sides of their face, if a line were dividing the face down the center.

Does this study really prove that facial symmetry defines attractiveness? What if knowing adults simply chose Denzel because they are aware that the media deems him sexier? Researchers wondered if the subjects' idea of attractiveness had been influenced by the cultural and media image of attractiveness. So to determine if facial symmetry is truly the key factor of attractiveness for subjects with no beauty bias, the research was conducted on babies. Clearly, babies have little or no exposure to media influence. In a research study conducted at the University of Texas at Austin during the mid-1990s, three-month- to six-month-old babies were shown photos of a variety of pictures of faces. The babies spent a longer time looking at the most symmetrical faces. Thus the researchers concluded that interest in facial symmetry is an innate factor that determines attraction.

Moreover, in various research studies on adult subjects, faces that were chosen as the most attractive were more closely examined. The women chosen had these features in common:

Sari Says

Typically, full lips are considered sensual in a woman, but in men, lips are thought to be sexier if they are not quite as fleshy. Of course, it's all a matter of personal preference. Some guys find full lips a turnoff; some women like men with full lips.

➤ Large eyes

➤ Dark eyebrows

➤ Long eyelashes

➤ Full lips

➤ High cheekbones

➤ Defined chin bone

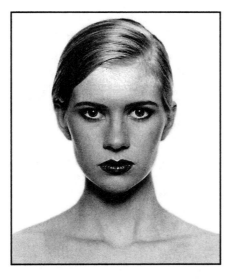

Photo by Johner Bildbyra.

The men had these sexy facial features in common:

➤ Small eyes

➤ Thick eyebrows

➤ Small lips

➤ Large chin

➤ Defined jaw line

Apparently, these male features are thought to display dominance and maturity. Other differences are hormonal. For example, the small jaw in women is a result of estrogen, the female hormone, and the large jaw in men is a result of testosterone, the hormone more abundant in men. Also, as I mentioned earlier, it was determined that people are both innately directed toward beauty, and that they have been socially conditioned to look for a certain "masculine" or "feminine" type.

Sari Says

While symmetry is the ideal of beauty, many people think symmetry is boring. They may find a not-so-perfect face much more interesting and yes, sexier, whether it's the trademark mole on Cindy Crawford's chin, Barbra Streisand's nose, or Lyle Lovett's unsymmetrical face. These quirky qualities make faces beautiful and interesting.

Your Fabulous Face

Women use makeup to make their eyelashes longer, which makes their eyes look larger; or to accentuate their lips, which makes them look more sensual; or put a blush in their cheeks to look healthier. But at some point, the makeup has to come off. And men don't wear makeup at all. So the key here is learning to accept your natural face as sexy. You've been looking at it in the mirror for as long as you can remember. Now, when you look in the mirror, start to look for things you like about it!

The fact is that most faces don't look like those so-called "ideals." We all have a unique look, and what's so wonderful about that is we all attract different types of people. No matter what your facial structure looks like, you can be sexy by being yourself and by loving what you see in the mirror.

Healthy Skin Is In

There is one thing that you could work on to make your face look sexier. That's your skin. It's our largest organ, and it's also one of our most sensitive. Age, stress, sun, even what we eat can make complexion wrinkle, break out, or just look dull. Everyone looks sexier with healthy skin. So to improve yours, here are some things to keep in mind:

➤ **Use sunscreen.** The sun affects you even when you're just going about your normal routine, and it can cause wrinkles, sun spots, and even skin cancer. If you must be outside a lot, also wear a hat. Don't sunbathe. If you must have a tan, use an artificial tanning lotion.

➤ **Drink lots of water.** You should have about eight glasses of water a day. Water keeps your skin hydrated and helps it stay clear and healthy from the inside out.

➤ **Develop a cleansing routine.** Wash your face every day with a mild soap or cleanser. Keeping your face clean can help prevent acne and rejuvenate your skin.

➤ **Use moisturizer.** Both men and women can reduce the risk of wrinkles if they properly moisturize their skin with a light moisturizer. If your skin is oily or tends to break out, try an oil-free moisturizer.

➤ **Exercise.** Sweating is good for your skin because it flushes out your pores (think of how good your skin feels after a sauna). Just make sure you don't wear make-up when you exercise, since that can clog your pores, and be sure to wash your face afterward.

➤ **Reduce stress.** In addition to all the other bad effects it has on your physical and emotional state, stress can have an affect on your skin, especially causing breakouts. Try going for a walk or taking a relaxing bubble bath when you feel stressed.

➤ **Fight acne.** If you have acne, wash your face with an acne-fighting soap or cleanser and try an over-the-counter medication such as Oxy, Stridex, or Clearasil. If you don't notice any improvement, make an appointment to see a dermatologist.

In addition to helping you fight acne, a dermatologist can help with other skin concerns such as age spots or wrinkle reduction. There are many methods (laser treatments, dermabrasion, facial peels, and glycolic acid treatments) that can make your skin look clearer, younger, and sexier.

Check Out That Body!

Who do you think is hotter, David Hasselhoff or David Schwimmer? Of course, every woman is attracted to a different type, but if you are just going on body alone, I'd bet that more women pick Hasselhoff's over Schwimmer's. There's something about a tall, strong man with his shirt off, running on the beach. That's because in our society, people tend to think tall, fit men look healthy.

When it comes to women, no matter how much you may wish that a full figured, voluptuous form would be the ideal of sexiness, in America today, it just won't get you the o-o-o-s and ah-h-h-s of a Victoria's Secret's bod. But as I will explain, while thin women and muscular men may be considered the ideals of our society, people of any shape and size are sexy.

Sari Says

The bods and faces in the ads and magazines are airbrushed or digitally manipulated by computer to *look* perfect. No one has that flawless a body, not even the top models or the most gorgeous actors!

Photo by Rieder and Walsh.

What's Your Type?

It's not just how people view others' bodies that determines attractiveness. It's how we think of our own bodies. Many average American women wish they could have what they envision as the "perfect" female body: 5'6", 120 pounds, and a size 6 or smaller. In reality, the average American woman is actually is 5'4", 140 pounds, and a size 12. Men on average fantasize about being 6 feet tall, but on average are 5'10". If people could accept their own bodies as ideal for them and not hope to fit some media image of ideal, they might be less judgmental of others and more inclined to see themselves as sexy.

The fact is that there are different body types. Technically speaking, there are …

➤ **Ectomorphs.** Very little body fat, small bones, and little muscle. Your basic supermodel.

➤ **Endomorphs.** Medium bone frame and more body fat. What we think of as "average."

➤ **Mesomorphs.** Think World Wrestling Federation. Large frame and big strong muscles.

No matter how much time you spend working out, you can not entirely change from one body type to another. You can reduce your body fat with exercise, and look more trim, but you can't change your bone structure and genetic muscle makeup. So exercise to stay in shape, but remember, you will stay in *your* shape.

You might not be able to have what you think is an "ideal" body. But because bodies come in different shapes and sizes, people have different tastes in what they think is sexy. That's why you have to love what you have, rather than trying to conform to some silly ideal.

Sexy Stats

Full-figured women are just as desired by men as thin women, and some research has found that they may even enjoy sex more than thin women. *Weight Watchers* magazine surveyed 6,000 women and found that 70 percent of full-figured women said they "almost always have orgasms," compared with only 29 percent of thin women.

The discrepancy that many people have in viewing their body as less than ideal causes many problems, from eating disorders like anorexia and bulimia to a general dissatisfaction with one's self that can cause inhibitions, including loss of sexual desire (see Chapter 6, "Getting Over Inhibitions About Your Body"). The best bodies are those that have confident people inside them—people who enjoy their bodies and know how to make the most of what they have.

Sexy Body Parts

There are certain obvious body parts that are considered sexy. In women, of course, the predominant symbol of sexuality is breasts. You don't need to go to a wet T-shirt contest to notice that breasts are seen as sexy in our culture. Breasts can be shown off in clothes by wearing something tight, sheer, or revealing. Some men say that they prefer women with large breasts, others like small breasts. The fact is that size or shape really shouldn't matter. If a woman feels good about her breasts, then her partner should enjoy the way they look and feel, too.

Flirt Alert

Anorexia, an eating disorder that affects more girls than boys, is characterized by an intense desire to lose weight. Anorexics have a distorted view of their bodies and deliberately starve themselves, obsessively exercise, or use laxatives to lose weight. Bulimia is an eating disorder characterized by self-induced vomiting. Both disorders have serious, even life-threatening consequences. Check Appendix C, "Resources," for referrals for more information and treatment.

While men's chests do not send the overt sexual messages that breasts do, they can still be displayed to look attractive. Shirtless muscular men are considered very sexy in our culture. Of course, just as breast size can cause insecurities in some women, chest development can be a concern to men. But the fact is, to some women, a body-builder chest is a turnoff. A guy who feels good about his body— no matter what it looks like—is always attractive.

Legs are another body part that both men and women often look at to determine sexiness. Women who want to show off their legs can wear pantyhose and high heels. Men don't show off their legs quite so much, but sometime at the beach, one can distinguish the guys with "chicken legs" from the guys who have muscular, fit legs. Of course, fewer women will probably notice a man's legs compared with his butt.

One body part that both men and women display (whether they like it or not) are their butts. From *Buns of Steel* workout videos to images of men or

Sexy Stats

According to a 1996 survey from *Intimate Relationships, Marriage and Families*, the features that men notice first about women are: figure, 44 percent; face, 33 percent; how she's dressed, 27 percent; eyes, 21 percent; legs, 6 percent. When asked what they notice first about a man, women said: how he's dressed, 34 percent; eyes, 30 percent; figure, 27 percent; face, 26 percent; legs, .5 percent.

women shaking their booty on the dance floor, butts have been sexual signals for generations. But as will all body parts, what is considered the ideal butt (tight, high, shapely) is not everyone's preference. There are plenty of guys who love a woman with a big, shapely butt. Whether you have a butt like Mel Gibson or Al Roker, Jennifer Lopez, or Camryn Manheim, if you're not self-conscious about it, your partner will enjoy it, too. (For more about enjoying your body, see Chapter 6.)

Sexy Hair

Sometimes it's what's on your head rather than in your head that people notice when they are checking out your sexy quotient. Many people think that long hair on a woman is considered the sexiest. And for a long time, long hair has been the ideal. For centuries writers and artists have depicted women with long hair draping over their bodies. This has some anthropological basis.

In Victorian times, long hair was seen as a sign of a woman's fertility. It was thought that long hair was proof that a woman was healthy and ready to bear children.

In the 1800s to the turn of the century, most women in the United States grew their hair long, because it was considered a sign of maturity to wear a bun of your hair on top of your head. Long, loose hair was thought to be a more private or sexy look. (Remember Ma from *Little House on the Prairie*—hair always in a bun, unless she was in bed with Pa?)

By the 1920s sexiness was often associated with a woman cutting her hair short, such as the hair style of Flappers. From then on, sexiness of hairstyles fluctuated with changing fashion trends. Also, from then on, men were more apt to have differing tastes in hairstyles for themselves.

Sari Says

In ancient Rome, women dyed their hair blonde to identify themselves as prostitutes. That's how the myth got started that blondes are sexually looser.

Not all men today prefer long hair on women. Hairstyles associated with sexiness change with time. We can even pinpoint changes by taking a look at some of the sexiest hair trends. Remember how hot Farrah Fawcett's feathered look was in 1976? Only a couple of years later, in 1979, Bo Derek's beaded locks were all the rage. At that time beaded hair became a sexual symbol, whereas today, beaded hair is not seen as overtly sexy—and of course feathered hair is thought of only as a throw back to the 1970s.

Today, sexy hair looks run the gamut. From a close-cropped cut to long, curly tresses, if a woman looks good and feels comfortable with herself, she can carry off almost any style. But remember, no matter what your hairstyle, clean, shiny hair in top condition is always in style and always sexy. Take good care of yours!

For the Ladies

The key to having sexy hair is finding a style, cut, and color that work best with your image and with your lifestyle. To do this ...

➤ **Look through magazines.** Choose hairstyles that you like, but be sure to choose models whose facial shape, skin tone, and hair type are similar to yours.

➤ **Try on wigs.** Wigs really let you see what different hairstyles will look like on you. Go to a wig store or a hair salon that carries wigs, and try some on. Choose one that will give you a new sexy look.

➤ **Watch a hairstylist at work.** When you go to a hair salon, don't just sit down with the first stylist who's available. Hang out; watch the stylists work, and see if they make their clients happy.

The best advice of all is to ask someone whose hairstyle you like for the name of her stylist. Bring in magazine pictures of hairstyles you like and ask the stylist to make your hair the sexiest it can be. (Just be aware that you won't come out looking exactly like the model in the picture!)

For the Men

For men, the most usual hairstyles are short cuts. But today, you see everything from entirely bald to Fabio-length long hair. It's a matter of taste. The biggest hair problem that men have is balding, or fears of balding. Some women find bald men very sexy (just look at Michael Jordan). So if you are losing your hair, don't cover it up. Instead, let your head show. Maintain a positive, sexy attitude, and think about all the sexy role models who have little or no hair.

Flirt Alert

While the hair on a woman's head is cherished, hair on other parts of the body is reviled. Women go to great lengths (pardon the pun) to shave, bleach, wax, depilate, and even laser it off. While so many women cave to the social pressure to be hairless, this also causes them pain and expense.

Sari Says

When a man's losing his hair, he might think that a hairpiece is a good way to go. Or maybe he wants to spend loads of time and tons of money getting hair plugs. However, most women consider hairpieces totally unsexy, and plugs often look fake. It's better to go bare than to wear fake hair or surgically implanted hair, and it's a lot less hassle and expense.

In the (Erogenous) Zone

Now that you know a bit about what looks sexy, what about what *feels* sexy? As I've mentioned, your skin is your largest and most sensitive sex organ. Just below the skin are nerve endings that detect touch. These allow you to feel hot, cold, pain, pleasure,

Lusty Lingo

Erogenous zones are the sensitive areas on your body that get you sexually aroused. They can exist anywhere.

and, well, any sensation. When certain nerve endings are stimulated in certain ways, they send a message to your brain about what's going on. If your genitals are being stimulated, your brain certainly gets the message.

But when other parts of your body are stimulated, your skin can send your brain the sexual arousal message, too. When you are eating, your lips send the message that food is incoming. But your nerves also know the feeling of a kiss, so at those times the food message doesn't come into play, and the arousal message does. That means that any area of your body can be an *erogenous zone*.

So what parts are the most likely to send that message of arousal? The obvious parts: your genitals. From there, it's all relative to what you think and feel.

Try the following exercise to find out what feels sexy to you. Circle the number that corresponds with how good each area feels when it's stimulated. Use the following ratings:

0	Uncomfortable
1	No sensation
2	Feels okay
3	Feels good
4	Feels outstanding
5	Brings you closer to orgasm

Face	0	1	2	3	4	5
Ears	0	1	2	3	4	5
Lips	0	1	2	3	4	5
Neck	0	1	2	3	4	5
Chest	0	1	2	3	4	5
Breasts	0	1	2	3	4	5
Nipples	0	1	2	3	4	5
Armpits	0	1	2	3	4	5
Arms	0	1	2	3	4	5
Hands	0	1	2	3	4	5
Fingers	0	1	2	3	4	5

Tummy	1	2	3	4	5
Sides	1	2	3	4	5
Back	1	2	3	4	5
Butt	1	2	3	4	5
Thighs	1	2	3	4	5
Behind knees	1	2	3	4	5
Calves	1	2	3	4	5
Feet	1	2	3	4	5
Toes	1	2	3	4	5

Once you have an idea of which areas feel good on your body when touched, you can figure out *how* you like those areas to be touched. You and your partner can experiment with sucking, licking, scratching, stroking, and so much more. Enjoy the way your body feels.

There's More to Sense

Touch isn't the only sense that arouses. The other four senses—hearing, sight, taste, and smell—can also get you in tune with what's sexy about a body.

To fully appreciate someone's body, allow yourself to experience all of the senses. Get your nose in there and really smell someone. Lick to taste everywhere. Listen to the timbre of his or her voice. And when you look at someone's body, don't judge it based on some ideals of facial symmetry, height, and weight. Instead, see it as the vessel that carries the mind, soul, and spirit of a sexy person. That's a surefire way to know that your lover looks sexy.

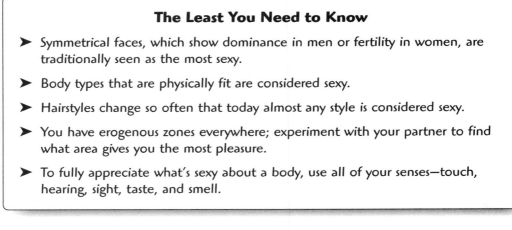

The Least You Need to Know

➤ Symmetrical faces, which show dominance in men or fertility in women, are traditionally seen as the most sexy.

➤ Body types that are physically fit are considered sexy.

➤ Hairstyles change so often that today almost any style is considered sexy.

➤ You have erogenous zones everywhere; experiment with your partner to find what area gives you the most pleasure.

➤ To fully appreciate what's sexy about a body, use all of your senses—touch, hearing, sight, taste, and smell.

Chapter 3

Attitudes That Define Sexiness

In This Chapter

➤ Why confidence is the key to sexiness

➤ How humor can help you be seductive

➤ Why acting mysterious can make you seem alluring

➤ Why sensuality adds to your sexy charm

➤ How your enjoyment of sex makes you sexy

Sexiness is much more than skin deep. As I discussed in the previous chapter, the way you look on the outside does account for a portion of your sexy persona. But it's your *attitude* that truly makes or breaks your sexiness!

Have you ever been at a party or a restaurant or even in a meeting and noticed one person who is so magnetic, so captivating, so powerful, that everybody seems to want to be around him or her? Don't you wonder what that person's secret is, what he or she has that you don't? The answer is simple and can be summed up in one word: confidence. If there's one lesson that I want you to take away from this book, it's that confidence is at the center of sexy. Along with confidence, other attitudes that make people sexy are humor, sensuality, mystery, and enjoyment of sex. All of these are covered in this chapter.

Sexy attitudes are the secret that all magnetic folks have. People aren't sexy because they have something extra in their DNA or that they necessarily work out for a couple hours every day. There is no magic sexy potion. But there are some secret ingredients to sexy attitudes.

How's Your Attitude?

In determining the attitudes that make people sexy, it's helpful to think about the general attitudes that people like about each other. What kind of person do you prefer to spend time with?

Someone who is ...

➤ Open.

➤ Engaging.

➤ Thoughtful.

➤ Excited about what's going on in his or her life.

➤ Interested in what's going on in your life.

➤ Confident.

Or, someone who is ...

➤ Closed-minded.

➤ Closed-off.

➤ Selfish.

➤ Constantly bored.

➤ Self-deprecating.

➤ Self-centered and who never asks you what's going on in your life.

Flirt Alert

There's a big difference between feeling "blue" and being clinically depressed. If you find that you have prolonged trouble sleeping (or sleep too much), seem to drag yourself through the day, experience a loss of appetite (or turn to food for solace), or find that your emotional state is disrupting your life, and these symptoms persist for an extended period of time, seek treatment from a doctor or therapist. Clinical depression is all too common and can be treated, so don't suffer in silence.

Unless you're a recluse who can't stand the human race in its entirety, I'm guessing you picked the qualities of the first list. And why wouldn't you? Who wants to spend precious time with a person who is negative, closed off, and disinterested? Think about it: How sexy is feeling sorry for yourself?

Think of a woman who is an absolute knockout, but, unfortunately, is the biggest stick-in-the-mud you could ever meet. She walks around all day long with a look on her face that is somewhere between disgruntled and melancholy. She constantly wonders why nobody is attracted to her. This isn't limited to attracting potential romantic interests. Friends avoid her, too. Her constant, negative attitude could suck all the fun and energy out of a room full of circus clowns!

Now think of a woman who, truth be told, is not very attractive, physically speaking. However, she can barely keep track of her phone messages. Admirers constantly surround her. She is also a breath of fresh air to be around. It may sound a little corny, but she has such a sparkle in her eyes that it draws you right in. She emits an energy that is fun, exciting ... and very, very sexy.

That's what it's all about. Sexiness is about being exciting inside, and part of that means having confidence in yourself.

Confidence Is Key

Confidence. It's the word that's going to keep coming up. You've heard that it's what makes people sexy. But what exactly is it?

According to *Merriam Webster's Dictionary*, confidence is "a feeling or consciousness of one's powers or of reliance on one's circumstances." Sort of like you trust in your surroundings. But that's general confidence—let's consider self-confidence: "confidence in oneself and in one's powers and abilities."

Now we're getting somewhere. This elusive concept is simply expressing that you feel sure of yourself, that you possess the power to be independent, and that you are proud of your abilities. In a nutshell, it means that you feel good about yourself and all that you can do.

Flirt Alert

Confidence may mean that you're self-assured, but don't go the next step to being conceited—that's obnoxious, not sexy!

Sari Says

You should love yourself as much as you love the other people in your life. If you'd cook a special dinner for your partner, then once in a while, cook one for yourself. If you'd buy a great gift for a friend, then occasionally buy a great gift for yourself. Treat yourself like you treat your own best friend—because in fact, you are!

Here are some more tell-tale signs that you have confidence:

➤ When you speak you are sure others care to listen.

➤ You know that you have a good look, and feel good about your body.

➤ You know you are going somewhere in life, and you are enjoying the journey.

➤ Making choices comes easily for you.

➤ You feel good about your accomplishments.

➤ You are proud of the fact that you can support yourself.

➤ People in your life are supportive of you.

Are you starting to see why these qualities are so sexy? When it comes to projecting sexiness, it means that you can walk into a room and know that you look great, feel comfortable in your surroundings, are genuinely interested in other people, and that you're an all-around great person. With that kind of confidence, others will surely be attracted to you.

The Good Humor Man (or Woman)

As I've mentioned, having a positive attitude is sexy. And what could be the most positive attitude of all? Humor!

Don't you love the person who's the life of the party? I don't mean the guy who walks around with a lampshade on his head, or the woman who monopolizes every conversation, but rather, the one who makes you laugh. When someone is witty, often it doesn't matter what he or she looks like, you just want to be around this person because laughing feels so darn good.

Having a sense of humor comes naturally to some people, and can be learned by others. That's right—you can learn to be funny by observing the things that make you laugh, and trying to emulate them (more on this in Chapter 8, "Developing a Sexy Attitude").

One problem with humor is that if you try to be too funny, you can end up being obnoxious—and there are few things that are less sexy. So where do you draw the line? This should give you some idea:

Funny	Not Funny
Telling a great joke	Telling racist, anti-Semitic, anti-gay, or misogynistic jokes
Doing a cute April Fool's prank	Making prank phone calls
Joking with your partner about sex in private and in a way that you are both comfortable with	Joking with your partner about sex in front of his or her parents

Funny	Not Funny
Surprising your partner by gently putting your arms around him or her and kissing him or her on the neck	Surprising your partner by jumping out of the bushes in the dark and grabbing him or her

If you need inspiration on how to use humor to be sexy, rent a romantic comedy movie in which the characters often joke around, such as …

➤ *When Harry Met Sally.*

➤ *Notting Hill.*

➤ *Four Weddings and a Funeral.*

➤ *The Philadelphia Story.*

➤ *Life Is Beautiful.*

➤ *La Belle Epoch.*

➤ *Forces of Nature.*

When you are flirting, having a sense of humor comes in quite handy. As you'll see in Chapters 8 and 12, "Sexy Flirting Techniques," you can work on being funny to be sexy.

The Mysterious Object of Desire

Think about the *mystique* that surrounded celebrities from the golden age of Hollywood: Greta Garbo, Jean Harlow, Marlene Dietrich, Clark Gable, Humphrey Bogart. They were strong, yet graceful. They were outgoing, but chose their words sparingly and their actions carefully. They were mysterious. They were sexy.

When you appear to be the strong silent type, it may be very attractive. That type of mystery lures people to want to learn more about you. You're not playing hard to get; you're not trying to hide anything. You're just being a bit more self-contained than most, and you're making sure that others want to know what's going on inside your sexy mind.

For more on this, again, I suggest that you go to the movies. Rent some classics that show mysteriously sexy men and women:

➤ *An Affair to Remember*

➤ *Sabrina*

Lusty Lingo

Mystique is an air or attitude of mystery and reverence around something or someone.

➤ *Casablanca*
➤ *Grand Hotel*
➤ *The Monte Carlo Story*
➤ *How to Marry a Millionaire*

Photo by Edward Holub.

For some activities to help you bring out your mysterious side, check out Chapter 8. In the meantime, practice your furtive grin and sultry walk.

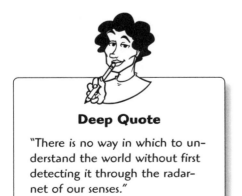

Deep Quote

"There is no way in which to understand the world without first detecting it through the radar-net of our senses."

—Diane Ackerman, *A Natural History of the Senses*

Sensuality: Soft to the Touch, Easy on the Eyes

Sexiness has a component that is calm, centered, romantic, and loving. That's sensuality. It's a way of expressing love and sexual interest that is deeper than just a sexy vibe.

Someone who is sensual …

➤ Enjoys touching and being touched.
➤ Loves eating succulent foods and feeding his or her partner.
➤ Feels comfortable with intimacy and expressing love.

➤ Makes many romantic gestures and acts of kindness.

➤ Sets a romantic mood, such as with candles and wine.

Being sensual means expressing your sexual attraction in more subtle ways than just wanting to have sex. Someone who is sensual emits an accepting, loving quality into the world and especially toward the object of his or her desire. In Chapter 8 I'll give you tips on how to express your sensual side.

Enjoyment of Sex

When a person has a positive attitude about sex, he or she feels comfortable with his or her sexuality, and thus can enjoy sex. If someone is not comfortable with sex, he or she may be afraid to get close, inhibited about his or her body, or afraid of not knowing what to do sexually.

Developing sexual confidence means getting over your inhibitions about your body and about sex in general. This may mean dealing with past experiences that were negative or repressive. See Chapters 6, "Getting Over Inhibitions About Your Body," and 7, "Getting Over Inhibitions About Sex," for more on this.

Having an enjoyment of sex also includes ...

➤ Allowing yourself to do what feels good.

➤ Knowing how you best achieve orgasms.

➤ Protecting yourself against pregnancy and sexually transmitted diseases.

➤ Feeling comfortable being naked, even with the lights on.

➤ Knowing that the amount and types of sex you like are healthy.

➤ Feeling free to make sounds or talk during sex.

➤ Being able to ask for what you want, and talk about sex with your partner.

Sexy Stats

While it's possible for everyone to feel great about his or her sexuality, many people have sexual problems at some point in their lives. Edward Lauman, a researcher at the University of Chicago, found that about two thirds of all Americans are affected by a sexual dysfunction. For information on treatment, please see Appendix C, "Resources."

Deep Quote

"The real meditation is the meditation on one's identity. You try finding out why you're you and not somebody else. And who in the blazes are you anyhow? Ah, *voilà une chose!*"

—Ezra Pound

It's sexy that you enjoy what you attract. Yet the sense of sexual enjoyment is an attitude, not a behavior. In other words, someone who enjoys sex does not have to flaunt it or discuss his or her sexual attitudes or experiences. Part of being sexy is being discreet.

An Exercise in Emulation

As you've just learned, a sexy attitude is defined by self-confidence, humor, mystery, sensuality, and enjoyment of sex. Now you can start examining yourself and those around you to see how you can be sexier.

Let's start with a little exercise. Think for a moment about the people in your life whom you most admire. Next, I want you list five individual qualities they have that make them people you like to spend time with:

1. _____
2. _____
3. _____
4. _____
5. _____

Now take these qualities and make them part of your ultimate sexy goal. Photocopy them out of this book and tack them up on your fridge, on the lampshade next to your bed, or on your PC—wherever it is that you can see them on a daily basis to remind you of the qualities to which you most aspire. Why? Because you need to have constant reminders to get you started building the characteristics that will be the cornerstone of your sexy foundation.

Flirt Alert

Seeing people for their negative attributes first is a bad trait. There is something to learn from everyone. Try to find the goodness in each person, and learn from it.

For instance, let's say one of the qualities you most admire is a positive attitude. If you have this on your list and the list is constantly in view, you'll start to take note of how you react to general questions like a simple "How are you?" Do you find that you frequently launch into the latest barb from your boss, gossipy comments about a co-worker or family member, or the hellish commute you had this morning? What do you think this is saying about you?

Instead of launching into the negative, make it a personal pact to speak only (or as often as possible) in the positive. When someone asks how you are, talk about how you're excited about a project you're working on, or the funny movie you saw last weekend that's still making you smile, or how the change in the weather has done wonders for your attitude. If you can't think of anything in particular to say, simply smile and respond, "I'm fine, how are things going with you?"

When you become aware of how you may be emitting the trait opposite of what you most admire, you will be able to pinpoint areas that need work. Those around you won't be able to help but notice the sexy difference.

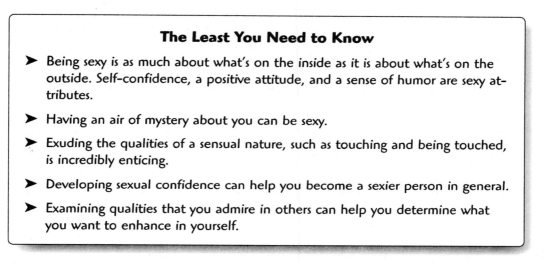

The Least You Need to Know

➤ Being sexy is as much about what's on the inside as it is about what's on the outside. Self-confidence, a positive attitude, and a sense of humor are sexy attributes.

➤ Having an air of mystery about you can be sexy.

➤ Exuding the qualities of a sensual nature, such as touching and being touched, is incredibly enticing.

➤ Developing sexual confidence can help you become a sexier person in general.

➤ Examining qualities that you admire in others can help you determine what you want to enhance in yourself.

Chapter 4

The Sexy Advantage

In This Chapter

➤ How being sexy can enhance your life

➤ Banishing negative stereotypes

➤ The ways that sexiness equates to power

➤ How being sexy can better your relationships

➤ How being sexy can heat up your sex life

Throughout this book, you may be thinking that being sexy is only for the bedroom, and it's not appropriate anywhere else. But the fact is that when someone is sexy, that person is sexy in all that he or she does, all the time.

Being sexy twenty-four-seven does not mean that you desire sex every minute of every day. You will some of the time, of course. But that is not what having a sexy attitude is all about. When you embody the attitudes of sexiness, you don't even have to flaunt it. It just becomes a part of who you are. It can make you seem confident, self-assured, and attractive. Because of that, it can actually improve your life—not just your sex life.

You may be more powerful and you may garner more attention. Being sexy is a great way to attract someone—for sex, or not. Sounds great, doesn't it? In this chapter, I'll explain more about how being sexy is an asset you don't want to (or have to) live without.

What Being Sexy Is *Not*

Before we get into how being sexy can improve your everyday life, I want to clear the air about something that may be troubling you. You bought this book, so I know that you want to learn how to be sexier. But is there also a doubtful little voice inside your head that says, "I don't want anyone to think I'm always trashy/stupid/slutty/easy!"? If so, you must learn Rule #1. Here it is:

Sexy does not equal immoral, distasteful behavior.

A sexy state of being has always been a sort of contradictory notion. Can sexiness be used with less-than-good intentions? Sure. But so can intelligence, strength, beauty, philanthropy, political power, love, ambition, and a slew of other states of being or gestures. There is good and evil in just about everything. Being sexy is not about being bad—it is simply about feeling good about yourself. So good that others stand up and take notice. What's so bad about that?

There is a lot of lip service paid to *self-empowerment*, but use the word "sexy," and people start wriggling around in their chairs saying, "Hey, now, I didn't say anything about sex." Which brings us to Rule #2:

Being sexy does not necessarily involve the act of sex.

Being sexy shows that you are happy to be alive—it doesn't mean you want sex all the time. Of course, you can use your sexy wiles to initiate sex (see Chapter 16, "If You Want Me, Just Whistle: Using Sexiness to Initiate Sex," for more on that particular topic), but that's just one aspect of sexiness. Being a sexy, magnetic person makes people listen when you talk, take interest in your point of view, appreciate your passion for life, and admire your inner and outer beauty. Being sexy does *not* translate into someone who is known on a first-name basis by every hotel in town with a day rate.

Once you knock these negative images from your perception of what a sexy person is, you are free to see how being sexy is a valuable attribute worthy of being cultivated.

As you learned in the last chapter, confidence, humor, a sense of mystery, sensuality, and an enjoyment of sex are all the traits that make someone sexy. Now that you've gotten the basics down and have started working out your own sexy traits, let's take this a step further—how can being sexy improve your life?

Lusty Lingo

Self-empowerment means to have influence over yourself so that you feel as if you're in control of your own life.

Power to the (Sexy) People

Sexy people are powerful people, but how you define powerful is the key to grasping this concept. Powerful has a much broader definition than you might expect. Does it include presidents of countries and companies, brokers of the economy, the wealthy, the famous, and the glamorous? Sure. It includes all of those—but most certainly isn't limited to them. Powerful is also …

➤ Someone who can get people to listen.

➤ Someone who is trustworthy.

➤ Someone who is determined.

➤ Someone who is dynamic and creative.

➤ Someone who is uninhibited.

➤ Someone who is outgoing.

➤ Someone who isn't hindered by outside opinion.

➤ Someone who seizes opportunities.

➤ Someone who can turn a negative situation into a positive one.

➤ Someone who has control over his or her life.

➤ Someone who is intelligent.

➤ Someone who is charismatic.

➤ Someone who is a leader.

Being sexy does not mean you use sex to glean power. It does not mean that you are sleeping your way to the top of the office food chain. But power *is* sexy and can indeed have its rewards in both your personal and professional life.

Being a powerful person is simply being an individual who has qualities that attract other people. Those qualities can be any or all that I listed earlier, and even a few others that I may have missed. Attracting the admiration of others puts you in a position of respect, whether for your thoughts, deeds, or just for the way you carry yourself. This is the ultimate power. Money can be squandered, looks are an objective issue and (unfortunately!) fade—the real power is in who you are and what you do with your good qualities.

Sari Says

How can being sexy get you ahead at work? Use your powerful qualities to be a leader. Initiate improvements, find alternate solutions to problems, express your well-thought-out ideas in meetings, and above all, be a good listener to your co-workers. There's no better way to earn power than to be a front-runner.

Flirt Alert

There is absolutely nothing wrong with being a powerful, sexy person—but there is something wrong with individuals who try to take advantage of you because of your sexiness. Sexual harassment is *never* okay. If you find that you are the object of unwanted propositions or advances at work, or if a colleague or boss is dangling rewards in front of you in exchange for duties that are most definitely not work related, go to your company's human resources department and report the harassment immediately.

The Power of Being Positive

There's nothing sexy about a bad attitude (unless, of course, you're an angry rock 'n' roll star or some kind of tortured poet, but I'm guessing that's not the case).

The problem with a bad attitude is that sometimes you don't even realize you have one. But if you know that you do, and you want your own sexy personality to shine through and help you find a new relationship, or enhance the relationships you have, you need to ditch that bad attitude, and fast! I'm going to help you get to the heart of the matter here. Answer the following questions as honestly as you can:

1. When you have a bad day at work, you …
   a. Try your best to shake it off. You don't like bringing your problems home.
   b. Tell anyone who will listen about what a jerk you had to deal with today.

2. It's Saturday night and you just found out the movie you've been dying to see is playing near you. You …
   a. Make a few phone calls to see if one of your friends is free. If no one's available, that's fine with you. You take yourself out to the movie alone. No big deal.
   b. Don't bother trying to find someone to go with you, and in fact, you forget the whole idea of going. Everyone probably has plans already and you wouldn't be caught dead alone at the movie theater. What would people think?

3. Your best friend and constant out-on-the-town companion just called you to say he or she got engaged. You …

    a. Feel overjoyed. You can't wait for the wedding—besides, everyone knows weddings are the best place to meet a possible Mr. or Ms. Right.

    b. Feel completely deflated. You're on your own. Who will you hang out with now?

4. Your colleague at work gets the promotion you were both gunning for. You …

    a. Feel a little down about it, but know that your co-worker worked equally hard. You try to learn from the experience and maybe see what he or she may have done that earned the extra points.

    b. Become irate and bad-mouth your colleague to everyone around the water cooler. You deserved that promotion and it wasn't fair that you lost out.

5. Your friend starts to tell you a story about something great that happened to her the other day. You …

    a. Listen intently, express enthusiasm, and congratulate her when she's done.

    b. Break in before she even finishes the tale and one-up her with a story of your own. This is the perfect opportunity to get the recognition you've been looking for.

You can see where I'm going here. If you answered mostly a's, you've got a healthy, positive attitude. You've got a great personality that is attractive to others, and you probably don't even realize how sexy that trait is.

On the other hand, if you answered mostly b's, it's time for a change. Being positive, outgoing, interesting, *and* interested are sure-fire ingredients to sexiness. People will desire your company so frequently, you'll need two Palm Pilots to keep track of the new phone numbers you'll receive.

Enhance the Romance

Now here's the one area where being sexy is the culmination of all your great attributes—tangible and otherwise. Being sexy in your romantic life can …

➤ Attract those you are attracted to.

➤ Rekindle the attraction of someone you already have a relationship with.

➤ Spice up your sex life.

➤ Keep the interest of your object of desire piqued and ongoing.

➤ Help you to initiate sex.

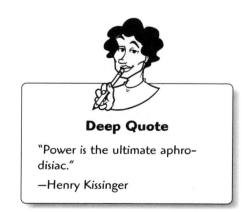

Deep Quote

"Power is the ultimate aphrodisiac."

—Henry Kissinger

As you saw earlier in this chapter, sexiness is multifaceted. Being a sexy person does not mean you are always sending out signals that you want to have sex. A large part of being sexy is how you are perceived—positive, engaging, powerful, and open. These are all qualities that make someone sexy and are appropriate in all settings. However, when it comes to romance, you get to pull out all the stops because this is the one area where sex comes into play.

When you behave in an explicitly sexy manner toward someone, you are making it clear that you want to be more than just a friend. That's another benefit from knowing how you use your sexiness: You can signal to whom you want to be closer.

Obviously, it's hard to resist someone who has an incredibly sexy personality. But couple that with someone who is physically alluring as well, and the object of your desire is the moth flying straight into your flame.

More than just the obvious attractiveness, though, being sexy shows someone else that you are putting forth an effort (even when it seems effortless). In addition to arousing the other person, being sexy makes the other person feel special to be the object of your attention.

There are many ways you can emit both emotional and physical sexiness. For example, flirting (which I give great tactics for in Chapter 12, "Sexy Flirting Techniques") can help you attract a sex partner. Also, you can put your sexy qualities to work in the bedroom as well. The way you and your surroundings look, smell, feel, and sound to another person all add to your allure and, thus, the sensuous nature of your love life (more on that in Chapter 13, "Sexiness Begins at Home: Creating a Sexy Environment"). From sexy talk to lingerie to new positions—these are all ways that using your sexiness can help you entice a potential sex partner, lead you to initiate sex, and add enthusiasm to your sex life (more on this in later chapters, too).

All you need to do to use your sexiness to its fullest is to know when and how to use it. There will be times for mesh stockings, and times to simply show your confidence without any hint of the sexual side of your sexiness.

The fact is, no matter what area of your life could use a little improvement—professional, social, or sexual—being sexy is the secret ingredient that can take it to a new level. Of course, you need to use the appropriate kind of sexiness depending on what the situation calls for. Being a vibrant, open, and attractive individual, however, is *always* appropriate.

The Least You Need to Know

➤ Being sexy does *not* mean that you want to have sex—although if you do, it certainly can help you send the right signals.

➤ Sexiness can help you to be perceived as more powerful.

➤ There's nothing sexy about sending out negative signals to others. If this is you, work on improving your attitude.

➤ Being sexy improves your personal life because it makes others enjoy your company.

➤ Being sexy definitely improves your sex life because it makes others desire you!

Chapter 5

Different Types of Sexiness

In This Chapter

➤ Find out if you are a true romantic

➤ Discover if you are naturally sexy

➤ Explore your flirtatious side

➤ Learn if your erotic elements run wild

➤ Knowing the difference between sexy and sleazy

➤ Determining your own sexy style

Have you ever thought about the fact that there is not just one look, attitude, or feeling that is considered sexy? There are many different styles of sexiness. Take clothing, for example. One woman can look completely sexy wearing a simple sundress, while another may look sexy wearing mesh stockings and a bustier.

The same goes for physical styles of expressing sexiness. Like ice cream, sexiness comes in a range of delicious flavors. You can taste all the choices, if you choose, or you can settle on a favorite one. Maybe you've felt how one sexy person's touch is gentle as he or she gives you back massages and tenderly kisses you all over, while another sexy person is into hot sweaty sex for hours with no kissing but a lot of moaning. Over the course of a night out, have you ever flirted with two different types of sexy people: one who is filled with jokes and sexual innuendo and the other who is just down-to-earth? Do you prefer one sexy style over another? Do you know which sexy style you possess?

I've isolated four different ways that one can express sexiness. Some people possess all these traits, and they can integrate them so that each comes up at a different time, or they can make their sexy styles appear simultaneously. Or perhaps each person likes only one sexy type. In any case, these types are part of the wide range of self-expressions that can be sexy. It's about how a person dresses, flirts, has sex, as well as his or her general personality. One thing's for sure, sexy types certainly don't have temperature in common with ice cream: They're all hot!

Sexy Stats

Romance is alive and well! According to a 1999 study conducted by the Romance Writers of America, 41.4 million adults (or 18 percent of the reading-age population) have read a romance novel in the past year. Three and a half million men and 37.9 million women read romance fiction. One in three women has read a romance in the past year, while one in every thirty men has read a romance in the past year.

Romantic Sexiness

Romance is a major part of sexiness, and it's a part that you can foster to increase your seductive powers. When someone has romantic sexiness, he or she does not display the sort of erotic sexiness that people think of when they think of S-E-X. Instead, romantic sexiness is more about expressing a sweet, loving notion toward someone.

Photo by The Picture Book.

If you display romantic sexiness, you'd be …

➤ Sending your lover flowers.

➤ Lighting candles around the bedroom.

➤ Using scented oils to give your lover a massage.

➤ Staying up all night drinking red wine with your lover.

➤ Talking about the meaning of life.

➤ Coming up with adorable pet names for your lover.

➤ Writing love poems to your lover.

➤ Reading romance stories to each other at bedtime.

➤ Going for moonlight walks on the beach.

➤ Giving your lover butterfly kisses by fluttering your eyelashes against him or her.

➤ Making love with your eyes open.

➤ Saying "I love you," and holding your lover after you both climax.

Deep Quote

"Oh baby what you've done to me,
You make me feel so good inside.
And I just wanna be close to you,
Because you make me feel so alive.
You make me feel, you make me feel,
You make me feel like a natural woman."

—Carole King, "(You Make Me Feel Like a) Natural Woman"

Being romantic is usually part of courtship. But having a sexy style that is predominately romantic means that you continue this sexiness throughout the relationship. If you're the romantic type, it's all about surprises, kisses, and love.

Natural Sexiness

Some people are so completely comfortable with themselves and their sexuality that they seem like they never have to try to look, dress, or act sexy. Their style is natural, cool, and casual. They may be a little rough and tumble and quite down-to-earth. Think Sandra Bullock or Harrison Ford. Someone who has a naturally sexy style says "Take me as I am."

If you want that down-home charm, give some of these naturally sexy traits a try:

➤ Skinny dipping with your lover

➤ Hiking hand in hand in secluded woods

➤ Having sweaty sex and lots of orgasms

➤ Laughing with your lover

➤ Playing sports together

➤ Walking around nude

➤ Speaking your mind with no editing

➤ Being honest about your feelings and not afraid to say "I love you"

➤ Wearing nothing at all to bed

Having natural sexiness is not usually something that you can strive for. In most cases, either you have it or you don't. That's what being natural is all about—expressing your sexuality without a second thought.

Photo by M. Yamaguchi.

Flirt Alert

You can be a flirt without being a tease, but you have to be careful that you are always giving clear signals. Don't lead someone on too far, unless you intend to follow through. Flirting shouldn't hurt anyone else. (See Chapter 12, "Sexy Flirting Techniques," for more.)

Flirtatious Sexiness

You speak in double entendres, suggestively tease people, use your mystique to attract someone you desire, and joke around a lot. You're a flirt, and that can be a real turn on.

Here are some things that are flirtatiously sexy:

➤ Having witty banter with your partner

➤ Surprising your partner with a thoughtful gift

➤ Feeding your lover with your fingers

➤ Tickling your lover

➤ Whispering sweet nothings in your partner's ear

➤ Having phone sex with your lover, with the promise of getting together later

➤ Sending flirtatious e-mails

➤ Smiling at your lover from across the room

➤ Lots of kissing during sex

➤ Enjoying a lot of foreplay

Being a flirt can be totally fun, and it's a great way to get things going with someone new. It can also be a sexy style to resurrect if your relationship needs a little attention.

Photo by David Perry.

Erotic Sexiness

Hot, wild, and sexy. *Erotic* sexiness is the most overt form of sexiness—like the way Ricky Martin moves his hips, or Tina Turner struts her stuff. It's down and dirty, hot and heavy, and it sure is a sexy way to be.

These are erotically sexy traits:

➤ Making sexually suggestive remarks

➤ Wearing outfits that show off your most overtly sexy features

➤ Delighting in turning on your lover

➤ Wearing sexy lingerie to bed

➤ Stripping for your lover

➤ Having hot passionate sex sessions for hours

Lusty Lingo

The word **erotic** is derived from "Eros," who is the Greek god of sexual love. All things erotic are said to encompass the sum of "life-preserving instincts that are manifested as impulses to gratify basic needs." In other words, erotic love dictates that we need sex to survive.

➤ Using sex toys during sex

➤ Combining food and sex

➤ Trying sexual variation, from exotic positions to consensual sadism and masochism (S/M)

➤ Having tons of spontaneity both in sex and in life

➤ Having a high sex drive

Photo by David Wise.

Sexy or Sleazy: Where Do You Draw the Line?

There is a distinction between being erotically sexy and being downright sleazy. Take a look at the following table to see the difference.

Sexy	Sleazy
Having hot sex for hours	Having hot sex for hours broadcast live on the Internet with a variety of people who won an online contest
Stripping for your lover	Pole dancing for 100 strangers on a greased-up pole
Wearing a shirt with cleavage (women)	Pushing your breasts so close together that they bulge out of your spandex shirt (women)
Wearing tight jeans (men)	Stuffing a roll of socks in your crotch, then wearing tight jeans (men)
Going to a motel for a steamy rendezvous with your husband	Going to a motel for a steamy rendezvous with your husband's brother

Sexy	Sleazy
Having sex with your partner under your desk in your office with the door locked on a weekend	Having sex with a co-worker during the workday on top of the copy machine
Wearing mesh tights, or four-inch heels, or a leather miniskirt, or having your nails polished bright red	Wearing mesh tights, four-inch heels, and a leather miniskirt, and having your acrylic nails polished bright red, then standing out on the street corner lookin' for some action
Whispering in your lover's ear that you're not wearing any panties while you're having dinner in a fancy restaurant	Waving your panties over your head so everyone in the restaurant knows you're not wearing them
Flirting with a cute co-worker after work	Hiring an attractive person so you can flirt with him at work

Flirt Alert

While for some people getting close to someone who is erotically sexy is highly exciting, for others, it can be intimidating. If you are erotically sexy, you may want to find a sex partner who really appreciates your sexual creativity, and avoid those who think it's too much.

What's Your Type?

Now that you have an idea of the four sexy types—romantic, natural, flirtatious, and erotic—let's see where you fit the best. Remember, they are all equally attractive and sexy.

Answer the following multiple-choice questions:

1. For women, whose style do you most relate to?

 a. Julia Roberts

 b. Meg Ryan

 c. Drew Barrymore

 d. Pamela Anderson

2. For men, whose style do you most relate to?

    a. Richard Gere

    b. Harrison Ford

    c. Mel Gibson

    d. Lenny Kravitz

Sari Says

People who enjoy alternative sexual lifestyles, like S/M, group sex, or exhibitionism, are not sleazy. They are just doing what feels right for them. However, they should be sure that they respect themselves and their partners, and everything is done with full consent.

Deep Quote

"Erotic is a feather. Kinky is the whole chicken."

—Unknown

3. What would you rather wear to a casual party given by someone you have a crush on?

    a. A cashmere sweater

    b. Jeans and a T-shirt

    c. A button-down top

    d. Leather pants

4. What type of lighting would you have at your place if your object of desire were coming over?

    a. Candles only

    b. Whatever lights are already on

    c. A small lamp with a scarf draped over it

    d. A red light

5. If you wanted to give your lover a gift for no special reason, what would you give?

    a. Flowers

    b. Home-baked cookies

    c. A great long kiss

    d. A sex toy and some lube

6. What's the best sex you've ever had?

    a. When your lover said "I love you" for the first time

    b. When you were outside under the stars

    c. When you undressed each other and kissed all over

    d. When you did something kinkier than even I could imagine

7. Where would you take someone for the perfect date?

    a. A small Italian restaurant to eat by candlelight

    b. An afternoon at the beach

    c. To see a sexy R-rated movie

    d. To your place, where the bed happens to be more comfortable than the sofa

If you answered mostly a's, you tend to be romantic; mostly b's, your style is natural; mostly c's, you're a flirt; mostly d's, you like to show off your erotic side. No matter what you chose, it all shows that you can be sexy!

Because sexiness can be expressed in so many different ways, you can surely find an outlet to be sexy in the way that fits you best. Or, for variety, try all the sexy styles at different times and for different reasons.

The Least You Need to Know

➤ Romantic sexiness helps you express your love and affection.

➤ Natural sexiness is the wholesome way to be sexy.

➤ Flirtatious sexiness is the sweet way to show that you're sexy.

➤ Erotic sexiness is the most overt way to express your sexiness.

➤ Don't cross the line between sexy and sleazy unless you really want to send out that kind of message.

Part 2

Looking and Feeling Sexy

Hey, hot stuff. Lookin' good. Yes, I'm talking to you. That's right—you! Wait a minute … what did you say? You think you're not very sexy? Well, my little hottie friend, do I have news for you. You're not just a little sexy, you're a hot commodity—you just need a dash of convincing and a pinch of Sexy 101.

By our very make-up, humans are sexual beings. To deny that is simply to stifle what comes naturally. But listen, I don't blame you for feeling like sexiness has gotten a little lost on you. Look at what you have to deal with every day—tons of contradictory images telling you at once that being sexy is the ultimate in power and yet is bad and immoral. But of course, sexiness is all good. To believe that, you just need to get over a few stumbling blocks, and learn how to bring out the sexiness already inside you.

And that's just what I'm going to help you do. In this part of the book, you can work on getting over your physical and sexual inhibitions by developing and defining your very own sexy attitude no matter what your age, using clothes (or lack thereof) to reflect your sexy image, and using body language to be the universal translator of sexiness.

Chapter 6

Getting Over Inhibitions About Your Body

In This Chapter

➤ Getting over the big "I"—insecurity

➤ How loving your nude body helps you become sexy

➤ Exercises to slough off that bad body image

➤ Getting in touch with your senses to feel good about yourself

➤ Getting over hangups about your body parts

➤ Freeing your mind of your body issues when you're around someone else

Remember when you were a kid and you used to run around all day in your bathing suit? You'd leap through sprinklers, dash around the beach, strut about eating ice cream. You wouldn't once think something like, "Oh no! Where's my T-shirt? I look so fat!" Now, why do you think that is?

I'll tell you why. You were comfortable with your body. You were sure of yourself. You were probably pretty happy, too. Sometimes it seems that very few of us get past puberty without some internal scars. Those can be turbulent years when your whole life changes—both physically and emotionally. Although it's a wonderful time of self-discovery, it is also the point where you get your first serious lessons in that bad "I" word—insecurity.

That "I" word is your main roadblock to feeling, and ultimately being, sexy. But, my friend, it's time to shake off those insecurities of the past. In this chapter, we're going to let it all hang out, and you're going to like it. Or at least I'll have you singing along to that song by Right Said Fred called "I'm Too Sexy"—and *believing* the lyrics!

Deep Quote

"To lose confidence in one's body is to lose confidence in one's self."

—Simone de Beauvior

Sexy Stats

According to the International Health, Racquet & Sportsclub Association, there are 22.5 million health club members in the United States. The fitness craze has caused many people to join gyms, whether they really exercise there or not.

Fighting Those Impossible Expectations

The getting-fit-and-staying-healthy craze that has taken the United States by storm over the last 15 years or so has made many of us more conscious of bad health habits and intent on improving our lifestyles. But it's not just health that drives many people to want to change their bodies. If you pick up any magazine, watch television, go to the movies, or even glance at a billboard, you can't help but be assaulted several times a day by so-called "perfect" body images.

It can be overwhelming: Christy Turlington's lithe, tanned body flaunted in Calvin Klein underwear; Antonio Sabato Jr. in boxer shorts with his muscles rippling; the babes and hunks of *Baywatch;* the cast of *Friends,* who seem to get thinner every season; and a million and one other icons impressing themselves daily upon your poor, unsuspecting self-image. Even if you have a fairly healthy body image, I'll bet you still stand in front of the mirror sucking in, doing the "Special K pinch," or just basically feeling inadequate. "If only I were a little more (or less) this …"; "If only I were a little more (or less) that …" These negative thoughts are like quicksand, sucking you down and immobilizing you until you eventually surrender to the muck. But if you want to feel sexy, you have to get rid of those impossible expectations. There are ways to do that! This chapter will help.

Sexual Healing: Working on Your Body Image

If you're really serious about wanting to be sexy, one of the most important things you've got to do is get comfortable with your body. Not just your clothed body, your *nude* body. Warts, love handles, freckles, and all. Always keep in mind something that's very important: You'll never experience great sex until you've experienced your own sexuality. You can't *be* sexy until you *feel* sexy.

I'm going to ask you to do something special for me in this chapter, so you're going to have to trust me. Ready? Take off all your clothes. Go ahead. Strip. I mean it. (Okay, if you're in a public place, keep your pants on, of course. This is strictly a home-based exercise.) You're not going to get over your physical inhibitions by just reading about them. You're going to have to get involved. So, take it all off, every stitch, before we go any further.

Now that you're good and naked, I want you to take a minute to think about how you feel:

➤ Awkward?

➤ Shy?

➤ Silly?

➤ Indifferent?

➤ Ashamed?

➤ Worried that someone's going to knock on your door or walk in on you?

➤ A combination of any or all of the above?

Whatever you feel is okay. These are all normal reactions. Think about how much time you actually spend in the buff each day: 10 minutes, give or take? In the shower; a few moments while getting dressed or deciding what to wear; a second or two while changing into your pajamas. For many people, that's it. Is that it for you? Since most states have laws about walking around in public in your birthday suit, that's not unusual. Of course, there are some people who walk around nude in their home all the time, and who wouldn't dream of sleeping with clothes on.

Sexy Stats

Think you're fat? Think again. Only 27 percent of women are actually overweight and 19 percent are actually underweight, according to the National Center for Health Statistics. If you're wondering what you should weigh, check out Metropolitan Life's Web site (www.metlife.com), in which you can browse a variety of health-related topics, including height and weight tables for men and women. Keep in mind, though, that these are *average* weights. I'm not telling you that in order to be sexy, your weight must conform to the height listed. Anyone of any size can be sexy—it's an attitude!

Deep Quote

"I have flabby thighs, but fortunately my stomach covers them."

—Joan Rivers

Photo by Joyce Tenneson.

The fact of the matter is that you may not be used to your body. It's hard to feel sexy about something that you're hardly familiar with. Let's change that, shall we?

The Naked Truth

I want you to find the mirror in your home that will give you the best full view of yourself. Find a hand-held mirror as well and keep it nearby because you're going to take a look at things from the rear, too.

Now, check out the goods. Stand in front of the mirror and take a good, long look. Start at your toes and work your way up. Then, turn around and, using the hand-held mirror, peruse your backside. Now, here comes the hard part: Don't criticize, just look.

It's hard to do, isn't it? That's because you're probably far more comfortable with self-criticism than self-love. Stop comparing yourself to fabulous models or actors. You don't look like them because you *aren't* them. You are your own fabulous self. To get you on the way to appreciating your physical assets, try this exercise. For every sentence you think or utter that's negative, I want you to add a positive "but." For instance …

My hips are too big ... *but* they are very feminine and curvy.

Or ...

My chest is too hairy ... *but* it is soft and feels good.

There are many tangible things that can add to being sexy—perfume or cologne, a great outfit, makeup that accentuates a pretty feature of your face. There is nothing wrong with using any one or all of these things to up your sexy quotient. However, if you don't feel confident, all the tips about fashion and body language in the world aren't going to teach you anything about sex appeal. You need to assess what you have and learn to feel good about it. If you don't feel good about yourself, all the slinky outfits in the world aren't going to help.

Flirt Alert

There is no such thing as the perfect physique. It just doesn't exist. Why? Because when it comes to physical beauty, "perfect" is in the eye of the beholder. It is entirely subjective, therefore it's impossible to come up with an example that would please everyone. The true "perfect" body is a healthy body.

Now, give it a shot. Use the fill-in spaces below to write down your negative body thought, and then add in the "but." The purpose of this is to start you on the road to feeling comfortable and confident about what you have got (so you can flaunt it later!):

1. My _____
   ... *but* _____
2. My _____
   ... *but* _____
3. My _____
   ... *but* _____
4. My _____
   ... *but* _____
5. My _____
   ... *but* _____

Just Between You and Your CD Player

Have you ever noticed how music can change your mood from bad to good, good to melancholy, melancholy to ... sexy? You know what I'm talking about. Music is a powerful medium. A little note here, a little note there, and you're dancing around your living room, belting out tunes, and feeling in love with life, and with yourself.

If you've ever watched the television show *Ally McBeal,* you'll remember how the notion of a theme song played a big role in the lives of a couple of the characters. They frequently used it as a confidence builder. Sure, it's a funny gag on TV and makes you laugh, but think about it. Have you ever had a song running through your head that put you in a great mood? Made you feel good? Made you smile? It's no accident that television and film use music to bring an audience to a particular emotional place. That's what music does: It touches us somewhere that words alone can't always do.

With this in mind, let's try a little exercise. I want you to think about the songs that make you feel—you guessed it—sexy.

This will be your sexy theme song (or songs). Go dig them out of your CD, tape, or record collection and put one on the stereo. (I am, of course, assuming you're still naked—did I *tell* you to put your clothes back on??? I don't think so.) Maybe it's a Barry White tune. Maybe it's Puccini. Heck, it could be Britney Spears or Barry Manilow. It doesn't matter, nobody's judging your musical taste here. What does matter is that it makes you feel good.

Sari Says

A sexy song doesn't necessarily make you want to have sex (although that's good, too!). It can be a song that just makes you feel confident, happy, and downright good to be in your skin. Remember, being sexy is all in the attitude.

Can't come up with a song? Here are a few good, ol' sexy standards to get your ego groovin':

➤ "Let's Get It On," Barry White

➤ "Do You Think I'm Sexy?" Rod Stewart

➤ "Vogue," Madonna

➤ "I'm Every Woman," Chaka Khan

➤ "Shake Your Hips," The Rolling Stones

➤ "Doo Wop (That Thing)," Lauren Hill

➤ "Peel Me a Grape," Diana Krall

➤ "Man! I Feel Like a Woman," by Shania Twain

➤ "Sexual Healing," by Marvin Gaye

Now, close your eyes and hear the music. Sing along or dance if that's part of what makes you feel great. Do air musical conductor. Whatever it takes to get you in a great mood. Stand in front of the mirror and think about the "but" exercise from earlier. While the song is playing, recall the "buts" you wrote down.

Now, this might feel a little silly, but stick with me. I want you to seduce yourself. While listening to your new theme song, savor how great the music makes you feel and concentrate on the positive aspects of your so-called negatives. Visualize yourself strutting your stuff to the music, and …

1. Think about yourself as a whole entity, moving and flowing with the song.

2. Concentrate on how good the music makes you feel with and about yourself.

3. As you experience how good you feel, start to visualize how good you look.

The whole point of this exercise is to learn to let go of your self-consciousness and feel good about the skin you're in. This isn't a one-shot deal, though. You may have to practice a lot, because there's more to come. I want you to work up to not just visualizing it, but actually doing it. I know what you're saying: "Dance around naked? Isn't that kinda weird?" It may well feel a little goofy, but it will accomplish a few very important things for you:

1. It will help you become comfortable naked.

2. It will help you become comfortable naked and moving around.

3. It will (most importantly) help you mend that bad body image you've cultivated.

Once you start to feel more comfortable with this exercise, you may feel more comfortable nude, and then more comfortable having sex. After all, what is sex but dancing lying down?

Flirt Alert

Unless you want to share your excellent body image with your neighbors, make sure you've closed the blinds or curtains before you start shakin' your naked groove thang!

Ego Mania

Okay, nudie (just kidding!), take a breath. That might have felt a little strange but there's a method to my madness. From now on, when you're in a situation where you want to be sexy but you're feeling less than confident about your body, I want you to think about your theme song and that sexy little dance you just visualized yourself doing (or actually did).

If you're worried about those shapely hips or that hairy chest, summon up your theme song and think about your "buts"—your positive attributes. Boost your *ego* by seeing yourself as a whole, fluid, sexy entity. By practicing this little positive visualization technique, you are learning to accept your body as a whole—not break it off into pieces that

Lusty Lingo

Ego is another word for self-esteem. It is one of three divisions of the psyche in psychoanalytic theory that mediates between the you and your reality, by helping you understand the world around you, and adapt you to fit into it.

you poke, prod, and (worst of all) critique. The "problem areas" of your body aren't actually a problem at all. It's all just part of the package that is the sexy and gorgeous you.

If you feel good about yourself, so will others. Yes, I know. Talk is cheap. That's why you've got to practice. It may not happen overnight for you. You may have to dance with Mr. Barry White every night for a month or more. It's not easy to exorcise a negative body image from your thoughts, but you can do it. Remember, body confidence and self-confidence are sexier than a six-pack of abs or fabulous legs!

Are You (Sensory) Experienced?

You can breath a sigh of relief—the aerobic part of this chapter is over. But, no, you can't put your clothes on yet. It's time to get self-indulgent. Now that we've taken steps to get you feeling good about what you've got, it's time for you to relax and enjoy it.

Why? I may be starting to sound like a broken record, but the fact is if you appreciate, like (dare I say *love?*), and feel comfortable with your body, then you've got the essence of sexy in the palm of your hand.

Some of the things I'm going to tell you to do may sound similar to the ideas I give you for setting a sexy scene later on in this book. That's not an accident. When you set a beguiling scene for the object of your desire—whether it is by wearing something that looks or smells great on you, using mood lighting, or putting on slow, sexy music—you are seducing that person through his or her senses. If you want to feel good about your body, you've got to do the same thing for yourself. When you finish this chapter, I want you to love your body (or at least be on the way to appreciating it a whole lot more than you do now).

Following are a few suggestions for getting the full sensory experience of your body and for seducing yourself. Try the ones that sound tempting, or try them all if you feel comfortable doing so. Whatever you decide, remember the key: You are learning to appreciate your body—and by doing so, others will, too.

➤ Fill a warm bath with bubble bath or scented oil (try rose or lavender if you don't have a favorite scent), light some candles, put on some great music, and soak. Feel the warmth of the water relax your muscles and the way your skin softens from the oils.

➤ After you bathe, instead of doing the usual quick dry with a bath towel, lie under a ceiling fan or near an open window (weather and neighbors permitting) and slowly dry off. Feel the velvety air as it blows on your skin.

➤ Slowly eat a meal of erotic foods. (Avocado, oysters, chocolate, strawberries, honey, and figs are a few.) As you nibble, experience the texture, smell, and taste of the food and think about how it makes you feel physically (the slow, thick sweetness of honey on your tongue; the cool softness of avocado; the tickling skin and luscious inside of a strawberry).

➤ Have a home spa night—give yourself a facial, manicure, and/or pedicure (yes, men, you can do this, too!). Slather yourself with some great, aromatherapeutic body lotion. Admire how great your skin looks and feels. When you're done, put on some slinky sleepwear that you've been saving for a special occasion. Feel how good it is to be in your own skin.

The Fun-House Mirror of Your Mind

There's nothing like those first moments when you meet someone to whom you are attracted. There's the flirting, the tingles up and down your spine, the great body language that says all the things you aren't quite ready to make audible. You might feel a little insecure during those moments and double-check your reflection in a mirror or window once or twice. For the most part, however, you're probably not thinking too much about love handles, cellulite, or stretch marks.

Most people don't start worrying about the way their bodies look until the first time clothes are shed in front of each other. They may be completely embarrassed to be nude in front of a partner, and they may even insist that the lights are turned out during lovemaking. They may try anything to avoid their partner getting a full-on look at their nude body, including sneaking around in the dark to get dressed.

While some people may feel most vulnerable the first time they are naked in front of a new lover, there are also couples who, after years together, still don't feel comfortable being naked around each other. They're insecure, worried about what the other thinks, and completely self-critical.

Although this kind of insecurity can be an issue of trust, more frequently, it goes back to that negative body image. I like to call this the *fun-house mirror effect:* You see only a distorted, negative view of your body.

You are the only person who can smash the fun-house mirror to bits. All the compliments in the world won't help you until you learn to accept your physical presence for what it is—a healthy, beautiful body that is uniquely your own.

Lusty Lingo

The **fun-house mirror effect** occurs when you see your body not as it is, but with a warped, distorted, negative view that results in insecurity and low self-esteem.

Feeling Comfortable About Your Sexual Body Parts

There are so many body hangups that people have when it comes to sex. A woman may worry that her breasts flatten out when she is on her back during sex, or that her vagina is not tight enough to please a man. A man may worry that he has too much hair on his back or shoulders, or that his penis is too small. Both men and women might worry that their bodies smell, taste bad, or will do things that they can't control (such as pass gas). They may also worry that their faces will contort in ugly ways during the moment of orgasm. But the fact is that having great sex is about getting lost in the moment, and not worrying about what your body is doing or what your body looks like. You need to get over these hangups to feel sexy!

In order to stop thinking about these things, you have to convince yourself that your partner is thrilled to be with you and loves your body, no matter what. You can enjoy your body more during sex if you enjoy the feelings in your body rather than focus on the negative thoughts in your head. Here are some ways you can do that:

➤ Don't draw attention to the things you don't like about your body by mentioning them to your partner. Your partner wants to enjoy you, not hear about your insecurities.

➤ Think about this: You are not scrutinizing your partner's body—so that means that your partner is probably not scrutinizing yours!

➤ Remember that all bodies are different and should be appreciated for their uniqueness.

➤ When you start worrying about your body, tell yourself, "Stop that!" Then focus your attention on what it feels like in your fingertips to touch your lover's body.

➤ Act like you are confident, even if you don't always feel that way. Confidence is sexy!

Overall, think of the wonderful feelings of the moment. Enjoy the pleasure that you feel rather than worrying about what you look like.

Flirt Alert

If your partner often criticizes your body or makes you feel inadequate, self-conscious, or, worse, downright unattractive, a warning bell should go off in your head. There's nothing wrong with you—but there is something wrong with someone who makes you feel there is. Perhaps it's time to reassess your relationship. Do you really want to stay with someone who makes you feel bad about yourself?

What You See Is What You Get—and Then Some

I'll say it again: There is nothing sexier than confidence. One of the best ways to feel comfortable nude in front of someone else is simply to be nude and not be shy about it. Easier said than done? Yes. But you've got to kick this self-image problem cold turkey.

The next time you are undressing with the object of your desire, don't turn out the lights, leap under the covers like a jack rabbit, or leave on an article of clothing to try to hide your body. Take it off with bravado. Even if you don't feel confident, act confident. You'd be surprised at how habit-forming confidence can be.

At first, it might be hard. That's when all those exercises from the beginning of this chapter are going to come in handy. Think about all those "buts" you wrote down earlier. Conjure up your theme song and think about how sexy it makes you feel. If you can't handle having the lights on during sex, at least light some candles. Most important, remember this: If someone is with you, chances are pretty darn good that the person is very attracted to you, likes what he or she sees, and is very excited about seeing more.

You get only one life and (short of surgical augmentation) one body. If you spend your whole life finding ways to hide it from others and, worst of all, from yourself, you'll be missing out on a whole world of sensory experiences. Being sexy comes from within!

The Least You Need to Know

➤ Insecurity is a major roadblock to feeling sexy. Fight insecurity by building confidence in yourself and in your body.

➤ Next time you find yourself criticizing a part of your body, add a positive "but."

➤ Come up with your very own theme song—something that you call up into your mind on the spot that will make you feel good, confident, and sexy!

➤ Get over your hangups about your sexual body parts—you're going to need to feel good about them to be sexy!

➤ Don't be shy about your body in front of the object of your desire; chances are, he or she is already sold on the goods you've got.

Chapter 7

Getting Over Inhibitions About Sex

In the last chapter, I talked about how difficult it can be to get over inhibitions about your body when everywhere you turn, icons of beauty assault your self-image. The obsession with looking good in this country has had an incredibly negative impact on the psyches of women and men from coast to coast. There's something else that this country is obsessed with, though, that, for some people, can be equally daunting and even harder to come to terms with: sex.

Perhaps you were raised to think that sex is dangerous, or that expressing your sexuality is "sinful." But then you were inevitably exposed to the explicit sexual messages that are perpetuated by the media. With a constant clashing of worlds, it's easy to have a hard time figuring out what *you* really feel comfortable with sexually.

In this chapter, I'm going to try to coax you out of your shell and open your mind to new sexual possibilities, as well as help you figure out where to draw your own lines. Let's talk about sex, baby!

The Lusty Room Next Door

A friend of mine told me a story a few years ago about her male roommate at the time. He was a good friend of hers and, generally, they got along famously—until one fateful night.

It was late and she was getting ready to turn in. She was in her bedroom reading when she heard the keys jingle in the lock, the front door swing open, and peels of laughter from three voices—two male and one female. She heard her roommate offer his guests a beverage, and then the tumbling of footsteps into his bedroom, which was next to hers.

She didn't really think much of it. He had friends over. Big deal. That was, until, the walls started shaking and moans and groans and giggles came through the thin plasterboard. This went on for hours. She was horrified. She tried putting pillows over her head. She tried putting her Walkman on. She tried everything to ignore what she knew was going on a few feet away from her. In a final moment of frustration, she banged a fist on the wall.

"Hey, could you keep it down in there?"

It got pretty quiet for a second. Then came the sounds of low giggling and the voice of the woman in the other room saying just loud enough for her to hear: "Maybe she'd like to join us." She could feel her face turning red. She pulled the covers up to her chin and stewed about the *ménage à trois* for the rest of the night.

Lusty Lingo

A *ménage à trois* is a sexual encounter between three consenting adults.

How Do You Feel About Sex?

When my friend relayed this story to me, she looked a little troubled. It seemed like she had more on her mind, so I asked if something else was bothering her about what happened that night.

"Well ..." she slowly began. "It's my boyfriend. He says that I'm sort of uptight about, you know, sex. He says I never want to try anything new. And he's right. I really dig my heels in on the issue; but something about the other night got me thinking more about this."

She went on to say that it seemed everything beyond lights-out-missionary-position sex made her uncomfortable and she didn't know why. She lumped all other sex into a sort of taboo category in terms of how far she was willing to take her own sexual experiences. She knew, though, that there was something beyond the surface of her discomfort with sex. She generally didn't judge others on what they did in bed. And she certainly wasn't a vestal virgin. Like over 90 percent of Americans, she engaged in premarital sex. So why was she so uptight?

After discussing it for a while, we got to the heart of the issue: She was worried about how she'd look to her boyfriend if he had the chance to see her from a different angle. She was worried that she'd be awkward and not "good" at something new. This grown-up, attractive, seemingly confident woman, whose family had always talked openly with her about sex, was actually worried that she wouldn't know what to do.

There's an ocean of difference between feeling something is morally wrong and feeling something is just not right for you personally. When it comes to decisions about sex under normal circumstances (no pressure, mutual trust being present), more often than not the decision is one of personal choice.

To make a choice about what you want to do sexually, you have to ask yourself: What *do* you feel comfortable doing? Is there more out there that you would be open to experimenting with? Here are a few determining factors to help you answer these questions:

➤ When having sex, do you feel uncomfortable about your partner seeing your body?

➤ After sex, do you frequently worry about your partner's satisfaction?

➤ Do you have difficulty climaxing because you are distracted? Or are you too distracted to climax at all?

➤ Do you feel apprehensive about telling your partner what you like and don't like?

➤ Do ever feel like there was a class on sex that you slept through and are too shy to ask someone else for the notes?

➤ Are you curious about trying different things (positions, role playing, using sex toys or other props), but feel that your partner might think you're weird for suggesting it?

Deep Quote

"The human mind, once stretched to a new idea, never goes back to its original dimensions."

—Oliver Wendell Holmes

Flirt Alert

Being pressured into a sexual act that you are not comfortable doing does *not* mean you are uptight sexually. It means that your partner is not thinking about your feelings. It's one thing to make a suggestion; it's quite another to make a demand. Don't ever let someone talk you into performing a sexual act that you're not comfortable with.

If you answered "yes" to any or all of these questions, you've come to the right book. It's time for a sexual-psyche adjustment.

Please Please Me

Before I help you figure out what other aspects of sex you are open to experiencing, let's take a look at upping your sexual pleasure quotient. You can try all the props and positions in the world, but if you don't know how to be happy, it's going to feel more like volunteer work than a mutually pleasurable experience.

What are your sexual expectations? Some people think that sex is supposed to be some incredible experience every time, that will flow perfectly and will always lead to immense pleasure. If it does not measure up, then one may think that it is his or her fault or his or her partner's fault, rather than realizing what the true problem may be: The person's expectations are too high, and might be based on cultural and media images of sex.

Many people concentrate a little too much on outside opinion—and there's a whole lot of it. On one end of the spectrum, for women, there's the "good girl" factor: Nice girls don't buy sex toys, read erotica, watch dirty movies, or do anything that would put them in singer Rick James's "Superfreak" category of women. On the other end, there are all the movies and television programs showing you how sex is *supposed* to be. Of course, many people overlook the fact that one, we don't have body doubles standing in for us; two, we don't have make-up artists making us appear so-called perfect every second; and three, we don't view our own sexual experiments through a rose-tinted camera lens.

The thing that makes good sex *good* is when both partners experience pleasure. This is not an area where being selfless is going to do you or your lover any good. The following are some suggestions for steps to help you lose your sexual inhibitions:

➤ **Know thyself.** If you don't know what you like, you're never going to be able to explain it to someone else. So, masturbate. Your partner doesn't have a map to your senses, so you need to take responsibility for knowing what feels good to you.

➤ **Speak up.** Once you know how to get your juices flowing (or, if you already do) speak up if your partner's not doing what works. This goes beyond clitoral or penile stimulation, however. If your partner is doing something that's a turnoff to you, it's going to distract you and make it that much harder—or impossible—to climax. And here's a little secret: A caring partner *wants* to know what turns you on! Wouldn't you want to know if your signature ear-blowing trick that worked so well on your last boyfriend really freaks out your new one? Of course! So speak up, or forever remain in a state of climactic limbo.

➤ **Welcome yourself to Fantasy Island.** Fantasizing is okay. In fact, it can be great. It doesn't mean that you're a million miles away and not concentrating on your partner. Fantasies can involve places, dreams, scenes, or even other people. So what if you think about the cute girl you saw on the street the other day or an actor you have the hots for? It's not real, so you can enjoy your fantasy.

➤ **Stop feeling guilty.** Thinking about yourself and your own pleasure is nothing to be ashamed of.

➤ **Sing your body's praises.** Being self-conscious about your body is just about the worst distracter during sex. If you're ashamed of your body, go back and read Chapter 6, "Getting Over Inhibitions About Your Body."

➤ **Have fun!** Your mother, priest, rabbi, Brahman, boss, and second-grade teacher with the ruler are *not* in the room with you and your partner. You are a consenting adult and you're allowed to enjoy the pleasure of your body and someone else's.

You have to take responsibility for your own pleasure. That may well mean breaking down those inhibitions you've been harboring all these years. It's going to take a little work, but it's well worth it. In the wise words of poet Maya Angelou, "We have it in us to be splendid."

Deep Quote

"We may think of sex as something we should do well, with skill and healthy motives. But health and technique, valuable as they may be, are not enough to evoke the depths of sex, which calls for imagination, reverence, and full presence."

—Thomas Moore

Take Me Higher

You can find even more pleasure in sex if you focus on a few things to free your mind and body. Most importantly, you need to be open to new ideas or experiences. The paradox is that if you are closed off to new ideas about sex, you may not even know that you are inhibited: You may have been going along all this time thinking, "Well, this is just the way sex is, and sometimes it's okay and sometimes it's blah."

Of course, it's unrealistic to think that every roll in the hay is going to be nirvana, but chances are if you're reading this chapter, you know there's room for improvement. If you are harboring inhibitions about letting go during sex, you are truly missing out. Just as I got you thinking about your mental sexual hangups earlier in this chapter, I want you to learn how to clear your head of inhibiting distracters during sex to help you on your path to a mind-blowing sex life.

Try some of the following techniques to de-clutter your mind. During sex …

➤ **Get rid of distractions.** Close the door to your bedroom, turn off the TV, close the window if it's noisy outside. Whatever outer elements are grabbing your attention, ditch 'em!

➤ **Experience the sensuality.** Feel what's going on between the two of you: the increased pace of your breathing; the way your bodies feel when they touch each other; the rhythmic movements you fall into. Be in the moment.

➤ **Find your visual.** Call up a mental picture that is the site of your fantasies. Maybe it's the moonlit beach in Mexico where you went on vacation last year, the shadowed spot under a vine-like balcony in New Orleans where no one could see, the peaceful peak of a mountain you hiked to once in the Sandias outside of Santa Fe. It doesn't really matter where. It does not have to be that exotic. It just should be a place that you found sensual and peaceful.

➤ **Trust your partner.** If you are constantly worrying about your partner's thoughts, you will not be able to experience your own sexuality. You're in this together. By trusting him or her, you will truly be able to let go and experience the pure sexiness of sex.

Photo by Johner Bibdbyra.

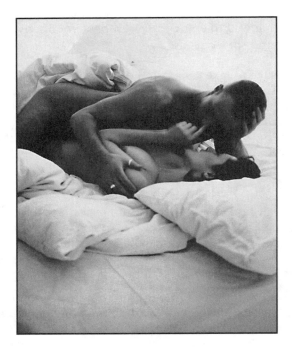

Sexual Enhancers: Turning on the Light Switch of Love

Remember back in school when there was that one great teacher who would always do something different or surprising to get you interested in class? It was that class that you enjoyed the best and got the most out of. Let's take that same theory and transfer it to your bedroom (or wherever it is you choose to get down).

There are a bevy of things from the outer world that can make your sex life a whole lot more interesting—and a whole lot sexier. You can be on your way to opening up to a whole new sexy world of lovemaking. It's time to start on your own personal journey to open your mind and find out what you truly aren't comfortable with and what might actually heighten your sexual pleasure.

I'm going to give you some suggestions for sexual enhancers to consider. As you go through them, I want you to use the blank lines underneath each item to write down three things:

1. One negative reaction

2. One positive reaction

3. A sentence or two on why this will or won't fit into your sex life

Don't just try to get through this like it's a task you need to complete. Really think about your reactions. The purpose of this is to get to the root of what you will and won't accept, and why. Sometimes you might have a negative reaction to something right off the bat, but when you think about it, there's no reason why you should feel that way. The point is to weed out your inhibitions from things that you truly find uncomfortable or distasteful.

Sari Says

Have you ever tried something—a food, new activity, or book by a writer whose work you've never read before—that you swore up and down you'd hate, but were surprised to find you liked it after all? It's the same with sex. To disregard something without giving it thought is to miss out. Before you say, "No way! I'll never try that!" think about the reasons why you feel that way.

Bedtime Stories

Steamy stories in some form or another have been around since people began telling tales. However, the underground literature of the nineteenth century is frequently cited as the beginnings of what we call erotica. Simply put, erotica is a literary or artistic work having sexual qualities or a sexual theme. Erotica goes straight to the heart of your fantasies, and can sometimes conjure up some new ones.

By today's standards, the *erotica* of the nineteenth century is pretty tame—for example, describing how a dainty beauty was ravished by a lustful man. In today's erotica anything goes, from bisexuality and group sex to S/M. The following list contains a wide variety of erotica in book form, so you can experiment with different types:

➤ *Best American Erotica*, edited by Susie Bright

➤ *Confessions D'Amour*, Anne-Marie Villefranche

➤ *Delta of Venus*, Anaïs Nin

➤ *Emmanuelle*, Emmanuelle Arsan

➤ *Lady Chatterly's Lover*, D. H. Lawrence

➤ *Sleeping Beauty Trilogy*, A. N. Roquelaure (Anne Rice)

➤ *The Story of O*, Pauline Reage

➤ *Tropic of Cancer*, Henry Miller

In addition to these books, I recommend that you check out the following Web sites. Not only can you view them in the privacy of your own home, but they also have great links to other sites and in-depth coverage and explanations of the various forms of erotica that exist:

➤ Amazon booksellers: www.Amazon.com

➤ Dreams Unlimited electronic books: www.dreams-unlimited.com

➤ The Erotica Readers Association: www.erotica-readers.com

➤ Nerve: www.nerve.com

➤ Red Sage publishers: www.redsagepub.com

➤ Scarlet Letters: *The Journal of Femmerotica*: www.scarletletters.com

➤ Silver Moon Books: www.silvermoonbooks.com

Lusty Lingo

Erotica is a literary or artistic work having sexual qualities or a sexual theme.

Sari Says

Some of you may be a little shy about checking out a store that specializes in sex or erotica, or even checking out the erotic section of your local bookstore. If that's the case, there are countless sources online that allow you to check out and purchase the books, gadgets, and toys you might be intrigued by in complete privacy.

Your Reaction to Erotica

1. Negative: _____

2. Positive: _____

3. How can this fit into/improve your sex life? Or why won't it? _____

_____

_____

Professor Gadget's Got Nothing on You

What's a passion play without props? Gadgets and extras aren't for everybody, and you may feel a little shy introducing them into your sex life, but think about it this way: When you were a kid and it was bath time, didn't an ample amount of floating toys make getting clean more fun? Well, the following items just might make getting down and dirty a little more entertaining, too:

➤ **Vibrators.** Electric or battery-operated devices that are designed as massagers to stimulate genitals, or anywhere on the body. They may be shaped like a penis or look just like a shoulder massager, such as the best-selling vibrator, the Hitachi Magic Wand. You can buy these in any adult sex shop and catalogs, or at many department stores that sell massagers.

➤ **Edible undergarments.** Panties that are made to be eaten, usually made of sugar or corn syrup molded into the shape of underpants (kind of like the consistency of "Fruit Roll-Ups"). They are sold in sex novelty stores and catalogs.

➤ **Dildos.** Cylinders of plastic, rubber, or latex that are inserted during sex (either vaginally or anally). They may be shaped like a penis, or just be a smooth oblong shape. Some are even shaped like animals. (Don't ask me why!) They are sold in sex novelty stores and catalogs.

➤ **Feathers.** You don't need to pick up a grimy ol' pigeon feather off the street. Instead, you can buy a feather boa, some feathers from a crafts store, or even use the tip of a clean feather duster.

➤ **Ben wa balls.** Solid metal balls that can be inserted into the vagina and may provide some stimulation when they rub together. These are sold in sex novelty stores and catalogs.

Your Reaction to Erotic Gadgets

1. Negative: _____

2. Positive: _____

3. How can this fit into/improve your sex life? Or why won't it? _____

_____

_____

It's Not Just for Breakfast Anymore

Food, glorious food. Who doesn't enjoy the sensual experience of a great meal, a fabulous dessert, or a sneaky midnight snack? Items from the kitchen can whet more than just your appetite for nutritional sustenance—they can also enhance your sexual appetite. Here are some suggestions for edibles that will turn your next sexual encounter into an unforgettable sexy snack:

➤ **Honey.** Thick, gooey, and sweet, when used in moderation, honey can add pleasure to task of the licker as well as the lickee.

➤ **Whipped cream.** When I was a kid, my parents had this album by Herb Alpert. On the cover was a beautiful woman in a dress made of whipped cream. Get out that can of whipped cream and whip up your own fashionably sexy creations—then let your partner "disrobe" you.

➤ **Passion fruits.** You'd be amazed at what you can do with the inside skin of a mango. Not to mention a peeled banana.

➤ **Body frosting.** Pop open a tub of cake frosting and spread it all over your lover. Or take some chocolate syrup and drizzle it on your lover. Or you can buy some specially made body frosting in great flavors like strawberry, passion fruit, and, of course, chocolate. Use the paintbrush provided with the jar, and become each other's edible work of art.

Sari Says

A movie that's bound to get you hungry for more than dinner is the beautiful Spanish film *Like Water for Chocolate* (1992). You might want to check out the book, too, by Laura Esquivel.

Your Reaction to Erotic Edibles

1. Negative: _____

2. Positive: _____

3. How can this fit into/improve your sex life? Or why won't it? _____

_____

_____

Using What You Have

You don't need sex toys, food, or erotica to enhance your sex life. If you're looking to expand your sexual horizons, there's plenty you can do with your own body parts.

Oral U.

Taking edibles one step further, oral sex is a fantastic way to give and receive pleasure. It allows you to be incredibly close to your lover and to experience a sensation that has no duplicate. However, some people feel inhibited about oral sex. The receiver may worry about his or her taste and smell, or whether the other person really wants to be doing it. The giver may be concerned about whether he or she is doing it well enough to please his or her partner.

If you are inhibited about giving or receiving oral sex, try to work on getting over your worries. Giving can be highly rewarding when you see your partner climax close up. And the sensation of receiving can be fantastic if you lay back and enjoy it. For more information on oral sex technique, see Chapter 18.

Your Reaction to Oral Sex

1. Negative: _____

2. Positive: _____

3. How can this fit into/improve your sex life? Or why won't it? _____

_____

_____

Get into Position

Following is a list and description of what I consider the most basic sexual positions for you to try. You can read about more advanced sexual positions in Chapter 17 of this book, "How to Have Sexier Sex," or check out my other book, *The Complete Idiot's Guide to Amazing Sex* (Alpha Books, 1999) for more in-depth coverage. Stretch out to get those muscles loosened up and give one or all of the following a go:

➤ **Riding High.** Just as it sounds, this position has the woman on top and the man on the bottom.

➤ **Doggy Style.** In this position, the woman is on her hands and knees and the man enters her vagina from behind.

➤ **Spoons.** With both of you lying down, you "spoon" each other (the way spoons fit together when placed on top of each other), while the man enters the woman's vagina from behind. You can also perform this position face to face with the woman parting her legs just enough for penetration.

➤ **Sitting.** Facing one another, both partners sit with their legs apart. Each person can control the thrusting by keeping their arms on the floor or bed and pushing, or by sitting close together and embracing.

➤ **Standing.** Although it can be a little tricky, the standing position is ideal for a "quickie." In order for the man to penetrate, the woman needs to be at the proper height or angle. This can be achieved by putting one leg up, or by wrapping her legs around his waist while he stands and thrusts.

Your Reaction to New Sexual Positions

1. Negative: _____

2. Positive: _____

3. How can this fit into/improve your sex life? Or why won't it? _____

_____

_____

Whatever you decide is pleasurable or uncomfortable for you is your own business. And again, never let anyone pressure or force you into performing a sexual act that you are not comfortable doing. However, I do urge you to keep an open mind and try to sort out the difference between what crosses the line for you and what simply makes you feel inhibited. We are all born with the same parts. You can't be naturally "bad" at sex. You have the potential to be a great lover—you just need to keep an open mind and shed those inhibitions that are holding you back in the sack.

The Least You Need to Know

➤ Closing your mind to other areas of sex or sexual enhancers without examining the reasons why can be holding you back from amazing sexual experiences.

➤ Learn the difference between what you are comfortable with and what you aren't—and never let anyone talk you into the latter.

➤ The best way to remain open to great sex is to clear away all inner and outer distractions, and to trust your partner.

➤ Explore areas that may add excitement to your sex life—try erotica, props and gadgets, oral sex, or simply a new sexual position or two.

Chapter 8

Developing a Sexy Attitude

In This Chapter

➤ How to power up your confidence

➤ Why being relaxed can help you appear confident

➤ Tickling the funny bone for sexual appeal

➤ How mystery can make almost anyone come hither

➤ How sexy, sensual thoughts can make you exude sex appeal

Remember back in Chapter 3, "Attitudes That Define Sexiness," I told you about the attitudes that can make you sexy? Humor, mystery, sensuality, and enjoyment of sex—all of these traits fall under the big umbrella of—that's right, you guessed it—confidence. I know, I know, you're sick of hearing about it! You are ready to scream at the top of your lungs, "Look! I'm me! I can't be all things to all people! I'm NOT every woman/man!" You want to crawl back into your comfortable zone, hunker down with a pint of Ben and Jerry's, and settle into what's familiar.

Now, now. We'll have none of that. In fact, I'm going to throw you a bone here—you may be right. You might *not* be able to master all of these qualities. Humor might not be your bag; maybe mystery is lost on you; maybe you're not the touchy-feely type. However, I'll bet you a Regis Philbin million that you've got the power to hone in on at least one of these attitudes. All you have to do is find that attitude within yourself. That's right. The secret ingredient has been in you all along. You just need to learn how to release it!

In this chapter, I'll get you all psyched up about unleashing your sexy potential through lots of exercises. First I'll help you become more confident, and then we'll zero in on your super-sexy zones so you can work it, baby. It's time to cop an attitude!

Confidence 101—the Basics

Before we get into specific attitude-enhancement exercises, let's work on the concept of confidence just a little bit more. Confidence is the foundation that you need to have as you start building toward getting sexier.

Deep Quote

"Beauty without self-confidence is less attractive than ugliness with self-confidence. If you are confident, you are beautiful."

—George Cukor

It might seem like overkill, but insecurity is something we have been weaned on in the good ol' USA. The fact of the matter is we are a country wracked by insecurities. Think about it—we always want everything we have to be bigger, better, faster, stronger. But you don't have to let that pressure get to you. So, without further ado, let's do some confidence warm-ups before diving into specific confidence "muscle" groups.

The first thing you need to do for this exercise is to create an "I like myself!" sheet. Find a picture of yourself that you like and tape it the center of a piece of paper. At the top, write "I like myself!" Make sure there's plenty of room around the picture for writing, because you are going to record the following confidence-boosters:

➤ **Make a list of all of the accomplishments in your life, no matter how ordinary you may think they seem.** For example: "I've raised a child who is well adjusted in the world," "I graduated from college," "I promised myself I'd read a book a month to keep my intellect sharp, and I've kept it up, more or less," or "I set my sights on getting promoted within three years of joining my company, and I did it!"

➤ **List your talents and skills, no matter how esoteric, and even if they are things you usually don't boast about.** It can be anything: "I am a good listener," "I am always fair in my judgments of others and don't rush into forming opinions," "I dress well," "I learned to play the guitar," or "I make great spaghetti sauce."

➤ **List the things about yourself that you think make you a good friend/ companion.** Ask your close friends or your partner to tell you three good things about yourself and write these down. For example: "I'm a good listener," "I'm generous with my friends and family," or "I'm always there for my friends."

➤ **Look in the mirror and force yourself to choose five things that you love about the way you look, no matter how small.** For example: "I think my freckles are cute," "I have really nice, friendly eyes," "I have a great butt," "I have a really attractive face," or "My skin is silky smooth."

Now, keep this somewhere handy, but private: your night table, taped inside your bathroom medicine chest, or even your sock drawer. Read this list every time you're feeling a little down or insecure. Or, if you feel like you need a big boost, make it a habit to go over your list each morning and night. Keep yourself aware at all times of the good things about yourself. Soon it will sink in: You're really a great person with qualities you should feel nothing less than confident about! You can like yourself— you can even love yourself.

Confidence 102—the Advanced Class

Okay, you sexy thing, how are feeling? A little boosted? A little better about the merit of some of your individual qualities? Good, because now we're going to take this one step further. These lists are good, but they're not quite enough. You need to put them to the test; exercise those skills to keep them sharp and make you confident in the sum of your parts.

Notice there are four items in that confidence-boosters list—just enough to give you one confidence-boosting exercise for each week of the month. Here are some weekly exercises that will help you concentrate on further upping your confidence quotient.

Week One: Climb Every Mountain

For the first confidence-booster, I asked you to make a list of all of the accomplishments in your life, no matter how small. Now I want you to add to that list. For week one, set a goal. A small goal is all you need, something that will make you feel better about yourself, no matter how silly it might seem. You have to change little things before you can change the big things.

Sunday night before you go to bed, think about what little thing you'd like to accomplish the following week. (Sunday nights are the best time to set your goals for the week ahead. On Monday morning you'll probably be rushing around getting ready for work or getting the kids off to school.) Write down your goal and then, beneath it, add some ideas for how to accomplish it. For instance:

Deep Quote

"No one can make you feel inferior without your consent."

—Eleanor Roosevelt

Joe Doe's or Jane Doe's Goal for the Week of January 1, 2000:

Goal: *To break out of my same-old clothes rut and look a little more appealing and less dowdy.*

Ways to accomplish this goal:

1. *Throw out at least five items from my closet that I haven't worn in over a month.*

2. *Think about colors that really bring out my eyes, accentuate my hair color, skin color, etc.*

3. *Plan and try on my outfits ahead of time so that I don't feel rushed or insecure about what I have on.*

4. *Add some new, affordable accents to brighten up the same-old duds—a new tie, a new scarf, etc.*

5. *Wear my clothes with confidence—be conscious of posture, body language, etc. I am what I project.*

End-of-Week Progress Report:

Did I accomplish my goal?

Yes! I feel much better about my style now, since I did most of the things on my list.

What else could I do to continue what I accomplished this week?

I can put away my clothes each week, send clothes to the dry cleaner when needed, and be more careful about what I buy when I go shopping for clothes and accessories.

You can mimic this list with your own personal goal for the upcoming week.

Week Two: Your Own Personal Talent Show

For week two, you're going to concentrate on honing your talents or finding new ones! No, you don't need to run around tapping people on the shoulder, shouting, "Look what I can do!" But you can subtly (or not so subtly, if you're feeling brave) put those talents on display.

For instance, if you think you're a good listener, look for opportunities during the week to use this skill, whether it be with a friend who needs an ear, a colleague who wants to bounce something off you, or a family member who just needs to blow off steam. If there is a talent you have that you are shy about, try to find ways to get out there and use it. Let's say you have a nice singing voice. You could check out your local community or church organizations to see if there's a choral group you could get involved with (which also is a great way to meet some new people!).

Sari Says

Record your "month of sexy confidence" in a private date book or journal. Keep track of what your goal is and the daily things you do to try to achieve that goal.

84

If you're up for a real challenge, try picking up some *new* talents. Maybe golf? Get out on that course, get some tips from the house pro, and start putting. Do you wish you were better at expressing your thoughts in front of others? Concentrate on making at least one point during a meeting or while hanging out with a group of your friends.

Use the following worksheet as a guide to help you hone your talents.

Talent Enhancer Worksheet

Talent I want to show off: _____

Or

Talent I want to improve on: _____

Things I can do to use/improve on my talent this week:

1. _____

2. _____

3. _____

4. _____

5. _____

Week Three: A Friend in Need

What's so sexy about being a great friend? That's easy—it's all about human relationships, baby. If you know how to be a good friend, you can also be a good lover. No, this doesn't mean you should go out and have sex with your friends! It means that the qualities that others admire in you and that you like about yourself translate well into romantic relationships: being kind, thoughtful, and generous.

During this third week, you're going to use your good-friend qualities on your significant other or, if you're not attached, on someone who you'd like to be with. Buy the object of your desire a cup of coffee, share your sandwich, and listen intently to what he or she has to say. Whatever it is, do your deed unselfishly without the expectation of getting something in return. Not only will this show the object of your desire that you are someone he or she wants to get to know better, it will make you feel pretty good!

Week Four: Get Over It!

Last but not least, to be more confident, you need to get over negative ideas that you may have about yourself, including your appearance, and learn to not be so hard on yourself when things don't go just right.

For this week, every time you feel like something went wrong and you start to blame yourself, write it down. Then write down why you are really not to blame for what's happened. Also, write down things that make you feel bad about yourself, and then write down how you can catch yourself when you start feeling bad. You will be replacing negative self-talk with positive self-talk.

Here's an example of the type of things you can write each day this week:

It's not my fault:

➤ I felt like it was my fault when *my daughter forgot to bring her lunch bag to school.* But it really wasn't my fault, because *she is 16 years old, and she should be more responsible.*

➤ I feel like it was all my fault when *I think about the fact that my ex-girlfriend broke up with me.* But it really wasn't my fault, because *it takes two people to create a good relationship and we were not right for each other.*

I am terrific:

➤ I feel like I am *stupid when people talk about politics and business.* But I really am *smart, just about other topics.*

➤ I feel like I am ugly, *when I am around lots of people who are better looking.* But I really am *attractive, just in an offbeat way.*

Now, you try. Fill in the following blanks with two of each for each day of the week so you can start feeling better about yourself.

It's not my fault:

➤ I felt like it was my fault when _____

_____

But it really wasn't my fault, because _____

_____

➤ I felt like it was my fault when_____

_____

But it really wasn't my fault, because _____

_____

I am terrific:

➤ I feel like I (something negative) _____

_____

But I really am (the positive of that) _____

_____

➤ I feel like I (something negative) _____

_____

But I really am (the positive of that) _____

_____

How to Beam with Self-Esteem

Now that you know how to boost your confidence, you have to work on looking confident. A bit of this has to do with what your body language says and what you wear, so read Chapters 10, "Body Talk: Using Sexy Body Language," and 11, "Dressing Sexy." But looking confident has more to do with what's going on inside your mind.

Remember: In *The Wizard of Oz,* the Cowardly Lion had the nerve all along, he just didn't know it. You don't need some phony wizard to unleash your confidence. You can do it yourself by simply acting confident. This might sound a lot harder than you think, but there's a secret I'm going to let you in on. Ready? *Relax.* That's it. Just relax. If you're thinking too hard about being confident, you'll probably seem like you're trying too hard to be confident.

Here's an exercise I want you to try. Stand in front of a mirror. Look at yourself for a sec with a blank thought in your head, keeping your mind clear of any thoughts (especially negative ones!). Think: I am looking at myself, big whoop.

Now, think of something really funny that happened to you, or something that you saw that cracked you up. Maybe it was when your best friend did a pratfall over your dog, some really funny bit that you saw on *Letterman,* or a dirty joke that your buddy told you. Whatever it is, think about it until you start laughing. Let yourself go—I know you can do it. There. Was that laughter I saw? Did you notice that just before you started cracking up, your whole face seemed to relax? You looked natural and calm. This is the way you want to look if you feel intimidated when you need to feel confident.

If you want to appear confident, put yourself in a playful mood, the way you did in this exercise. Even if you are just walking down the street. If you are bouncing down the street, smiling, and

Deep Quote

"There came a time when the risk to remain tight in the bud was more painful than the risk it took to blossom."

—Anaïs Nin

Deep Quote

"Sex appeal is 50 percent what you've got and 50 percent what people think you've got."

—Sophia Loren

observing the people around you, you will come across as happy and spontaneous. If you're a woman, you may worry that if you appear too open and accessible, you may attract a guy who is looking to take advantage of you because your guard is seemingly down. The fact is that if you appear fearful and withdrawn, you may be *more* likely to get negative attention. It's okay to be relaxed and be yourself—just make sure you stay alert, feel empowered, and allow your instincts to guide your comfort level.

To relax and show your confidence, try some of the following:

➤ **Think about a place where you feel totally comfortable and happy.** It could be your living room, your favorite coffee shop, a park, your car, or really anywhere you feel confident enough to relax and be yourself. Whenever you are in a situation or place where you feel out of sorts, bring up a mental picture of "your place" and the way you feel when you are there. In order to look relaxed you have to feel relaxed. Thinking of an environment that you are used to can calm you.

➤ **When you are in public, don't primp.** No matter how messy you may think your hair looks, don't whip out a comb to fix it. Don't check your face in your pocket mirror every 15 minutes. Stop fidgeting—you look fine! If you start tugging and poking at yourself in public you'll look insecure. Be sure of yourself. Or, if you must, excuse yourself to go to the bathroom and check it all out in the mirror. Just don't let anyone know.

➤ **Say positive things about yourself.** Too often people are too modest about themselves. Or worse, self-deprecating. Of course, you don't want to sound like you're totally conceited and self-absorbed, but you do want to sound like you are proud of yourself and happy with yourself.

Flirt Alert

Too many people lose self-confidence because they are overly critical of themselves or self-deprecating. If you think of negative things about yourself before you think of positive things, you need a major attitude adjustment. Stop the negative self-talk, and learn to love yourself.

Sexiness Takes More Than Confidence

Now that you've had all this great confidence prep, my dear reader, it's time to focus on honing the other sexy attitudes we touched on in Chapter 3: humor, mystery, sensuality, and enjoyment of sex. Even if you don't think that all of these areas are up your alley, read each of them anyway. You never know when they might come in handy.

Funny Strange, or Funny Ha-Ha?

Did you hear the one about the nun, the mule, and the dildo? I hope not, because that sounds like the kind of joke that is offensive rather than sexy.

You learned in Chapter 3 how humor can be sexy. But there are different types of humor, and not everyone finds them all funny. The safest best is to stick with good, clean fun. Avoid crass, low-brow humor at all costs—it's better to keep your lip zipped if you can't think of anything amusing to say rather than risk offending someone.

It might be fun to tell dirty jokes to your pals when you're sitting around drinking a beer. But if you want to project an image of funny sexiness, then lay off the dirty jokes, and try some flirty, sexy talk instead.

Here are some examples of ways you can sound sexy without being a potty mouth:

➤ **Tell a funny story about something that happened to you during the day.** Use cues to get your audience to participate—whether that audience is one person or ten. Ask questions like, "Can you guess what happened next?" or "What do you think he/she said?"

➤ **Retell a funny scene from a movie.** If you find that others know it, don't clam up or be selfish—let them join in and tell it with you. There's nothing like making others feel included and laughing together.

➤ **Be animated when you talk to make funny stories come alive.** Don't be afraid to act out the story if using physical gestures or movements will add to the punch.

➤ **Keep a yarn going.** If someone tells a story that reminds you of something funny, you've got the perfect opener: "Oh, that reminds me of a really funny story!"

➤ **Use a little poetic license and exaggerate just a bit.** This doesn't mean lie, but sometimes good stories are a little exaggerated for entertainment value. Feel free to spice it up a little.

Deep Quote

"Among those whom I like or admire, I can find no common denominator, but among those whom I love, I can: All of them make me laugh."

—W. H. Auden

Finally, exercise caution when trying out sexual jokes. They can constitute sexual harassment if they are told in the workplace or to strangers. Be careful about how you treat people. Say overtly sexy things, including jokes, only if you know the person, you think that he or she will appreciate it, and it is in the right environment.

Silent and Mysterious

Sexiness is not all laughs and lingerie. It's also about creating a sense of mystique. In Chapter 3, we talked a little about understanding what mystique is, and some films that give good examples of actors and actresses with this quality. But now we're going to take this quality off the silver screen and into the real world.

Imagine that you're at a party and you notice a tall dark stranger. If the person comes right up to you and starts talking, that's cool. But if the person lingers around the room, occasionally throwing furtive glances your way, doesn't it make you curious? Does it make you play a sort of "cat and mouse" game with the mysterious stranger, trying to catch his or her eye without seeming obvious? Does it suddenly make a boring party very, very interesting? Most of all, isn't it sexy?

There is something about desiring someone that enhances that desire for that person. What I mean is, if you want to entice someone, the person has to want to get to know you. The process will have the person riveted if you reveal yourself gradually.

Don't Share It All

Of course, being mysterious doesn't mean being untruthful. You must still be honest, but that does not mean that you must disclose everything about yourself immediately. Here are some things not to talk about, at least not right away:

➤ Your ex, especially sex with your ex

➤ The disappointments you face at work

➤ Problems with your family

➤ Whether your outfit looks good or not

➤ Your confusion or anxiety about your future

➤ What you talk about in therapy

➤ That you weren't always the way you are now

Poise and Grace Win First Place

Besides just knowing when to not talk, having a sense of mystery is also about how you look and move. There is something about looking "sultry" that means more than just looking sexy. Here are some things it also means:

➤ Making prolonged eye contact, mixed with subtle glances.

➤ Walking slowly, consciously.

➤ Standing up straight and tall.

➤ Smiling or grinning, rather than laughing.

➤ Speaking with a calm deep voice.

➤ Wearing dark solid colors, such as navy, deep jewel tones, and, of course, black.

➤ Being well groomed in a well-put-together outfit.

➤ Having a trademark item of clothing or accessory, like a hat or scarf. Everyone will wonder why you wear that trademark item, and that's the point: making people wonder about you.

If you really want to heighten the air of mystery around you, you can try a few parlor tricks. Leave the party a little early, but pass your phone number to the person you've been making eye contact with all night with a note that says, "Must leave, but would like to talk sometime—call me." You could also try doing a little "touch and go"—brush up against the person or get close a few times, then quickly disappear, leaving him or her wondering where you ran off to.

Remember, to come across as mysteriously sexy and exude an air of quiet confidence, you need to block out the insecure part of you. Someone who appears to be mysterious in a sexy way is someone who looks calm, mature, and extremely sure of him- or herself.

Exuding Sensuality

Showing off an attitude of sensuality means that you have sexual charms, without immediately making someone think of S-E-X. This is where the flirtatious, romantic, and natural styles come in much more than the erotic style.

In order to show off your sensuality, do things like the following:

➤ Take baths instead of showers.

➤ Always have fresh flowers at home.

➤ Wear clothes that look soft and inviting.

➤ Smile and laugh sweetly.

➤ Be relaxed, still, and calm.

➤ Be a friend and confidant to a lover.

➤ Use the power of touch.

Speaking of touch, it may be one of the best ways to be sensual. Just a gesture, like touching someone's hair or brushing his or her cheek, can send shivers down the spine. Giving a back massage or spontaneously reaching for someone's hand while

Flirt Alert

Be mysterious, not shady. If someone you like asks you direct questions, answer them. You don't have to tell everything (maintain some mystique), but tell enough that the person won't think you are rude, aloof, or avoiding talking about yourself.

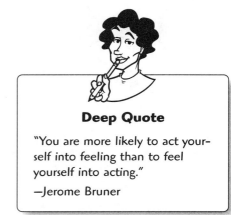

Deep Quote

"You are more likely to act yourself into feeling than to feel yourself into acting."
—Jerome Bruner

walking goes even further. If you enjoy and are comfortable with touch, this is a great asset to coming across as sensual—and that's so sexy.

Photo by The Picture Book.

There are other things you can do to bring out your sensuality. Let's go back to the mirror for a minute, but this time, instead of funny thoughts, focus on sensual thoughts. If you are at a loss for what to think about, here are some suggestions to put you in a sexy frame of mind:

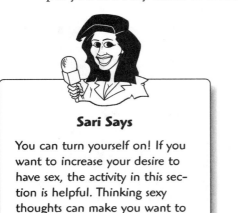

Sari Says

You can turn yourself on! If you want to increase your desire to have sex, the activity in this section is helpful. Thinking sexy thoughts can make you want to have sex.

➤ How it feels when someone runs his or her finger tips on your thigh, teasing you, not quite touching your genitals.

➤ What you feel like when you get dressed in sexy underwear. Imagine yourself slowly putting it on.

➤ A moment in sex that you really enjoyed. Imagine that you are feeling it again right now.

➤ What your lover looks like when he or she looks the sexiest. Maybe think about a part of his or her body, or a way he or she moves.

If you want to look sultry, *think* sexy!

For the Love of Sex

Besides confidence, humor, mystery, and sensuality, another sexy attitude is having an enjoyment of sex. The best way to project this attitude is by having a positive outlook on sexuality.

In Chapter 7, "Getting Over Inhibitions About Sex," you learned about how to get over your sexual inhibitions. That is the first step in being positive about sex. Then you should try to determine if you feel good about your current sex life, and if not, what you are willing to do to improve it.

Answer the following questions to help examine your attitudes about sex:

1. Who was the first person you remember talking with about sex? How did you feel about that conversation?

2. How did you feel when you got your very first period (for women), or had your first wet dream (for men)? Did you confide in anyone, and how did this person make you feel?

3. Growing up, did you have someone to talk to when you had questions about sex? How did this person make you feel?

4. What values about sex did your religion give you? Were those positive or in any way helpful to you?

5. What values did your parents give you about sex? Did that make you feel good about your sexuality?

6. When did you first experience sexual feelings toward someone else? How did you feel about that?

7. Why did you have sex the first time? Do you think that was a good reason?

8. Does your body image hold you back from enjoying sex? Are you willing to work on improving the way you feel about your body exactly the way it is now?

9. Do you feel as if sex is fun and creative and that you can express yourself during sex? Are you willing to explore what can make the most fun for you?

10. Have you had sexual problems that have interfered with your sex life recently? Have you received help?

Sari Says

Sex therapists are specially trained to help you improve your attitudes toward sex, and improve your sex life. You can find one by getting in touch with the American Association of Sex Educators, Counselors, and Therapists (see Appendix C, "Resources").

To have a sexy outlook, you need to come to terms with negative attitudes about sex that were perpetuated in your childhood. Then you need to deal with disappointments about sex that you've had as an adult. Finally, you need to seek help if you have sexual problems. If you have a negative attitude about sex that is getting in the way of your expressing your sexiness, see a sex therapist.

To project an attitude of being comfortable with sex, you really must be comfortable with it. If you're not, then what would happened when your sexy charms lead you into the bedroom, and you just don't know what to do once you're there? Make sure that you understand and appreciate your sexuality in order to be sexy.

The Least You Need to Know

➤ Remembering great things about yourself can increase your confidence.

➤ Thinking happy thoughts can make you appear more confident.

➤ Sexy thoughts can make you look and feel sexy.

➤ Acting quiet and mysterious can be seductive and sexy.

➤ It is imperative that you feel comfortable with your sexuality in order to be sexy.

Sexy at Any Age!

In This Chapter

➤ Feeling great about getting older

➤ How staying fit can keep you looking sexy at any age

➤ Dressing to look youthful no matter how old you are

➤ Having sexy sex in your golden years

Have you heard the slogan, "I'm not going to age gracefully—I'm going to fight it every step of the way?" Well, any man or woman who adopts that attitude will certainly be interested in this chapter.

In our society the media put so much emphasis on youth as beauty that growing older is something many people dread. The stress over getting older usually starts around age 40, and for some people, it gets worse after each milestone year passes: 50, 60, 70. One of the biggest myths about aging is that one's sexiness falls away with each birthday. But nothing could be farther from the truth. Age is a stage of mind. You can be a vibrant, tantalizing, *sexy* human being no matter what your age!

You're Not Getting Older, You're Getting Better

The 40th anniversary issue of *Playboy* magazine featured layouts of former Playmates, then and now. For all to see were women over 50 years old, Playmates from the first decade of the magazine. They exhibited just as much pride in their bodies now as they had when they were originally in *Playboy* when they were in their 20s.

In fact, it's not just on anniversaries when *Playboy* celebrates older women. In the past few years, the magazine's cover models have included Nancy Sinatra at age 55, Farrah Fawcett at age 48, and Shari Belefonte at age 45. It's testament to the fact that once someone is sexy, he or she can always look sexy.

It used to be our society dictated that only youth was valued and considered sexy. However, these days it is much more accepted that people of any age can be seen as sexy. Celebrity women including Oprah, Sela Ward, and Susan Sarandon have been quite vocal in assuring women that they can be sexy at any age. Famous men such as Sean Connery and Paul Newman have shown that men can also stay sexy as they age (something that has traditionally been more accepted in our society).

When it comes right down to it, it's not just that with age it is possible to still be sexy. In fact, getting older can mean that you actually get *sexier*. If you've always enjoyed flirting, dressing sexy, demonstrating sexy body language, and copping a sexy attitude, then your sexiness could have increased with your experience. On the other hand, if you haven't been so sexy all your life, then maybe you need a few more lessons about sexy styles and how they relate to aging. That's where this chapter can help.

Mature, Fit, and Happy

Do you remember when you first noticed wrinkles at the corners of your eyes, when your laugh lines first set in, or when you plucked your first gray hair? You may have felt fear or helplessness when you reached those firsts. But after a while, aging just becomes a way of life. And after all, it *is* part of life—we all do it.

For women, the first hurtle to adjusting to aging may be dealing with *menopause*. Their bodies have a tendency to gain weight more easily, and they may feel uncomfortable with hot flashes and other symptoms. The fact is that women can get past the discomfort of this natural process, and break out their sexiness. In fact, for many women menopause has a positive effect on their sex life, since they can no longer get pregnant from sex. Not having to use birth control can make them feel free and sexy.

Deep Quote

"No spring nor summer beauty hath such grace,
As I have seen in one autumnal face.
If we love things long sought, age is a thing
Which we are 50 years in coming passing."

—John Donne

Lusty Lingo

Menopause is the cessation of menstruation in women and the natural decline in female sex hormones, which usually occurs for most women during a two-year period starting as early as age 35 or as late as age 60.

For men, losing their hair and gaining a gut can have a large effect on their self-esteem. Just as women can, men can also find ways to boost their image and work towards sexiness. Or perhaps I should say, workout toward sexiness.

The best way for women and men to deal with these changes is for them to try to stay fit. Exercise makes people look and feel sexier.

To stay in shape, try …

➤ **Walking.** Whether it is on the treadmill, around your block, or at the mall, walking will keep you fit and healthy.

➤ **Swimming.** It does not put a strain on your aging joints, and feels great, too. Many gyms offer water aerobics classes; give them a try.

➤ **Low-impact aerobics.** Grooving to the funky beat not only can help you stay in shape, it can also be tons of fun. Along with elevating your heart rate, it can also elevate your mood.

➤ **Yoga, tai chi, or pilates.** For poise, balance, and strength these forms of fitness can help your body get lean and help your mind stay clear, calm, and focused.

Give all these types of exercise a try to see which you like the best. Then start a regular exercise program, combined with a healthy diet. In addition to keeping you fit and healthy, you'll be surprised at how good exercise makes you feel about yourself!

Keeping Up Appearances

How can one 70-year-old look 70, and another look 50? Is it genetic? Could be. Plastic surgery? Maybe. But I bet that 9 times out of 10, it stems from attitude. The 70-year-old who plays tennis every day, reads the most current books, and even surfs the Net gets a jump on his or her peers with a more contemporary attitude. That outlook affects the way this person dresses and carries him- or herself. This energetic and up-to-date 70-year-old still feels confident about letting his or her sexiness shining through.

Sexy Stats

Because men die an average of eight years before women, many widows are looking for new sex partners. Eighty percent of widowers remarry. Women, on the other hand, remarry in far smaller numbers, partly because there are fewer available men their age.

Deep Quote

"To resist the frigidity of old age, one must combine the body, the mind, and the heart. And to keep these in parallel vigor one must exercise, study, and love."

—Bonstettin

If you want to keep up your sexy appearance for years to come, here are some things that can help:

➤ **Get naked.** Look at your nude body in the mirror, and instead of focusing on all the things that have aged, see how beautiful you are. Take note of your positive attributes.

➤ **Dress fashionably.** I don't mean you should raid your children's or your grandchildren's closets, but do keep up with the latest styles. Ask for help at a major department store. The sales people can show you the newest looks and help you find the styles that look best on you.

➤ **Get a great hairstyle.** Cut and color can take years off your look. Find a hairstylist who knows how to do tasteful, easy-care styles that will bring out your sexy spirit.

Sari Says

You don't have to look at magazines that only feature young models to get ideas for current clothing styles. In fact, if you don't want to see images of young perfect bodies, then forgo perusing *Cosmo* and *Glamour*. Today, you can find great fashion magazines aimed at a more mature crowd, such as *More* or *Redbook*.

Men and women who keep up with the styles and exercise to stay fit feel better about their bodies, and that means feeling better about aging in general. It's really true: You're not getting older, you're getting better!

Sari Says

If you have grandchildren who are teens or adults, or adult children, ask them to help you get into the youthful swing of things. Go shopping with them to choose fashionable, current outfits for your wardrobe. Ask your child or grandchild to teach you how to use a computer and surf the Net. Find out what books they recommend from their recent reading list. Listen to the kind of music they like, or watch their favorite TV shows with them.

It's All in Your Head

Aging is not only about what is going on with your good ol' body. It's also about what's going on upstairs. Your thoughts about aging greatly affect how you age. In order to be sexy at an older age, you have to raise your self-esteem and your self-confidence. That comes from some things that don't even have to do with sex, like the following:

➤ **Getting a job or doing volunteer work.** Helping others will make you feel better about yourself. Realizing that others value your skills is a huge self-esteem booster.

➤ **Making some younger friends.** Maybe you won't really care when they talk about the hot new MTV video, but, then again, maybe they can turn you on to new ideas.

➤ **Listening to music.** Try to find new pop music, or at least listen to your old faves. But whatever it is, music will energize you and make you feel good all over.

➤ **Keeping up with technology.** You're never too old to get a computer and explore the Internet. You can even bypass getting a computer, and sign up with a Web provider that uses only your television set. Once you learn how to go online, you'll love being able to send and receive e-mail, especially if your children and grandchildren are also online.

➤ **If you're single, going on dates.** Older people on the dating scene experience the same hopes, fears, and excitement as younger people do. Don't let your age get in the way of meeting new people. Ask friends to introduce you to people, or go to social gatherings and flirt to the point that you can ask someone out yourself. Then review Chapter 14, "Sexy Dates," for some creative, fun date ideas.

Sexy Stats

More and more older people are discovering the vast wealth of information online. In fact, seniors age 60 and over make up the fastest growing group on the Internet.

Sexy Stats

According to the Hite Report, 57 percent of men between the ages of 61 and 75 said that their desire for sex either remained steady or increased with age. When asked how age affected their enjoyment of sex, only 11 percent reported decreased satisfaction. Similar results were reported for women.

All of these things will help you keep up a confident attitude in general. For more tips, review Chapters 3, "Attitudes That Define Sexiness," and 8, "Developing a Sexy Attitude." And remember, the advice in this book applies to people of all ages. You have the same needs and desires to be sexy, so keep that sexy attitude alive forever.

Sexy Sex at Any Age

When you were young maybe you never wanted to imagine your parents or grand-parents having sex. But now that you are getting older, you know that seniors can have amazing sexy sex just as well as young people can; some say even better.

Of course, there are some ways that you can improve your aging sex life:

➤ **If you need extra lubrication, use it.** After menopause many women have problems with vaginal lubrication. There are many over-the-counter lubricants that are perfect to make sex more comfortable and fun. Try a brand like Astro Glide or KY-Liquid.

Lusty Lingo

Impotence is the inability of a man to get or maintain an erection. It is also called erectile dysfunction.

Deep Quote

"Sex is a very important part of my life. Having the right partner, as I do, means a lot. Sex keeps me young. The more you want it, the more youthful you become."

—Dick Clark

➤ **Enjoy the spontaneity of not having to use birth control, if you are a post-menopausal woman.** To make sure that you can no longer get pregnant, see your doctor, who may recommend that you still use birth control for 12 months after your last period, just to be sure. Of course, you will still want to use condoms for disease protection. Age does not deter AIDS and other sexually transmitted diseases.

➤ **If you have trouble getting a firm erection, get help.** If an aging man is *impotent*, then he should see a doctor or a sex therapist. If the problem is physical, he can easily get help in the form of a pump that is used to bring blood flow into the penis to get the erection going. Or he can get help in the shape of a little blue pill: The drug Viagra works for some men by increasing blood flow to the penis. However, Viagra does not work for all men, and can even have life-threatening side effects for some. Consult your doctor.

➤ **Change sex positions if you need to.** If you are experiencing aches and pains due to aging, or any of the illnesses or surgeries that may come along in older age, then you shouldn't be trying most of the wild sex positions like the ones in Chapter 18, "Super Sexy Sex." You might be better off in restful sex positions, like sitting face to face. However, you can still have fun experimenting.

➤ **Use more loving physical gestures.** Hold hands, put your arms around each other, hug, snuggle, and kiss. Those sexy, loving ways of being physical become much more important during old age. People of every age need physical affection. Yet if sexual activity is decreased due to old age, then the desire for affection may become ever greater.

➤ **Create steamy moments.** At any age, you need to create sexy moments. Get into candlelight, champagne, and lingerie, no matter what your age.

Photo by Barbara Singer.

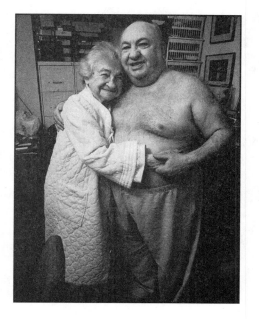

Golden age men and women can stay sexy, as long as they think sexy, and act sexy. There is no age limit to sexiness!

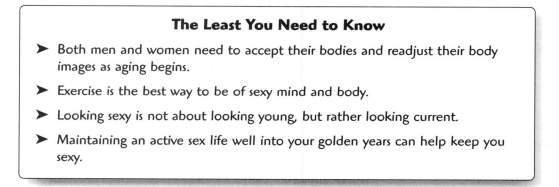

The Least You Need to Know

➤ Both men and women need to accept their bodies and readjust their body images as aging begins.

➤ Exercise is the best way to be of sexy mind and body.

➤ Looking sexy is not about looking young, but rather looking current.

➤ Maintaining an active sex life well into your golden years can help keep you sexy.

Body Talk: Using Sexy Body Language

In This Chapter

➤ Picking up on body language cues to tell if someone is attracted to you

➤ Using your body to express your interest in someone

➤ Understanding what occurs during nonverbal communication

➤ Personal space: How close is too close?

➤ Using your eyes and smile to signal interest

➤ Mirroring each other's body language

Imagine you're at a party and you see a man walk into the room (or if you're a man, reverse this scenario and imagine you see an attractive woman). Aware that your eyes are upon him, he moves briskly through the crowd toward you. He is standing tall, shoulders back, head held high. You think he is quite attractive. You catch his eye, grin, then glance away. You look again, and then establish eye contact as the stranger approaches you. He smiles, extends a hand, and introduces himself. While you talk, you cock your head slightly, moisten your lips with your tongue, and then smile. You both move closer to each other. When you gesture, your arm casually brushes against his. He smiles, then runs his fingers through his hair.

Any words that were spoken in that scenario are far less important than the body language of seduction. Postures, movements, gestures, smiles, and eye contact speak volumes. You can learn to use body language to help increase your sexual attractiveness.

And you can learn to understand which nonverbal cues signal that someone is sexually attracted to you. The intricate dance of body language can sweep someone off his or her feet. So, as Olivia Newton-John sang in "Let's Get Physical," "Let me hear your body talk!"

What Is Body Language?

Generally, when people first meet, they do not blurt out their honest feelings about each other. Sure, sometimes you can say flat out, "I find you very attractive." However, most of the time when you first meet someone, it would seem inappropriate if you just said something like that. That's where *body language* comes in. It can be more revealing than what someone actually says, or it can express what is unspoken. It is usually unconscious, involuntary, and automatic—but if you think about it, you can learn to use it intentionally.

Lusty Lingo

Body language is the way people express themselves nonverbally through facial movements, gestures, posture, and eye movement. It's how people show their feelings of comfort or insecurity, power or submission, interest or indifference, and attractiveness or awkwardness. **Kinesics** is the scientific study of body language.

The scientific study of body language, or *kinesics,* was pioneered in 1952 by anthropologist Dr. Ray Birdwhistell. Kinesics has become an important area of study, because understanding body language can help people's relationships in so many ways—from job interviews to courtroom defenses to singles-bar flirtations!

Now that you know that body language is a fact of life, you need to learn the specifics about how to understand others' body language and how to make your body language sexy! If you become aware of how you move, where you look, how you gesture, and how you smile, then you can find ways to entice someone using the power of your body.

The Sequence of Body Language for Love

When two people are attracted to each other, their bodies take over and follow a pattern that illustrates their attraction. Many research studies have found that most people follow a similar sequence. Think about the scene at that party that I mentioned at the beginning of this chapter. In a setting like that, the most common ways that people's body language shows their interest are in the following order:

1. Establishing intimate space

2. Holding their bodies erect with their chests out

3. Preening themselves, such as fixing their hair

4. Smiling

5. "Accidentally" touching the other person

6. Making eye contact and holding each other's gaze

7. Cocking their heads

8. Moving their legs toward each other

9. Pointing a finger toward each other

10. Mirroring each other's movements

In the following sections, I'll explain how you can recognize and perform each step of this dance of love.

Sari Says

Did you believe that men usually make the first move? Guess again! According to research by sexologist Timothy Perper, women most often make the first eye contact, although men most often make the initial approach.

A Space to Call Your Own

Have you ever noticed that when you like someone and are generally friendly with that person, you don't mind (or you might not even notice) if he or she stands quite close to you? But if you dislike someone and that person stands very close to you, you may feel that your space is being invaded. We all have an invisible boundary directly surrounding us that is our *personal space.*

Photo by Marc Tauss.

In the 1950s, researcher Edward Hall coined the term *proxemics* as the science behind how and why we define the territory around us. The amount of space around people makes them feel either more relaxed or anxious. Proxemics research found that the most common reason why a person allows someone into his or her personal space is sexual attraction.

When people are attracted to each other one of the first things they do is enter each other's personal space. First, by standing side-by-side, then eventually moving face-to-face. If you are attracted to someone and you want to begin sexy body language, the first thing you need to do is to move closer to that person. But how close is close enough, and how close is too close?

People perceive a distance that is appropriate for the relationship they have, which nonverbally defines how they feel about the person. If they feel the same way about each other, they will automatically position themselves with a mutually accepted amount of space between them. If one of them is more interested in the other, then one might move in closer than the other, and they may become conscious of their space issues. The person who disagrees with the other's feelings, will usually nonverbally and often unconsciously, change the distance between them. (If they are fighting and one gets too close, the other person might actually say, "Get out of my face.")

Research has estimated the distances that people leave around them depending on who their interacting with. Personal space seems to range from about two to four feet. This is the typical amount of space that most people leave between themselves and friends and family members if they are standing up and having a typical conversation. *Social space* is a larger range of 4 to 10 feet, and that is the space most people leave between business associates and strangers in public areas (at a bus stop, for instance). Finally, *intimate space* is about six inches to two feet and probably includes touching, whispering, or hugging.

If someone who you don't like (or someone with whom you don't have a close personal relationship) stands in your intimate space, then you would back away, trying to regain your social space. Or you may

Lusty Lingo

Personal space is the area that immediately surrounds a person, two to four feet. **Proxemics** is the study of how the space around us affects us. **Social space** is further apart, 4 to 10 feet. **Intimate space** is defined as quite close together, six inches to two feet.

Sari Says

Personal space differs in different cultures. In Saudi Arabia you might find yourself nose to nose with a business associate because, in that country, social space equates to our intimate space. If you were in the Netherlands, you would find that people stand farther apart, and you would be the one moving in on others, because their personal space equates to our social space.

even find yourself turning your back to avoid having the other person invade your invisible boundary for intimate space. Nothing is less sexy than invading someone's space!

If you want to get closer to someone you are attracted to, do the following:

➤ When you approach someone's personal space, move with grace and poise. Think of an image from an old movie like Cary Grant approaching Deborah Kerr in *An Affair to Remember* or Audrey Hepburn gliding across the floor toward Humphrey Bogart in *Sabrina*. Stand tall, proud, chest out, shoulders back, and head high.

➤ As you move into the person's space, at first approach from a 45-degree angle, rather than head on. This makes others feel more comfortable.

➤ As you talk for a few minutes, assess if this person is as interested in you as you are in him or her so that you can move a bit closer.

Be ready to move away, just in case. If not, you can move to the next step: body positioning.

Body Posture and Positioning

After the initial approach, the next step in body language is posturing your body to show interest. The most appealing way seems to be displaying your best features, using "open" body language, and mirroring the other person (which I'll talk more about a little later).

First of all, displaying your best features means that you will be facing the person, standing tall, with your chest out and head up. Think about the way a bird puffs out its chest to attract the attention of a potential mate. You don't have to strut around like a bird, but you should try to look proud as a peacock. (Yes, that's how the expression was coined!)

Sexy Stats

Based on an estimation of many research studies, we know that at least 70 percent of all communication is nonverbal communication. That means that on average, a person may give hundreds of thousands of nonverbal cues a day.

Legs and Feet

Observing the feet is one of the best ways to gauge if someone is interested in you. People unconsciously angle their legs and feet toward someone they are interested in. Look where the feet are pointing, and that could be an indication of where the person wants to go. Feet pointed toward the door, away from you, is not a good sign. Feet pointed toward you is promising.

If you want to attract someone, the way you move your legs may be key. Crossing and uncrossing of legs is thought to be a seductive way to draw attention to the genitals. However, if someone repeatedly crosses or uncrosses his or her legs, this may be a sign of agitation, much like when a person swings a leg or taps a foot.

Arms and Hands

When someone is interested in you, his or her hands are most often relaxed and they will often point toward you. To use your body language to show that you are interested in someone, you can allow your hand to extend toward the person. I don't mean pointing "I want you!" like Uncle Sam. Instead, place your hand in a practically undetectable way: If you are sitting at a table, rest your hand on the table (palm down) so that your hand is aimed at the person.

There are some times when casual finger pointing is used to show sexual attraction. Especially when casual finger pointing emphasizes the genitals. A person could place three fingers of his or her hand in his or her front jeans pocket, and leave the index finger or thumb out of the pocket, casually pointing toward his or her crotch. Or someone could hang his thumb in his belt loop and point all four fingers toward his crotch. This evokes an image of a sexy cowboy or rebel, like John Wayne or James Dean.

Photo by Christopher Wadsworth.

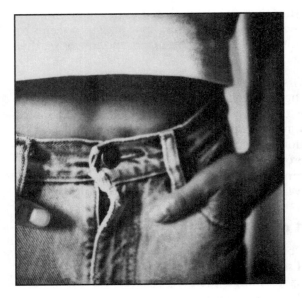

Tightly clenched hands, drumming the fingers, biting the nails, rubbing or wringing the hands, or rubbing the back of the neck are signs that someone is uncomfortable or agitated. That's not sexy! Also, when someone is not interested, the person may try to put a physical barrier between the two of you. It could be something large, like standing behind a chair, or something more subtle, like holding a drink up near his or her face. When someone is trying to be sexy towards you, the person would put the drink down. Or, to be even sexier, the person may gently circle the rim of the glass with a finger.

Crossed arms are often a sign that someone is not interested in you, or a good way for you to send someone the signal that you are not interested in him or her. Crossing your arms does a couple of things. First, it covers your chest. Since a protruding chest is a sexual sign of attraction in both men and women, covering the chest indicates a person's disinterest in showing you a sexual signal. Second, it shuts off your personal space, as if you are holding yourself away from the other person by crossing your arms.

Also, preening behavior—a man straightening his tie or a woman brushing the hair out of her eyes—occurs when a couple is flirting. Rather than being a sign of fidgeting, it is more a sign of sexual attraction. Similarly, watch for "accidental" touching, which may be the greatest sign of sexual attraction. It is totally sexy to touch someone when you gesture, or to momentarily brush up against the person to bridge the physical gap, and show your interest.

Flirt Alert

Sometimes body language may not mean what you think. For example, if someone has his or her arms crossed, you might think that this is defensive posture, showing protection and no sexual interest. However, maybe it's just cold in the room, and crossing his or her arms helps the person feel warmer. Consider the obvious before you jump to conclusions.

The Eyes Have It

"You have beautiful eyes!" It might sound like a classic pickup line, but in fact, the eyes are the features that most people notice first when they look at someone they are attracted to. The eyes carry much allure. You communicate thoughts with each look. Sometimes your looks may be intentional—other times, you can't control what your eyes reveal. The eyes confess the secrets of the heart.

Here are some ways that you can decipher what different types of eye contact mean:

➤ **Downcast eyes, then looks at you.** The person is acting coy and flirtatious.

➤ **Looks away for a prolonged period, then glances at you, then looks away again for a prolonged period.** Sign of disinterest that shows there is something, or someone, more interesting than you; especially if the person is looking out a window, or looking at his or her watch.

➤ **Glances around your body, especially looks in your eyes, then to your lips, then back to your eyes.** Sexual signal showing that the person would love to kiss you or touch you.

109

➤ **Stares at your body, especially breasts, butt, or genital area.** Disrespectful sign, showing in a very unsexy way that the person has blatant sexual interest, but no interest beyond that.

➤ **The blank stare.** Complete disinterest, just waiting to make an exit.

One more important key to attraction is a person's pupils. People look more attractive when their pupils are dilated (meaning when the black part of their eyes looks large and round). A person's pupils automatically dilate when he or she is in a dark or dimly lit room. Turn off the lights and have a candlelight dinner if you want to look more attractive! And by a wonderful stroke of luck, sometimes when you see someone you are attracted to, your pupils dilate automatically if you are in a room with moderate lighting. Psychologist Michael Argyle found through his research that pupils dilate when people are interested in what they are looking at, almost as if they are trying to see as much as they can of it.

As the saying goes, "The eyes are the windows to the soul." When you gaze into someone's eyes you can feel connected, in love, and even sexy. We think of people as having sexy eyes when they know how to use them to grab attention and to make you feel closer. Think Bette Davis or Omar Sharif—those deep, soulful eyes and intense gazes. Show the sexy side of your soul by using your eyes to express yourself.

Sari Says

Peek-a-boo is one of the first games infants learn to play. Interestingly, this is a one of the most alluring games that adults can play, too. When you are attracted to someone, catch the person's eye, then look down. Make eye contact once more, and then lower your gaze again. Soon you'll find you have that person cooing like a baby.

Deep Quote

"There is a smile of love and there is a smile of deceit."
—William Blake

Turn the World on with Your Smile

If Mary Tyler Moore could do it, then surely you can! A smile is the simplest way to show someone that his or her presence makes you feel good. When a smile is genuine, a person's whole face and body seem to light up. On the other hand, when a smile is phony, that deceit comes shining through, too. If you want to come across as sexy, you need to smile, but make it a real smile. To do that, have a pleasant thought in your mind, maybe just about how nice it is to meet someone new, or how glad you are that you are looking at someone attractive. Then your smile should come naturally.

Beyond smiling, the mouth and lips also tell a lot about sexual attractiveness. When someone is flirting, he or she may draw attention to his or her mouth.

Putting something in your mouth can be very sexy. Maybe you could tease your lips with a drinking straw, or place your pinkie finger at your lips. But keep it natural—you don't want to look like Dr. Evil and Mini Me in the movie *Austin Powers*.

Wetting your lips is a sexy way to show someone you're interested. When lips appear glossy, as if they're constantly wet, it's very sensual. That's why lipstick looks appealing on women.

Mirror Me

When two people feel as if they are both somewhat interested in each other, remarkably, they will start to mirror each other's body language. For example, if you are sitting with your right foot flat on the ground, your left leg crossed over your right knee at a 90-degree angle, with your hands in your lap, the other person would be sitting facing you with his or her left foot on the floor, and right leg crossed over the left leg at a 90-degree angle.

When two people are attracted to each other, even as they shift their positions, they follow each other without even being aware of doing it. Mirroring is a profound reflex action that puts two people's bodies in synch. Sometimes, it even goes as far as creating other unconscious similarities: two people walking in step with each other, or breathing at the same pace. The power of love can make your body feel as if it is one with your partner's.

Sexy Stats

Facial expressions often tell more than the spoken word, according to research done in the 1970s by Dr. Albert Mehrabian, a pioneer of the study of nonverbal communication. He found that words provide 7 percent of the meaning of a message; tone of voice, 38 percent; and facial expressions, 55 percent.

Flirt Alert

Don't give mixed messages with your body language. If you know that someone is interested in you but you're not interested in that person, make sure your body language says that you are *not interested*. Do not stand face to face. Don't smile excessively. Do not accidentally brush up against the person. Don't allow your body to behave as if you are attracted to someone if you are not.

Reading the Signs

In the past sections, you got an idea of what is sexy about body language, and what is not. The following table sums it up.

Unsexy Body Language: Signs That Someone *Is Not* Interested	Sexy Body Language: Signs That Someone *Is* Interested
Looking at wristwatch or glancing out the window	Makes eye contact
Tapping foot	Matches your posture
Drumming fingers	Fingers point toward own genitals
Swinging leg	Uncrossing legs
Hand on side of face	Preens hair
Head in hand	Arms gently gesturing
Crossed arms	Chest out
Holding drink high, or drinking or eating a lot	Holding drink low, or puts it down
Feet pointing away	Feet pointing at you
Never touches you	Brushes up against you

The Least You Need to Know

➤ Following the usual sequence of exchange during nonverbal communication can help you determine if there is a mutual attraction.

➤ When you're attracted to someone try to enter that person's personal space, while noticing if the person responds positively.

➤ Use your eyes and your smile to be more alluring.

➤ Mirroring is a reflex in which two people mimic each other's body language, and it makes them feel more intimate.

➤ Be aware of your body language so you do not send mixed signals to anyone.

Chapter 11

Dressing Sexy

In This Chapter

➤ How your inner personal style adds sex appeal to your outer appearance

➤ Quiz: What does your personal style say about you?

➤ The four types of sexy dressing

➤ How clothing or accessories from a different era can add mystery and sex appeal to an outfit

➤ What types of lingerie can look great

➤ How to take it all off!

Clothes make the man—and the woman. It's undeniable that a woman walking down the street in a tight skirt, silk blouse, and fabulous heels is going to turn heads. And plenty of women will give a sly second glance to a guy dressed just right in a classy suit.

When you dress to impress, you not only exude sexual energy in general, but you also send particular messages depending on what type of sexy dressing you've chosen. In this chapter, we're going to dress up for sexiness—and learn how to take it off to tantalize, too. So, throw open those closet doors, dear reader—it's show time!

Differing Views of What's Sexy

We've all seen reruns of the old TV show *Gilligan's Island*. But did you know that actress who played sweet, girl-next-door Mary Ann got just as much steamy fan mail as the actress who played the voluptuous and glamorous Ginger? It's true. Both women received more proposals, propositions, and party invitations than 100 women could handle in a lifetime.

It just goes to show you that there are many different kinds of sexy looks. There might be one in particular that is already your signature look, or maybe you like to experiment with different types depending on your mood and the company you'll be keeping. Perhaps you're not really sure if you have a sexy look at all. Don't be fooled: What you wear can speak volumes about who you are (or who you want people to perceive you are).

Before we go any further (or dig any deeper into that closet of yours), let's try to pinpoint your own personal sexy style. Sexy dressing can be divided into four categories, which are the same as the categories of sexiness that I discussed in many places in this book, and in depth in Chapter 5, "Different Types of Sexiness":

1. Romantic
2. Natural
3. Flirtatious
4. Erotic

You might fall solidly into one of these categories, or you might be a combination of several or all of them, depending on your mood. Take the following quiz to see where it is your personal style falls in the spectrum of sexy dressing.

Flirt Alert

It's fun to play around with what you wear and your general outer appearance and, yes, you can suggest different aspects of your personality or moods, depending on what it is you want to convey. However, clothes, make-up, and so on, should never be used as a mask to hide the real you, only to accentuate your many facets.

Deep Quote

"Style is not neutral; it gives moral directions."

—Martin Amis

I'm Too Sexy for My Wardrobe!

The following two quizzes—one for women and one for men—can help you determine which kind of sexy dressing you fall into naturally.

If you complete the quiz and feel a little disappointed because you fall securely into one or another category, don't worry. First of all, you have your own style and that's what makes you unique and gives you your own personal flair. Secondly, this isn't GrrrAnimals dressing—you can change your clothes to fit your mood. If you're the natural type and want to be an erotic babe, you can—all it takes is some imagination, or a helpful department store sales person.

Got your pen ready? Okay, let's get to it. Women, what kind of sexy are you?

Quiz: The Feminine Mystique

Put a check mark next to the answer that best describes your personal style.

1. It's a hot, sunny day outside. A good friend of yours calls up and asks you to go for a walk in the nearby park. You put on ...

    a. A floral sundress. ___

    b. Your favorite pair of cut-off Levi's and a white cotton tank top. ____

    c. Your old well-worn denim mini skirt and that cool new pink blouse you just bought. ___

    d. A red tube top, second-skin capris, and a pair of strappy four-inch heels. ___

2. You've been asked to a cocktail party given by that really cute new guy at work. You wear ...

    a. A demurely fitted cashmere sweater and an A-line skirt with a slight flare at the bottom. ___

    b. Faded jeans and a black turtleneck. ___

    c. A sheer blouse with a fitted double-side-slit skirt. ___

    d. A tight sleeveless V-neck top with faux leopard-skin pants. ___

3. You are about to leave for a dinner date with a guy you've been seeing and in whom you're interested. A half an hour before he's about to show up, the below-calf-length, straight, black skirt you're wearing rips on the seam dead center in the front. The rip is about six inches high. You ...

    a. Break out the emergency needle and thread and sew up the rip. ____

    b. Change into a pair of attractive but comfortable black slacks that you really wanted to wear anyway. ____

    c. Take the needle and thread and secure the point where the rip stopped. The skirt sort of looks better like that and shows a little leg. ____

    d. Rip it to mid-thigh height. You've got great fishnets on—why waste the view? ____

4. If you were a famous actress and nominated for an Academy Award, which designer's clothes would you wear to the ceremonies?

    a. Vera Wang. ___

    b. The Gap (hey, Sharon Stone did it!). ___

    c. Calvin Klein. ____

    d. Versace. ___

5. You are going to the beach. After putting on your bathing suit, you try to decide what to wear over it for traveling to and from the sandy shore. You select …

   a. A demure cotton summer dress that hits just above the knee. ___

   b. Shorts and your favorite T-shirt. ___

   c. A cute, short sarong that you just got from Victoria's Secret. ___

   d. Um, cover up? Why did I spend 100 bucks on this fabulous bikini to cover it up? ___

6. If you were about to go on vacation, what would you wear on the plan ride there?

   a. A picture hat, a twin set in a pastel color, and a long, flowing skirt. ___

   b. Khakis and a comfortable button-down cotton shirt. ___

   c. A formfitting top that hits your curves nicely and a pair of cute capris. ___

   d. Red leather pants and a black rubber top. ___

7. Your husband is about to come home late from work, and he's going to want to have a little fun, if you know what I mean. You greet him at the door wearing …

   a. A silk nightie with lace panties underneath. ___

   b. Your favorite comfy T-shirt and boxers. ___

   c. Only his pajama top. ___

   d. A corset with a garter belt and stockings and high heels. ___

8. The color you feel best wearing is …

   a. Pink. ___

   b. White. ___

   c. Purple. ___

   d. Red. ___

Deep Quote

"If clothes make the man, then naked men must have little or no influence on society."

—Mark Twain

If you answered mostly a's, you fall into the *romantic* category of dressing; mostly b's, you fall into the *natural* category of dressing; mostly c's, you fall into the *flirtatious* category of dressing; mostly d's, you fall into the *erotic* category of dressing.

If your answers were scattered, you have a smattering of the other categories, too. That means that you can pick and choose what makes up your dressing style.

Okay, men, now it's your turn!

Quiz: The GQ Quotient

1. Your best buddy asks you to go shoot some hoops. You wear ...

   a. Your good-luck Michael Jordan numbered jersey. ___

   b. Whatever you have on at that moment in time. No need to change clothes to play a few games of one-on-one. ___

   c. Your cool new Adidas workout pants with the side zips at the ankles and a tight white tank—you never know who's going to be hanging around the park. ___

   d. Black bike shorts and a tight, black tank. ___

2. You need to go to the bookstore to pick up a copy of the how-to manual you've been meaning to get to teach you how to use your new computer software. You've noticed that there are always a lot of attractive women at this store. You wear ...

   a. A soft, finely tailored corduroy shirt, thin wool slacks, and a sports jacket. ___

   b. Comfortable jeans and a gray sweatshirt touting your alma mater. ___

   c. Tight jeans and a colored T-shirt. ___

   d. Black jeans and a tight black turtleneck. ___

3. Complete this sentence using one of the following selections: The type of clothes I feel best in are ...

   a. A cashmere sweater and nice slacks. ___

   b. Khakis and a polo shirt. ___

   c. A button-down shirt and jeans. ___

   d. Leather pants a la Jim Morrison. ___

4. You are taking the woman you've been eyeing for months out on a first date to a nice restaurant. You wear ...

   a. A tailored suit. ___

   b. Khakis and pullover sweater. ___

   c. Blue jeans and a button-down shirt. ___

   d. Black jeans, a black button-down shirt, and a leather jacket. ___

5. If you were to play one sport professionally based solely on the uniforms, which one would you pick?

   a. Polo. ___

   b. Bowling. ___

   c. Baseball. ___

   d. Swimming. ___

117

6. You are going to the beach. What do you wear with your bathing suit?

   a. A short-sleeved button-down shirt and a straw fedora. ___

   b. Your favorite T-shirt and a baseball cap. ___

   c. A tight tank. ___

   d. Nothing. ___

7. You want to turn your lover on, so you come to bed wearing …

   a. Silk boxers. ___

   b. Nothing at all. ___

   c. Colored boxer-briefs. ___

   d. A snug leopard-print bikini. ___

8. The color you feel best wearing is …

   a. Blue. ___

   b. White. ___

   c. Red. ___

   d. Black. ___

If you answered mostly a's, you fall into the *romantic* category of dressing; mostly b's, you fall into the *natural* category of dressing; mostly c's, you fall into the *flirtatious* category of dressing; mostly d's, you fall into the *erotic* category of dressing.

Sari Says

You may think that romantic dressing relates more to women than men. But the fact is, men can look totally romantic, too. Perhaps if you think of romance fashion as soft and sensual rather than something frilly, you'll be better able to picture romantic-looking men.

As with the women's quiz, if your answers were scattered, you have a smattering of the other categories in your dressing style, so you like to choose different looks.

The Fabulous Four Fashion Styles Defined

You may be wondering why I started you off earlier in this book helping you to feel good about your body and getting over your physical inhibitions. Why not just learn how to dress sexy? Isn't that what being sexy is all about?

The answer is yes and no. Yes, clothes, accessories, makeup, and so on, can turn anyone into a Cinderella or Cinderfella. But you've got to lay a solid self-image foundation first. Think about it. You can get compliments all day long on how great you look, but if you're not feeling so fabulous about yourself, they won't mean diddly.

Now, think about a day when you've woken up in a great mood, feeling confident and happy. You probably got dressed with attitude. You put on the color that you know looks great on you. Or maybe you even pulled out an outfit or an accessory that you'd stashed away for a special occasion. Well, guess what? You *are* a special occasion.

What you wear can say a lot to those around you about how you feel: Demure? Coy? Free spirited? Flirty? Bold? Steamy? You can express all these things with your physical appearance (and, of course, a little attitude!).

Even though you have determined which of the four areas of sexy dressing your personal style falls into, it doesn't mean that you can't mix and match. Some days you might feel flirty, others you might feel naturally great. And some nights you just may feel the erotic beat of the world around you. No matter. You are not relegated to one quadrant of the sexy dressing spectrum. Dress according to your moods for the best results.

Now, let's take a closer look at types of ensembles in each of the sexy dressing quadrants.

Deep Quote

"I base most of my fashion taste on what doesn't itch."

—Gilda Radner

Sari Says

The men of the nomadic Wodaabe tribe of Niger, Nigeria, and Cameroon are no strangers to the romantic lure of fashion. During Geereol, a weeklong annual festival celebrating the end of the dry season, male members of the tribe participate in two competitive dances to charm the women. In the second dance, the men are judged solely on their beauty—they paint their faces, plume their hair with ostrich feathers and cowry shells, and decorate their chests with white beads placed in a crisscross pattern.

Romantic: Soft, Sensual, and Downright Sexy

If you're a true romantic at heart, you probably express this in your choice of clothing and colors. Romantic clothing is soft to the touch and easy on the eyes. It says, "Touch me."

Some examples of romantic sexy dressing are the following:

Women	Men
Silk blouses	Cashmere sweaters
Floral sundresses	Well-tailored suits
Off-the-shoulder peasant blouses	Fine corduroy shirts
Flowing skirts	Lightweight wool slacks
Soft colors like pink, rose, and lavender	Muted colors like evergreen, baby blue, pale yellow, and tan

In most of the categories, certain "period pieces" also work well and add a unique and sometimes mysterious touch. For romantic dressing for women, look to the Victorian era (lace and long skirts), the Romantic era (ruffled blouses), a picture hat reminiscent of the antebellum South, or even the bubble-gum fashions of the '50s (swingy skirts, a scarf in your hair).

Men can follow a similar trail to the past: a fedora from the '40s a la Frank Sinatra, the clean-cut look of the '50s good guy, or the buttoned-up perfect suit of a nineteenth century English dandy. Whether you choose a classic piece or a department store selection, adding some romance to your wardrobe can put you in that sensual state of mind.

Deep Quote

"Nothing prevents one from appearing natural as the desire to appear natural."

—Francois de La Rochefoucauld

Natural: Keeping It Simple

Makeup? Accessories? Hair products? If you are the natural style, it's all an unnecessary albatross around your neck. And as far as fabrics go, it's cotton or nothing at all. Your theme song is Aretha belting out "You Make Me Feel Like a Natural Woman," or an earthy Bob Dylan growling out "Like a Rolling Stone." The natural prefers faded jeans to Fendi and cut-offs to Chanel. This style of sexy dressing says, "Take me as I am." More often than not, the natural can be found wearing the following:

Women	Men
Soft T-shirts	T-shirts or tanks
Khaki slacks	Faded, worn, comfortable blue jeans
Linen dresses or skirts	Soft flannel shirts
Cut-offs made from worn jeans	Unlined cotton or linen blazers
Earth-toned hues like taupe, sage, sky blue, and brown	Classic colors like navy, white, and tan

As far as period pieces go, the natural is pretty timeless. Think Adam and Eve. Or you could go for a 1960s Woodstock look with bare feet and a daisy tucked behind your ear to top off your casual, comfy jeans and T-shirt. The bare basics (or just simply being bare) are the best ways to show off your natural style.

Flirtatious: Guess What I've Got on Underneath?

Ah, the flirt. Who can resist? They speak in double entendres and hushed voices, and when they throw that devastating come-hither gaze in your direction, they look away as quickly as they looked over, leaving you wondering until you find yourself playing that hypnotic game of hide and seek all over again.

The flirt is playful and, although not afraid to show a little skin, he or she knows the intense power of leaving something to the imagination. If you opened a flirt's closet, you'd likely find the following:

Sari Says

In Japan, the position of the obi, or sash, that ties around the middle of a kimono is an indicator of a woman's innocence or lack thereof. The younger and more sexually inexperienced the female, the higher the obi position. An experienced, married woman's obi sits closer to the hips. Geisha often wear their obi lower as well, signifying their sexual experience.

Women	Men
Sheer blouses	Button-down shirts
Long, formfitting skirts with a slit up the side or in the back	Tight blue jeans
Miniskirts	Formfitting T-shirts
Low-back dresses	V-neck shirts and sweaters
Warm colors in rich tones like cranberry red or deep ocean blue	Warm or mildly bold colors like royal blue or berry red

Women can try the flare of a 1940s-style skirt, or a fringy, low-back dress fit for a flapper. Men can play around with the pocket-watch style of a 1940s gangster or the charm of cowboy boots straight out of the Old West. It'll put a sexy grin on your cowgirl's face.

Erotic: A Devil in Leather Pants

With moves like a black cat sneaking across a dark, steamy city street, someone with an erotic style is in touch with his or her sexuality—and definitely not afraid to show it. The erotic's choice of clothing exudes a primal sexiness that screams like a red fire engine on its way to a five-alarm blaze. The second skins you'll find the erotic dresser wearing might include the following:

Women	Men
Leather anything	Tight black jeans
Animal prints (leopard being a favorite)	Leather pants
Tight, short skirts	Leather jacket (a staple)
Formfitting, low-cut tops, maybe with some kind of extra sexy detail, like lace-up sides or cutouts	Tight-fitting shirts
Black, black, and more black; red	You guessed it—a black wardrobe, of course

Although the erotic style tends to go toward the urban or a slightly futuristic, modern appearance, women can try the red lipstick, tight capris, and heels of the 1950s bad girl, the bohemian chic of Anaïs Nin's underground Paris of the 1940s, or the corseted undergarments of anything before the turn of the twentieth century. And for you men out there, two words: Jim Morrison (see Chapter 22, "Sexy Men We Can Learn From").

Flirt Alert

Erotic dressing is totally hot, but it can get you more unwanted attention than other styles. The way you dress makes a statement about you. If you dress provocatively, you may get the kind of sexual attention that some would assume you are looking for. Of course, you should be able to dress any way you want, any time, any place, but that's not the reality of our society. Give careful thought to where you are going and what you are wearing, and the kind of sexual messages your outfit sends.

Dress You Up in My Love

Even if you took the quiz and found out you were a tried-and-true romantic or a hard-core erotic, no matter. There is no rule that says you have to stick with one look all the time. You may find you fall more frequently into one particular area of sexy dressing because you find you express your sexuality best in that vein. That's fine. But there's no need to limit yourself.

People use different sexy styles to affect the mood on dates. For example, they may mix it up depending on whom they're dating or how many dates they've gone on. Perhaps, starting with romantic and, if the first date goes well, moving on to flirty for date number two. If a third date is in order, then sticking with one of these areas until the time comes to give out more obvious sexual signals. Then moving on to the erotic outfit. Some people save natural for last. It can be quite revealing, sending the message that they're really comfortable with themselves around the person they are involved with.

You can control the signals that you want to send out simply by changing your shirt. Have fun with it—you are your own blank canvas.

Lingerie for Him and Her

What you wear underneath your clothing will add to your sexy style, too, of course. Lingerie (for women) or sexy underwear (for men) comes in all different styles, which we can fit into our Fab Four categories.

For romantic sexiness, men can wear silk boxer shorts. To be flirty, try attractive colored briefs. To be erotic, wear tight bikinis. For the natural look, you might prefer nothing at all.

Women in lacy bras and matching panties are quite romantic. In the flirtatious style, wear a short silk robe. To be a natural, wear nothing at all, and gently drape yourself in a white cotton sheet. More elaborate lingerie, such as a teddy or corset, is erotic, as are a racy garter belt and stockings, or a push-up bra and a thong.

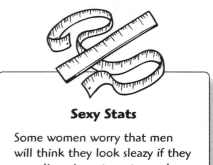

Sexy Stats

Some women worry that men will think they look sleazy if they wear lingerie, yet most men love it. A recent *Redbook* magazine survey of 40,000 men found that over 80 percent of men are turned on when women wear sexy lingerie.

Lingerie is usually intended to be shown off to turn your lover on. But you can also wear it just to make yourself feel sexy all day long. If you are hard at work, and you pause and remember that you're wearing red lacy panties, you'll recapture your sexiness, even in the middle of a busy work day. Wearing something sexy under your clothes helps you feel sexy. Feeling sexy in turn makes you look sexy by helping you project confidence and pride. Sexy underwear can do a lot for your self-esteem—as well as your sex life!

Take It Off, Take It All Off

A chapter on dressing sexy would not be complete without a little discussion on how to take it off like you mean it. Although the boldness of stripping off all your clothes at a moment's notice definitely has its appeal, the subtlety of a slow striptease can be hotter than blacktop in the August sun.

Photo by Gen Nishino.

The idea of stripping might make you a little nervous. What if you look foolish? What if you get tangled up in your clothes? What if you try to add a few dance steps and fall flat on your face?

Stripping doesn't have to entail choreography. Stripping can be as simple as a slow, simmering disrobing. Here are some tips for stripper-friendly clothing as well as ideas for heating things up by taking it off:

➤ Clothing with multiple buttons *in the front* works really well. The tease of a blouse, dress, or a pair of button-fly jeans being ever so slowly undone is always fun to watch. If it's a shirt or dress you're undoing, try leaving just one button closed in a strategic place (for women, across the breasts on a blouse or at your hips on a dress; for men, at the navel in a button-down shirt), and let the member of your captive audience undo it.

Flirt Alert

Avoid clothes that button or hook in the back, because they are way too complicated to undo gracefully. A zipper is okay in the back, but just make sure you can reach it!

➤ Zippers in the front, side, or back of dresses, skirts, or shirts, as well as on jeans or slacks, work well for a steamy undressing session. Always ease the zipper down using one controlled, flowing movement. Don't just whip the thing down.

➤ Dance around to some sexy music, if you like, emphasizing your chest, butt, and legs. You can lift up your leg, and brush your lover's thigh with your foot. (See Chapter 13, "Sexiness Begins at Home: Creating a Sexy Environment," for some music tips.)

➤ Flash a little skin intermittently. A shoulder here, a leg there, a bit of hip action are the preview to the full-main event. Be tantalizing!

➤ Use props. A hat, gloves, or sheer scarf can be an incredibly sexy asset when taking it off. Use your imagination and think about how you could use props to add an extra sensual element to your performance.

➤ Gently toss your clothes at your lover, one piece at a time.

➤ Make sure you wear great underwear! Anything soft or silky or slinky will be perfect, depending on your personal sexy style, of course.

➤ Roll your hips. Stand with your feet firmly on the floor, and your legs shoulder-width apart. Pretend that a single beam of light is shining out from your genitals. Then roll your hips in a circular motion, so that you are drawing an imaginary circle of light on the floor. Go around and around in one direction several times, then switch directions.

➤ When all your clothes are off, move around seductively for a little while longer, for more "look but don't touch" excitement. Then finally, touch your lover and let the real show begin.

Sari Says

Break out the popcorn and do a little fun research. Check out some of the better stripping scenes that movies have to offer to get a few cinematic pointers. Try *9¹/₂ Weeks, Erotica, Blaze,* or *Striptease.*

Whether you are taking them off or showing them off, clothes are an incredible asset to your sexy quotient. Your personal style of dressing up—or stripping down—are part of the sex appeal that is yours alone. Don't be afraid to experiment with different looks if you feel they mirror a facet of your personality. Most importantly, have fun! Clothes aren't for hiding in—they're for expressing yourself.

The Least You Need to Know

➤ Each of us has our own, distinct style—reflect what's inside you with what you wear.

➤ You may fall into a particular facet of sexy dressing, but that doesn't mean you are stuck there. Explore different styles depending on your moods.

➤ You can use a particular style of sexy dressing to send a message to the person you're with.

➤ Your undergarments can add to your sexy style, too.

➤ Taking it off can be just as fun as putting it on!

125

Part 3

Sexiness in Dating and Relationships

Congratulations! If you've made it this far, you've stripped off those layers of bad attitude and know what's what. You've got it goin' on now—you know what sexiness is and isn't, you know how to work your own sexy attitude and put out the right sexy signals. Now let's put it to good use.

Getting attention is nice, but you need to learn how to set your sexy sights on the person you most desire (whether that's someone new in your life or the person you've been waking up next to for the last decade or so). Here you're going to learn about the ever-fun art of flirting, how to get your home in tip-top sexy shape, how to arrange the perfect hot date, and, if all is going well, sexy gifts to give when you've surrendered to love's (or lust's) spell and care enough to give the very best—you!

Chapter 12

Sexy Flirting Techniques

In This Chapter

➤ Learning sexy flirting techniques

➤ Picking up tips on pickup lines

➤ Discovering the sexiest ways to flirt

➤ The truth behind playing hard to get

Hey, baby, you're looking kinda hot right now. I see you sittin' there reading this with those big eyes. Once you put the book down, how 'bout we go out for a drink? Yes, you!

Okay, not really. I just thought you could use a little flirting to spice up your reading and set the stage for what I'll talk about in this chapter.

Flirting is the way that you show your interest in someone, and establish yourself as a sexy person. People flirt when they meet for the first time if they're attracted to each other. And people also flirt even if they've been together for years and years, just to keep showing their love, affection, and sexiness for each other.

If you are comfortable talking with others, then flirting may come naturally. If not, this chapter will give you the basics. Then, for those of you who are flirts to begin with, I'll go beyond the basics to explain some of the sexiest flirting techniques you could ever imagine.

What Is Flirting, Anyway?

The thought of *flirting* flusters some people. But the fact is that flirting is not all that different from talking. Flirting is basically talking while you are acting extra interested and smiling a lot.

Besides just acting charming, when people flirt they like to flatter each other. Or flirts might try to make the other person laugh. Some people even make sexual innuendoes. Here are some examples of how flirting is not such a stretch from simply asking, "How was your weekend?"

➤ Flirting: "I thought about you this weekend. What did you do?"

➤ Flattery as flirting: "I saw the most beautiful sunset this weekend, and I thought of you. The sky looked as radiant as your eyes."

➤ Humor as flirting: "Did you see *Saturday Night Live* this weekend? Let me tell you about the funniest thing on the show …."

➤ Sexual innuendo as flirting: "The weather was so hot this weekend—almost as hot as you make me, baby."

Lusty Lingo

Flirting means playfully gaining the attention and admiration of others, often someone you're attracted to.

Really, all you have to do to flirt is start talking with someone you like. Approach the person the same way you'd go up to talk with anyone. Then say whatever comes naturally.

Don't be self-conscious, and don't be shy. Be light, fun, and relaxed, and if he or she likes you, he or she will respond. There are ways to make flirting really sexy, but before we get to that, I want to make sure that you have down the basics.

Flirting 101

So you see a gorgeous stranger and you want to let him or her know that you're interested. Or maybe you see someone every day on your way to work. You've said "Hi" a million times, but now it's time to kick it up a notch. You'll have to start flirting if you ever want things to progress. So what are you waiting for? The best time to flirt is … now!

Here are flirting basics for the first flirtatious conversation:

➤ **Talk.** Say something, anything to get the ball rolling. You can start with "Hi," and move on from there.

➤ **Have great body language.** Smile. Make eye contact. Mirror the other person's body

Flirt Alert

Using sexual innuendo can be a great way to flirt; however, be careful when and with whom you use it. If you come on sexually to someone you just met, that person may think all you're interested in is sex. Or, the other extreme, if you make sexual overtures to someone who finds it offensive, you may have lost your chance to flirt with that person.

130

positioning. Do all those wonderful things that I talked about in Chapter 10, "Body Talk: Using Sexy Body Language."

➤ **Be flattering.** Mention something that you like about the person's look, outfit, hairstyle, or whatever seems unique or catches your eye. Make sure you're sincere.

➤ **Ask lots of questions.** You are interested in getting to know this person; so, get to know this person! Ask whatever you can think of. Where is the person from? What does he or she do? Ask about his or her background. Try to get stories about this person's life.

➤ **Listen.** People feel as though you're interested when you are listening to them. Really listen. Don't think about what you're going to say next. Pay attention and try to remember what you're learning about the person.

➤ **Be nice.** Be extra nice, in fact. You should be carrying on a conversation, but never debate or challenge someone when you intend to flirt. If you ever disagree with someone early on in the flirting process, just let it go for now. You can deal with those things if this progresses; but for flirting, just focus on being friendly.

➤ **Laugh.** You can even tell a few jokes (clean, tasteful jokes), and ask the person you're flirting with if he or she knows any jokes. Laughter is so sexy, and it helps people bond and really like each other.

➤ **Be honest.** It might sound impressive to say that you live in a five-bedroom house on a lake. But if the truth is that you live in one bedroom in your parents' five-bedroom house (that has a small Koi pond in the back yard) then tell the truth—or just don't mention it.

➤ **Make an impression.** Try to say something interesting or do something memorable. You want to express something unique about yourself that this person would like or at least remember. For example, if you're at a party, and there's a piano, maybe you could play a short song. Whatever you do well, try to do it—without showing off too much, though.

Deep Quote

"I don't remember anybody's name. How do you think the 'dahling' thing got started?"

—Zsa Zsa Gabor

Flirt Alert

In some cases, flirting on the job can be construed as harassment. A safe policy is to never flirt at work. If you're in a more social setting with someone you work with, such as at lunch or at an office party, you might try some mild flirting. But use discretion—you don't want to be labeled the office flirt!

➤ **Be a "closer," or at least try to be.** After you've flirted for a few minutes, if this is someone you want to see again, you must ask for his or her phone number or e-mail address. Try to close the deal. Never be afraid to ask! Remember, for Babe Ruth's record numbers of homeruns, he also had a record number of strikeouts.

By the way, at the end of the flirting, don't think that the guy always has to ask the woman for her number—it goes both ways. In fact, sometimes it's very sexy when a woman asks the guy for his number. The bottom line is, you just need to find a way to get in touch with each other again.

A final thought about this first conversation: Don't be afraid of rejection. Think of it this way: When two people aren't right for each other, there's a good chance one of them will realize it before the other does and end the relationship or potential relationship. Sometimes it will be you who rejects the other person, and sometimes you will get rejected. But if your instincts tell you that this could be a cool person, then you always should try.

Sari Says

No matter where you go or what you do, if you're single and looking for love, always keep a pen and piece of paper on you at all times. You can flirt and meet people anywhere, and you always want to be prepared to write down a phone number.

Pickup Lines: The Good, the Bad, and the Ugly

Usually the best way to start flirting is to just go up to some one, say "Hi," and then talk about whatever comes to mind. But other times, it can work if you use a line to start things off.

There are many different types of lines. Some are classics; some are so contrived and cheesy that they're silly; some are downright offensive or sexually vulgar and should be avoided. Let's take a closer look at some opening lines that may get you a chuckle—and those that may get you a slap in the face.

Classic Lines: Use Only If Said Tongue-in-Cheek

Here are some classic pickup lines that will definitely let the person know that you are trying to pick him or her up. Use these lines in a playful, tongue-in-cheek way:

➤ What's a nice person like you doing in a place like this?

➤ Haven't I seen you somewhere before?

➤ What's your sign?

➤ You look so familiar. Are you a model?

➤ Your place or mine?

Cheesy Lines: Use with Caution!

There are some lines that are so cheesy, the only way they'll work is if the person laughs at the line and then talks to you, sort of out of mercy. However, be careful if you want to use one of these to get a laugh, because some people might find them annoying rather than funny:

➤ Do you have a quarter I can use? My mother said I should call her when I find my true love.

➤ I'd like to rearrange the alphabet so I can put U next to I.

➤ Do you believe in love at first sight or do I have to walk by you again?

➤ Is it hot in here, or is that just you?

➤ Are you tired? Because you've been running through my mind all day.

➤ Excuse me, can I have your phone number? I seem to have lost mine.

➤ Every person in this place seems to want to meet you, so I came over to find out what's so special about you.

Offensive Lines: Do Not Use!

Here are some examples of pickup lines that are considered offensive and should be avoided (unless you know the person well and you think he or she would get a kick out of it):

➤ Is that a mirror on your pants? Because I can see myself in them.

➤ If I said you had a beautiful body, would you hold it against me?

➤ Do you want to have breakfast? Should I call you or nudge you?

➤ I like your pants, but I'd like them more if they were in a pile on my bedroom floor.

➤ Let's play carpenter. We'll get hammered, and then I'll nail you.

➤ Hi, my name is Pogo. Do you want to jump my stick?

➤ That's a nice shirt. Can I talk you out of it?

➤ I may not be Fred Flintstone, but I bet I can make your bed rock.

Most people think that pickup lines are so silly! But, the fact is, sometimes when you want to meet someone, getting him or her to take notice of you is a triumph—and a way to continue flirting.

Sari Says

I often ask people to tell me the worst pickup lines they've ever heard. Here are some real stinkers. "If you were a booger I'd pick you first." "Hey, baby, wanna go halves on a bastard?" Don't even think of using these!

What Should You Talk About?

Without using a line, you can just begin a conversation by speaking the way you would to anyone. An easy opening topic is why you are both at the same place. Use your surroundings for topics of conversation:

➤ If you're at a party, talk about how you know the people who invited you. Did the same person invite you?

➤ If you're at a club, you could discuss why people like going there. What's so cool about the place?

➤ If you're browsing in a bookstore, talk about your favorite books. Which recent books have you loved?

➤ If you're flirting in the produce aisle of supermarket, don't be shy about bringing in a little subtle sexual innuendo. Does he or she thinks the tomatoes are ripe?

Wherever you are, talk about the people, places, or things around you. It's a more specific way of asking, "What's a nice person like you doing in place like this?" Once you get the ball rolling, try to make the conversation a bit sexier.

Try revealing some things about yourself and eliciting some intimate revelations from your new potential partner. Listen attentively and ask follow-up questions to keep the conversation going. If you two are a good match, your conversation will probably flow naturally after that.

The Most Sexy Flirting

So now you know the basics of how to flirt, what lines could work, and how to get a conversation started. But you're reading this book so you can be sexy. So I'm going to let you in on a few secrets about how to make flirting sexier.

These are things that don't just work for someone you are meeting for the first time. Flirting continues throughout an entire relationship—even after years of marriage!

➤ **Touch the person you're flirting with.** In Chapter 10, I explained that brushing up against someone or casually touching while you gesture are signals of interest. When you are flirting, be sure that you find a way to touch. Some ideas include commenting on the person's watch, and when you do, gently take his or her wrist in your hand to look more closely. Or brushing a piece of hair out of his or her eyes. If you've known each other for a while, a shoulder massage is always a great flirtation tool, too.

➤ **Raise the general subject of sex.** Find a way to work some sex topic into the conversation. Nothing that could bring up negative feeling: nothing too personal (not about what your ex liked in bed), nothing controversial (not abortion). Try mentioning something like an R-rated movie that you saw recently that was sexy and asking if this person saw it and what he or she thought of it.

➤ **Make a romantic gesture.** If you're at a party or bar, offer to get him or her a drink refill. If you're outside, pick a flower and give it to him or her. If this is someone you've just met, write down your phone number along with a one- or two-line flirty note—even just "I loved meeting you!" If this is someone you've been married to for a dozen years, leave Post-it love notes around the house. Any little thing like that is sexy!

➤ **Ask the person to dance.** Of course, this works best if you're actually at a place where music is playing. Asking someone to dance is a great way to escalate your flirting to the next sexy level, because when you dance you can hold each other and move your bodies in all sorts of sexy ways.

➤ **Feed the person.** If you're at dinner with a date, share a dessert with one fork. Or during dinner with your partner, casually say, "You should try this." Then hold up a small forkful of food from your plate for your date to try. Feeding someone is such a sexy way to flirt.

Flirt Alert

If you try these sexy flirting techniques on someone and that person does not seem interested in you, take note and back off. There is no greater turnoff than someone who keeps making advances after he or she is signaled to stop.

Sexy flirting is about being creative and coming up with great ideas to make the person feel wanted and attractive. So let your imagination run wild to get someone wild over you.

Playing Hard to *Guess*

Imagine this: You're a guy who's been chatting up a woman all night. You've flattered her, made her laugh, and even had a lively discussion about what different politicians would be like in bed. All the groundwork seems to be in place to take this sexy flirtation to the next level—getting her phone number and asking her out. She has given you all the signals that she's interested, but then, when you finally ask for a date, she turns you down flat! What's up?

Is she the following:

➤ Feigning interest in you just to pass the time?

➤ Married or in a serious relationship but she couldn't resist flirting with you?

➤ Playing hard to get?

It's very tough to know what someone is doing in this scenario. The only way to find out would be to ask. But would she really be honest? If she were playing hard to get, it would defeat her purpose. That's why I call it "playing hard to *guess*." If someone tries to play hard to get, he or she leaves the other wondering what to do next, and that is certainly not a surefire way to get to the next step.

The theory behind playing hard to get is that people want what they can't have. If someone you like has to work to get your attention, then supposedly the person will like you more. However, I think it's a high-risk strategy that can easily backfire.

I always tell people that if someone is acting aloof or ignoring you, move on. So if people have been taking my advice, then, by playing hard to get, you'll be forcing others to leave you alone.

I think it's totally sexy to be spontaneous and to make it known that you are interested in someone. Make the advance, or accept the advance if you are interested. If you want to move things along, play like you want it, not like you don't.

Deep Quote

"When you realize you want to spend the rest of your life with somebody, you want the rest of your life to begin as soon as possible."

—Harry (Billy Crystal), *When Harry Met Sally*

That having been said, you can play around a bit with being coy and showing the mysterious side of your sexiness (as I discussed in Chapters 3, "Attitudes That Define Sexiness," and 8, "Developing a Sexy Attitude"). That means you don't want to totally disclose every little thing about yourself. But that does not mean screening your calls when you think the hottie you like might be calling.

Bottom line: Playing games, including hard-to-get games, is not sexy. How can you get what you want unless you let yourself be gotten? If you want to get closer to someone, then don't waste any time playing games. Say "yes" when someone you like asks you out.

Flirt Alert

It's okay to show someone you're interested, but don't go overboard. If you seem extremely eager to see someone all the time at the beginning of a relationship, you might seem too needy or even obsessive.

Being a sexy flirt is about being excellent in someone's presence. It's all about showing the best sides of yourself, while you simultaneously make the other person feel great about him- or herself. It's also about making your interest known. Flirting is about getting closer to someone, being sexy yourself, and about making the object of your desire feel sexy, too.

The Least You Need to Know

➤ The basics of flirting mostly involve being really nice and acting very interested when you first talk with someone.

➤ Some pickup lines do work, but be careful when trying anything too contrived, and avoid sexually vulgar lines altogether.

➤ Try some very sexy flirting techniques to show off how sexy you can be.

➤ If you play hard to get, you might not let anyone get you.

Chapter 13

Sexiness Begins at Home: Creating a Sexy Environment

You've just come home from work. You've had a lousy day. To snap yourself out of your bad mood, you head straight to the stereo and flick on some soothing tunes. Maybe you even go for a little aromatherapy and light a scented candle that reminds you of the smell of fall, your favorite time of year. Then you change out of your monkey suit into something less constricting and flop down on your comfy couch. Ah. Instant sensory healing!

See? You already know how to use sensual details to change the mood of your surroundings when you see fit. Creating a sexy scene in your home is no different. In this chapter, I'm going to help you create your very own little love nest.

Kick Your Surroundings Up a Notch

Whether you are stoking the fire of someone new, or just trying to keep the love alive with your old flame, you go to some trouble to look—and feel—your best. You turn up your personal sexy quotient by dressing a certain way (see Chapter 11, "Dressing Sexy," for a detailed discussion on dressing sexy), taking extra care with your hair (and makeup if you're a woman), and probably even spritzing on a little cologne or perfume to add an alluring scent to the mix. Why wouldn't you do the same with your home?

Picture this: You walk into a room. The walls are plain white. The lighting is fluorescent and harsh. There are no pictures or books. There is no music playing, let alone a stereo to play it on. The furniture is drab and rough to the touch. The air smells stale and old. It's even a little chilly. The only thing you want to do is turn around and walk right out.

Now picture this: You walk into a room. The walls are a warm, inviting color. The lighting from the lamps is soft and a few flickering candles cast dancing shadows around the room. There are interesting photographs and prints on the walls that make you curious about the person who lives here, telling you something about his or her interests and tastes. The sultry sound of Nina Simone drifts from the stereo, immediately relaxing you and making you want to lie down on the nice, soft sofa with one of those plush throw pillows behind your head. There is a subtle, earthy, almost wood-like scent in the air that reminds you of a crackling fire. It is warm and cozy. You feel like you never want to leave.

Deep Quote

"A comfortable house is a great source of happiness. It ranks immediately after health and a good conscience."

—Sydney Smith

This is a no-brainer, my friend—you want what's behind the door to the second room. You don't have to expensively remodel your home. All you need is a few bucks and a little imagination. And the easy thing is you can apply the same principles you learned about dressing sexy in Chapter 11 to creating a sexy scene. You can create a scene that is one of the following:

1. Romantic.
2. Natural.
3. Flirtatious.
4. Erotic.

The key to fleshing out these interior fantasies is paying attention to the sensory details: sight, touch, smell, taste, and sound.

Easy on the Eyes

In the same way what you wear and how you present yourself can send out a particular type of sexy message, so can the way you choose to decorate your home. You want to have soft lighting, telling colors, and special touches that say something about *you*.

Light the Way

Lighting is one of the most important components of a sexy scene and one of the easiest to change. You're not going to feel much like getting cozy in a room that's lit like the inside of a shopping mall. The lighting should be soft and low. Believe it or not, you can control the type of scene merely by what kind of sexy lighting you choose:

➤ **Romantic.** Choose low-voltage, tinted light bulbs (pink adds a nice, rosy hue). If you have a dimmer (and if you don't, they are very easy to install and available at your local hardware store), keep the lights a little on the low side. Not so much that you can't see, but enough to make the room reminiscent of your favorite romantic trattoria. If using candles (which I highly recommend you do), candelabras give the impression of the romantic past. You can also find candles with flowers and herbs pressed into the wax, which are not only pretty but smell great, too.

➤ **Natural.** Go for the soft white bulbs with a low wattage (no higher than 40 watts). For candles, use pure white or off-white. One large, triple-wick white candle in the middle of a dining table or coffee table is a nice, simple addition to a natural setting.

➤ **Flirtatious.** You can use either soft-hued, tinted light bulbs or the soft-white, but try adding touches like a sheer piece of material draped over a lamp shade. Depending on the color and pattern, it can completely change the mood and cast interesting shadows. For candles, try medium-sized clusters around the room. Purple- or wine-colored candles add a flirty touch. Also, try floating candles.

➤ **Erotic.** For erotic lighting, I recommend foregoing the electric lights and using candles only. Transform any room into your own sexy love den by using lots of them placed in several strategic spots. Go for red—it's always the right signal in an erotic setting.

Flirt Alert

Be very careful when placing material over a lamp—make sure it doesn't touch the bulb, otherwise it is a serious fire hazard. Never drape on a halogen lamp, since a fire will be the guaranteed result! Never leave a burning candle unattended, and make sure the flame isn't near something (such as curtains) that can catch fire.

Color Me Impressed

Speaking of color, try for a moment to imagine your world without it. No indigo, pink, and purple sunsets. No yawning, bright green buds in early spring. No gazing into someone's eyes and discovering the intricate deepening hues that you'd never noticed before you got that close. Just one big blank canvas. Pretty boring, right? A world without color would be as interesting as staring at a snowy TV screen all day, every day.

Many people claim they don't have an eye for color or that they just don't have the confidence to experiment with it. Get over any fears about using color. You can't escape it. You respond to it every day. You "see red" when you're angry or impassioned. You feel "green" when you're inexperienced or envious. You're "blue" when you're sad.

The colors you use say a lot about your emotions, your personality, and, when it comes to setting a sexy scene, the kind of signals you want to send. You can follow the same rules for coloring your environment as you do for choosing your clothing:

➤ **Romantic.** Soft pastels in rose, pale yellow, baby blue, and lavender.

➤ **Natural.** White, off-white, and earthy hues.

➤ **Flirtatious.** Jewel tones in purple, wine, deep blue, or vibrant green.

➤ **Erotic.** Red! Although black works well with erotic clothing, avoid too much of it in your decor. It can give a gothic feel to your surroundings or, worse, remind your guest of a funeral.

Obviously, you are not going to repaint your entire home every time you want to change the mood. That's why the accessories that decorate your abode are the key place to work with color.

Every Home Tells a Story

If you've ever stayed in a bed and breakfast, you know that it's the little things that make it such a great, memorable experience. A picture on a wall, the books on a shelf, the texture of the materials that you sit or lie down on. Keep this same idea in mind when you are setting the scene in your home.

➤ Set the mood with candles.

➤ Enhance both the look and smell of your home with fresh flowers, which add an attractive, sensual element.

➤ For upholstery and furniture use soft, inviting fabrics and colors that range from demure to downright luscious.

➤ Cover your couch or chairs in slipcovers. This is an inexpensive, convenient way to change the look of a room to suit your needs. If a slipcover is still too far out of your budget, buy a large piece of material or sheet in a great fabric and color and drape over a couch or chairs. Add throw pillows in complementary tones to give it a more put-together look. (Use the sexy-scene color guide in the previous section.)

➤ Try moving things around a little to create a cozy atmosphere. Even break the rules a little. Try positioning some pieces catty-corner, or, if you have the space, put a couch or a large chair in the middle of the floor and position other pieces around it to build a conversation area.

To learn more about how your environment can improve your well-being, you might want to check out some books on the ancient Chinese art of *feng shui,* which has to do with arranging your home so that it enhances your spiritual goodness.

➤ Place a book or two on your coffee table or somewhere visible to suggest the mood you are going for. Try one of these literary lovers: *Don Juan,* by Lord Byron; *Sonnets from the Portuguese,* by Elizabeth Barrett Browning; *Lady Chatterly's Lover,* by D. H. Lawrence; *The Lover,* by Marguerite Duras; *Lolita,* by Vladimir Nabokov; *Delta of Venus,* by Anaïs Nin.

Lusty Lingo

Feng shui is the ancient Chinese art of arranging one's surroundings so that they are in harmony with one's spirit.

Romancing the Nose

To create a sexy scent-sation, ditch the potpourri air freshener and go for something more sensual and pleasing to the unsuspecting nose. Scented candles in every aroma under the sun are widely available and easy to find: from fireside scent for the immediate toasty smell of a crackling fire to chocolate scent to get the object of your desire thinking about what's for dessert! You can even find candles that smell like freshly baked banana bread or apple pie for that natural homey feeling.

In addition, you can spray your favorite cologne or perfume strategically (but *sparingly*—you don't want to stink up the place) on areas where you might be cozying up: Spritz throw pillows on the sofa, or cushions of the love seat. Or dab a scent on a light bulb; the warmth of the bulb will spread the scent throughout the room.

Flirt Alert

Spraying perfume on your sheets may seem like a good idea, but if you're not sure if your lover likes the smell, skip the spritz. You want him or her to sleep there all night—not run out choking, sneezing, and screaming, "Ah! I can't breathe in your bed!"

If you don't have a favorite scent, you might try these suggestions:

➤ **Romantic.** Try Carolina Herrera or Paris for women; Eternity or Tiffany for men. Light florals such as lavender or freesia also set a romantic mood.

➤ **Natural.** Try CK by Calvin Klein (for both men and women). Patchouli oil or any type of musk also works well.

➤ **Flirtatious.** Try Poison or Byblos for women; Cool Water by Davidoff and Polo for men. Lively scents such as citrus and honeysuckle also set a flirty mood.

➤ **Erotic.** Try Coco by Chanel or Jil Sander for women; Obsession by Calvin Klein or Anteus by Chanel for men. Heady scents such as jasmine and spices also set an erotic mood.

Fresh flowers not only smell great, they look beautiful, too. Depending on what's in season, try lilacs or roses for romance; white tulips or daisies for a natural look and smell; calla lilies or pink carnations for a flirty flavor; or orchids or bird of paradise for an erotic feel.

Sexy Is in the Ears of the Beholder

As you discovered in Chapter 6, "Getting Over Inhibitions About Your Body," music is a powerful mood enhancer. Just as films have a soundtrack, your sexy scene should have its own musical score. Remember to keep the volume high enough so you can hear it, but low enough so that it doesn't distract conversation. Here are some suggestions for sensual music in each sexy-setting category.

For romantic:

➤ Chet Baker, "The Best Thing for You"
➤ Billie Holiday, "Love Songs"
➤ k. d. lang, "Ingenue"
➤ Sarah McLachlan, "Fumbling Toward Ecstasy"
➤ Harry Connick Jr., "We Are in Love"
➤ Elvis Costello and the Attractions, "Almost Blue"

For natural:

➤ Lucinda Williams, "Car Wheels on a Gravel Road"
➤ Cat Stevens, "Greatest Hits"

Sari Says

If you don't have a multi-CD player (or any CD player) but don't want to keep getting up and down to change the music, try recording your favorite sexy tunes on tape. You can do one from each category and label them accordingly (romantic tunes, erotic rock, and so on), or you can mix it up and put some on from each category. Mixed tapes also make very sexy gifts!

➤ Sting, "Nothing Like the Sun"

➤ Spencer Lewis, "A Sense of Place"

➤ Various Artists, "A Winter's Solstice"

➤ Eric Clapton, "Unplugged"

For flirty:

➤ Frank Sinatra, "Love Is a Kick"

➤ Paco de Lucia, "Solo Quiero Caminar"

➤ John Coltrane, "Blue Train"

➤ Teddy Pendergrass, "TP"

➤ Erykah Badu, "Baduizm"

➤ Stevie Wonder, "Songs in the Key of Life"

For erotic:

➤ Luscious Jackson, "Natural Ingredients"

➤ Prince, "Dirty Mind"

➤ Madonna, "Erotica"

➤ Nina Simone, "After Hours"

➤ Barry White, "Ultimate Collection"

➤ Patti Smith, "Horses"

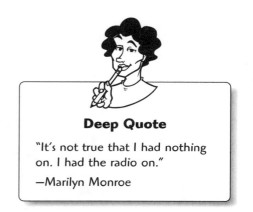

Deep Quote

"It's not true that I had nothing on. I had the radio on."

—Marilyn Monroe

The Way to Someone's Heart

How would you feel if you went over to a new boyfriend's apartment for dinner, and he served you a steaming plate of Chef Boy-R-Dee? Some women might think that he is showing his sense of humor or his great level of comfort with you. But you have to admit, if he gave you a sensual surprise it might be a bit more appreciated.

How would you like it if when you arrived, the lights were low, the candles were flickering, and he'd painstakingly prepared a meal that was clearly made to tempt more than just your rumbling stomach? Perhaps he greeted you at the door with a glass of Grand Marnier, and from that point on it was a delight of the senses. Not only was the food great, but there was something so sexy about this guy cooking up a storm in his tiny kitchen, that he became instantly irresistible to you. It worked like a charm.

Food is sexy on so many levels: It is the fact that someone has taken the time to do something so time consuming for you; it is the phenomenal aromas that naturally fill the air; it is the allure of taste and the sensuality of texture. Even if you're an inexperienced cook, there are many sensual foods you can easily prepare to enhance the mood of your date. Try some of the following:

➤ Sliced avocado.

➤ Strawberries with champagne or a bowl of homemade whipped cream for dipping.

➤ Seedless grapes.

➤ Fresh figs.

➤ Steamed artichokes with melted butter.

➤ Chilled shrimp or oysters.

➤ Chocolate fondue.

Sari Says

Looking to prepare a meal that's as hot on the brain as it is on the flame? Pick up *Intercourses: An Aphrodisiac Cookbook,* by Martha Hopkins and Randall Lockridge (Terrace Publishing, 1997). It presents a whole array of sensual delights to whet all kinds of appetites. Also, check out chef and artist Bob Blumer's cookbooks, such as *Off the Eaten Path: Recipes, Illustrations, and Objects D'Art* (Ballantine, 2000). He shows exciting, gorgeous ways to create memorable meals—and Bob's a really sexy guy, too!

Notice the one thing that all the foods in this list have in common: They can be eaten with your fingers if you choose. There is something so very sensual about edibles that can be eaten this way. Try feeding each other—and feel free to lick your fingers (despite what your mother may have told you about that).

Setting just the right scene to create a sexy atmosphere takes a little ingenuity. By using just the right lighting, soft fabrics, great scents, soothing sounds, and other special touches, you can infuse your home with the passion and personality that would make anyone want to come in and stay awhile. Everyone has a little romance, a little *au naturel,* a little flirtatiousness, and a little eroticism in them. How you choose to express it within your four walls is up to you—and that's half the fun (the other half happens when your company arrives!).

Sari Says

You might be wondering if there are any foods that are aphrodisiacs (substances that are alleged to stimulate or increase sexual desire). The fact is, there's really no such thing as a food that makes someone more sexually aroused. The only way food can turn you on is by the way you use it. Feeding an oyster to someone can be a turnon. The properties of the oyster itself are too minute to make a difference all on their own.

The Least You Need to Know

➤ Creating a sexy scene requires you to get a little creative—think about the mood you want to create (romantic, natural, flirty, erotic, or a combination of these) and work from this idea.

➤ Lighting is a key element in setting the mood—keep lights soft and low, and don't forget the candles.

➤ Don't be afraid of color—use it to send sexy messages to your guest of honor. And don't forget to use materials in soft, touchable textures.

➤ The nose knows—use scent, whether from perfumed pillows or an aromatic meal.

➤ Although used in the background, music is a vital element in setting a sexy scene.

➤ The way to someone's heart truly is through the stomach. Food—especially food that can be eaten with the fingers—is sexy on many levels.

Chapter 14

Sexy Dates

Which sounds sexier to you: dinner and a movie or a picnic and lingerie shopping trip? Of course, the latter! When you are dating someone, you want to make every effort to have a great time on your dates, right? You also want to make sure that your dating will progress. There may be a ton of sexual chemistry between you and your date. You may feel sexy and act sexy, just because you are around someone who turns you on. But even with sexual chemistry, you may still need to create sexy settings for your dates.

Creating sexy dates can help your dates progress to a stronger relationship—and possibly to a sexual relationship. And if you have been with the same partner for years, going on dates can add a spark to your relationship. There's no reason to settle for going on typical dates. In this chapter I'll give you lots of great ideas for different types of sexy dates—whether you're on your first date with that person, or married or in a committed relationship with that person. Sexy dates are for everyone to enjoy!

What Are Sexy Dates?

When you consider what makes a date with someone sexy, does your mind automatically think s-e-x? Sure, having sex on a date can be sexy, but having a sexy date is about much more than that. Sexy dates create interest and desire. You are setting the scene to tantalize your date. Dating needs to foster the development of love and possibly sex. Creating a sexy date will do that.

Sari Says

While spontaneity is sexy, when you are dating, you need to make some plans. So get to know your neighborhood restaurants, so you can choose a romantic one at the spur of the moment. Keep a bottle of champagne in your fridge at all times. Buy some sexy outfits that you wear just on dates.

Sari Says

There's a fun area on America Online (AOL) that helps people figure out things to do on dates. Go to Keyword: Date Planner. Click on the Q and A, then answer the questions about what you like to do on dates, and it will give you a long list of creative suggestions. The more flexible your choice of answers, the more dates will be suggested.

Sexy dates can be anything that you and your date enjoy, where you will feel relaxed enough to let your personalities shine through. On a sexy date, you'll do lots of flirting, flattering, handholding, hugging, and kissing to increase your intimacy and feeling of sexiness. Most of all, you'll have lots of fun!

Daytime Dates

Daytime dates may be the best way to get to know someone new. They work great for first dates, because then there is not as much pressure about whether or not you're going to have sex. They also work well if you and the person have gone on a dinner date or two, and now you are looking for a way to do more interesting activities together—and to see what the person looks like in the light of the day. Also, daytime dates can help recharge a long-term relationship, especially if you play hooky from work to have a special day together. In order to be sexy during the day, make romantic dates and have fun together. Here are some great ideas.

Picnic in the Park

Pull together a picnic basket with the emphasis on sensuality and romance. That means including a bottle of wine (if you and your date drink it), wine glasses, a candle and matches, and some delicious finger food, such as strawberries, chocolate, cheese, and bread. Use a red and white checkered blanket for a classic romantic touch. You can bring a portable CD player for some mood music. You might even bring along a rose to give to your date.

Choose your picnic location carefully. You don't want a place where you'll get hit in the head with a Frisbee, or where a nearby group is having a noisy family barbecue. If it's a new date, you shouldn't choose a place that's too isolated, so your date doesn't feel threatened. If you're with a longtime partner, go revisit a place that evokes a romantic memory that you share. Then lounge, lunch, laugh, and enjoy your sexy date.

Flirt Alert

Beach dates are not for everyone. If you or your date have body image issues (see Chapter 6, "Getting Over Inhibitions About Your Body"), you or your date may not feel comfortable in a bathing suit. Or if you or your date have a wandering eye and can't deal with seeing others in bathing suits—then a beach date might not be the best option for you, either. You will both need to feel secure enough with your bodies to be comfortable on the date. You need to be interested enough in each other that you will not gawk at others, or get jealous if your date does.

Day at the Beach

Going to the beach can be a great date, because it can include play time, relaxation, and romance. Scout out a romantic, not-too-crowded beach. The two of you can go for a long walk in the surf, swim, and jump in the waves. You can play volleyball, Frisbee, or catch. Bring a pail and shovel to build your dream house as a sandcastle. You can go for a run, or just lay back and enjoy the warmth of the sun. Enjoy the sexy feelings of rubbing sunscreen on each other. Create memories by collecting some shells and other beach treasures. If you enjoy walking on the beach at sunset, you can even make a night of it.

Photo by The Picture Book.

151

Pottery Class

Like the sexy scene from the movie *Ghost,* you can help each other spin a pot on a potter's wheel. Or you can just paint ready-made mugs or plates at a paint-your-own pottery place. You could have fun using each other as creative inspiration. Also, you can learn about each other: how you each paint, how imaginative you are, and how you express yourselves.

All the time that you'll spend painting will also give you an opportunity to talk and get to know each other, or if you've been together for years, to reconnect. One more thing about pottery painting that can be really fun is that you might even have a little flirtatious paint fight! Finally, going to pottery class can be a great date because you have to come back in about a week to pick up your finished products. That means that you'll have to make one more date.

Amusement Park

Winning the big stuffed lion at the dart game and presenting it to your date. Grabbing your partner tightly while you whoosh around the hairpin turns on a roller coaster. Sharing a sweet kiss after eating cotton candy. What could be more fun than a day at an amusement park? Enjoy this fun date with someone new, or as a way to feel young at heart with your longtime love.

Photo by The Picture Book.

Workout Buddies

Working out together can be a great date and can keep you in shape, too. If you or your date belong to a gym, go there, or you can always get a day pass to any gym. You can lift weights, help each other adjust the equipment, and do the Stairmaster side by side. Or you can forgo the gym and have an outdoor workout: Go in-line skating, hiking, or do any sort of physical workout together. Once your endorphins kick in, you'll surely feel sexy for each other.

Sexy Fun Around Town

There is so much that you can do to have fun, laughs, and a good time. Go for a walk hand in hand with your date. Take your dog to a dog park, then sit with your date, and watch the pooch get acquainted other dogs—how romantic! Go to an outdoor concert and pick one song to be "your song." Browse at a flea market, crafts fair, or street festival—then buy one thing each to give to each other. Enjoy a sporting event—kiss every time your team scores. Go to a museum and steal a kiss or two when no one is around. Don't forget to bring a camera on your jaunt to preserve the memories.

Sari Says

Always be on the lookout for great date ideas in your town. Read your local newspaper and keep your eyes open for fliers and posters announcing upcoming events, such as concerts, arts and crafts fairs, sporting events, touring plays or comedy troupes, dog or cat shows, car or boat shows, or food expos.

Sexy Shopping Trip

If you both like shopping, you can really make a great date of it. Each of you can pick a favorite store to introduce to the other person. Have some fun at the mall: Play with the gadgets at the electronic stores, try samples of ice cream flavors in the food court, and people-watch. If you pass a flower store, ask your date to wait a sec while you go in to buy one for him or her. Pick an outfit for each other at the clothing store. The more you shop together, the more you'll learn about each other's likes and dislikes—and that kind of intimacy is sexy.

If you're with someone for whom shopping is not a favorite activity, then put a sexy spin on it to pique his or her interest in this type of date. What if you go shopping for lingerie? Or even for sex toys in an adult store? Going on a sexy shopping trip with a date can lead to a night of excitement.

Sari Says

Men have different tastes in what style of lingerie they like to see women wearing. See Chapter 11, "Dressing Sexy," for ideas about the variety you can choose from to look natural, flirtatious, romantic, or erotic. Then have your own lingerie fashion show (more about that a little later in this chapter).

Nighttime Dates

Most couples go out to dinner on a date. That's okay, but there are loads of other creative ideas for sexy nighttime dates. One key to planning a sexy nighttime date is to use the night to create a sexy mood. For example, rather than driving somewhere on your date, try walking to a nearby park so you can gaze up at the stars. A date on a night with a full moon can be especially sexy. But no matter what the cycle of the moon, you can create a sexy date by trying some of the following ideas.

Dinner and Dancing

If you're used to a typical dinner-and-a-movie date, try something instead of a movie for a little added excitement: dancing. If you don't feel like you are good enough dancers to hit the floor right now, try taking a dance class together first. This can be especially sexy for a couple in a long-term relationship.

You can vary the type of restaurant you go to and the type of dancing you do. Go out to eat barbecue food, then go country line dancing. Or dress up in your finest, then go out to dinner at a four-star restaurant followed by swing dancing at a club or waltzing in a grand hotel ballroom. Or have a romantic picnic under the stars and slow dance together (who needs music?). Whether it's dancing to disco or big band, dancing together is sexy because you can see how your date moves, and you can touch, flirt, and laugh.

Hot Tubbing

For a sexy date that will make you really hot, try relaxing in a hot tub. The warm bubbling water can really turn you on. You'll have an opportunity to talk with each other and to see each other wearing next to nothing (or nothing at all). Even suggesting a hot tub date is a sure-fire way to signal to your lover that you're in the mood to sex up your relationship. And don't forget the bottle of bubbly.

Theme Dates

Theme dates are a great way to show off your creativity and sexiness. Think about some sexy themes, such as "Italian night." You can eat dinner at a dark, romantic restaurant, rent an Italian film, and maybe even wear those sexy Italian leather pants. Or try Mardi Gras night, when you eat Cajun food, wear brightly colored beads, dance to Zydeco music, and do a little love spell to get things really hot. Come up with as many creative themes as you can, and you'll have lots of great ideas for nighttime dates.

At-Home Dates

When you really want to turn on the sex appeal, what could be better than having a date at home? You have access to many sexy things—including the bedroom. Spruce up your home so it looks and feels warm and inviting (for some tips, see Chapter 13, "Sexiness Begins at Home: Creating a Sexy Environment"). You can have the home-date advantage.

Candlelight Dinner

Show someone that you really care for him or her by cooking dinner at your place. Carefully plan the meal, timing it so that you don't have to do much work in the kitchen once your date gets there. When your date arrives, have candles and wine all ready to go on the table. It'll be so romantic! The dim light will even make your and your partner's pupils dilate, which will make you both seem more attractive to each other.

Champagne in Bed

This is the type of date that's a little bit more than just a date. Maybe it follows cooking dinner for a special lover at your place. Or perhaps it's a way to show off that lingerie that you bought on your sexy shopping date. Drinking a bottle of champagne together often leads to one thing. So if that's where you are with your relationship, it might be the perfect date for you!

A Date in Front of the TV

Maybe watching television on a date doesn't seem so sexy to you. But if you're starting a new relationship, it can actually lead to more intimacy. Watching TV together gives you plenty of time to see what the other person is like when you're just around the house. Or if you've been together for years, it can be a way to feel closer, without having to plan an elaborate night out. You can snuggle next to each other on the sofa. Just don't have too big a love spat over who gets the remote control.

Flirt Alert

When you're watching TV with your date, don't get so comfortable that you fall sound asleep and start snoring right there on the couch. This is not sexy at all.

Lingerie Fashion Show

Another great reason to stay at home on a date is to have a sexy lingerie fashion show for your partner. Set your partner up in comfortable spot, maybe on the sofa in the living room, or even on the edge of your bed. Then try on all the lingerie you have, one piece at a time, prancing in front of your partner to show off each of your different outfits. If you and your date went shopping for lingerie, now's the time to show it off.

Sex All Night

This kind of date would certainly not be a first date. This is the kind of nighttime date for people who have been going out long enough that they have already had sex with each other, or they are married, and they are looking for a little sexual thrill. Making a date to have sex all night is a way to plan for sex, without taking away spontaneity and excitement. After all, you have all night to think of different ways to do it!

Sari Says

For couples who have children, making a date to have sex all night, either when the children are away or you can get away, is a great way to be sexual in a way that you can't be when the kids are home.

Weekend Dates

If things are going well in your relationship and you want to get even closer, or if the sexiness is waning between you and your partner and you want to invigorate your sex life and your relationship, try a great weekend date. It will be a mini-vacation, and a way for the two of you to focus on each other.

Exploring Sites in Your Own City

You can enjoy a sexy, romantic weekend without going far from home. Call your local chamber of commerce to find out about the different sites that you can explore in your city. Read a travel guide to your own area, or search your own town on a travel site online. Then live like a tourist for a day and enjoy the attractions.

Country Inns/Bed and Breakfasts

For a weekend getaway that will be totally relaxing, go to a romantic country inn or bed and breakfast. You can sleep late in a calm setting, on a big old feather bed, maybe in a room with a fireplace. Spend the days hiking, horseback riding, antiquing, or just recharging your batteries. The inn may offer elaborate meals or close access to a small romantic restaurant, which can be a nice start to a sexy night.

Camping

Ahhh, the great outdoors … that feeling of fresh air, the smell of pine needles, the little tent in which you need to snuggle to keep warm. Camping can be such a sexy way to get closer to someone, especially if you have a sleeping bag meant for two. Plan the trip together; call ahead to reserve a campsite. Shop together for all the camping equipment you'll need, and even for the peanuts and raisins for your trail mix. Camping can be good for your relationship. When you're hiking in the woods, you need to communicate and trust each other. Those things make for a sexy relationship.

Island Getaway

Flying off to an island in the Caribbean, for example, or to Hawaii can be the perfect sexy getaway. Spend your days on the beach, snorkeling or scuba diving, or sightseeing. Spend your night enjoying tropical drinks and the warm ocean breezes. If you live in a cold climate, it's a great way to feel warm again. Also, getting away from it all to a romantic island is a sexy way to reconnect and have time to enjoy sex with your partner.

Ski Trip

Whether it's the exhilaration of swooshing down the slopes with your love, or sipping hot chocolate near the fire in the ski lodge, a ski vacation can be very sexy. The physical activity of skiing all day can invigorate you. Most ski towns have romantic restaurants and clubs in which to dine and dance the night away. After a long day of skiing, you can also soak in a hot tub together or massage each other's sore muscles.

More Tips to Fire Up Your Dates

No matter where you go on your date, there are some things you can do to always make it a sexier date:

➤ **Dress in a sexy style.** What you wear can set a sexy mood. Whether it's an erotic outfit, like leather pants and a tank top, or a romantically sexy outfit, like a flowing skirt (for women) or soft corduroy (for men), choose something that says "I want you to touch me!" Review Chapter 11 for more details on dressing sexy.

➤ **Talk about positive topics.** The things you say on the date can make or break the sexiness factor. Discuss topics that you have in common. (But not negative things like why you both hate your jobs.) Talk about your lives. (But don't talk about your ex or past

Flirt Alert

If you're in a new relationship, make sure that you have spent several days in a row together at home before you take your new love on the road. Some couples who have never spent more than one night at a time together find out that they bicker nonstop when they spend a whole weekend or a week together. It's better to learn that at home rather than on vacation.

Sari Says

If you are on a second, third, or later date, it can be very sexy to bring your date a small gift. Flowers are always welcome. Or you could choose something more creative, like some chocolate chip cookies that you baked yourself, or a book you just know your date would love.

sexual conquests.) Share information about something the other person might not know. (But don't sound condescendingly preachy.) Discuss issues in the news or current events. (But don't debate, argue, or complain.) Flirt, too! Read Chapter 12, "Sexy Flirting Techniques," for more about flirting.

➤ **Don't sweat the little stuff.** For example, don't freak out if your CD player jams when you wanted to play some sexy Billie Holiday, or if you forget the wine glasses on your picnic. Laugh it off and improvise. You can always sing a song together, or take turns drinking right out of the wine bottle.

➤ **Treat your date with respect and show interest.** Showing up on time is the first sign of respect to your date. Throughout the date, be polite and courteous. Say "please" and "thank you." It shows that you care enough about your date to really pay attention to his or her needs. Also, really listen to what your date talks about, and ask follow-up questions. You should really want to get to know your date. *That's* sexy.

➤ **Use sexy body language, but don't come on too strong.** Let your eye contact say that you are into your partner. Casually touch your partner to show your interest, but do not grope further than you know your partner wants. Review Chapter 10, "Body Talk: Using Sexy Body Language," for more on making your body talk.

➤ **Give good follow-up.** Give your date a good-night kiss. Then call the same night after the date, just to say that you had a great time. Or call the next day. Either the man or the woman can call—just as long as one of you calls.

The sexiest thing about a date with someone new is wanting to have another date with that person. The sexiest thing about a date with someone whom you've been with for a long time is feeling like you really reconnected and had a great time with each other. With a little planning and attention, all your dates can be sexy dates!

The Least You Need to Know

➤ Anyone can have a fun, sexy date!

➤ You can come up with creative ideas for many types of sexy dates.

➤ You can have sexy dates at home, out at night, during the day, or over a weekend.

➤ Remember to keep it sexy throughout the date by what you wear, say, and how you treat your date.

Chapter 15

Sexy Gifts for the One You Love

In This Chapter

➤ When should you give a gift?

➤ Choosing from the variety of store-bought sexy gifts

➤ Sexy gifts that don't cost a thing

➤ Composing a love letter

➤ Compliments that will make your lover feel sexy

If actions speak louder than words, then gift giving is a surefire way to show your partner how sexy and loving you can be. From the most traditional, like flowers or sexy underwear, to the more creative, like a homemade scrapbook showcasing the highlights of your love affair, gifts can touch your lover's heart, and spark your lover's desire.

Contrary to what you may think, you don't have to spend a lot of money on a gift that shows your sexiness. A simple bouquet of handpicked wildflowers can mean just as much as something bought at a store. It's not the amount of money you spend, but the *thought* that counts!

In this chapter I'll tell you about the best times to give gifts and the best ways to surprise your lover, as well as tons of great ideas for sexy gifts—including gifts that won't cost you a dime.

Honey, I Have a Surprise for You

How would you feel if on your birthday, your lover filled your room with a hundred balloons, presented you with a gigantic bouquet of fragrant flowers, and then gave you a little something special in one of those aqua boxes from Tiffany? Or if he or she cooked a romantic dinner for just the two of you and served it on a candlelit table? You'd probably feel excited, valued, thankful, and, yes, lustful! Gift giving at the right time can really make someone feel great, and can make a relationship. On the other hand, forgetting to give a gift at appropriate times can break a relationship. So when are the all-important times to give gifts?

There are the times when you should always give a gift to your lover—no excuses:

➤ Birthday

➤ Wedding anniversary

➤ Anniversary of the day you met

➤ Valentine's Day

➤ Christmas (or each night of Chanukah)

➤ Mother's Day or Father's Day if you are parents

Here are some times when it can be extra sexy to give a gift:

➤ The day after you say "I love you" for the first time

➤ The anniversary of the first time you had sex

➤ When you had great sex the night before

➤ When you are on vacation

➤ When you are attending a wedding of someone in your partner's family

➤ When your partner is going through stress at work or in his or her personal life

➤ When you are apologizing for doing something that upset your partner

➤ To cheer up your partner when he or she is feeling blue

➤ The first night in your new home together

➤ When you feel great about how the relationship is going in general

➤ Just because you see something you know your partner would like

If you haven't given a gift to your partner yet, then you have to start. But you may be wondering, "How soon is too soon?" Giving a gift too early in a relationship can throw it off whack, seeming confusing to the person you are dating. For example, if you gave someone an expensive piece of jewelry after only three dates, the person may think that you are rushing things, that you don't understand the natural progression of a relationship, or that you are trying to buy love.

On the other hand, not giving a gift soon enough could make your partner think that you are not romantic enough, or that you just don't care. The basic rule of thumb is that you should give a small gift or two (such as flowers or a CD of music that he or she might like) when you are establishing your relationship, such as after the first or second month. Then give a larger gift (such as lingerie, jewelry, or anything personal) on special occasions when you are fully established as a couple (between three months and six months), whichever comes first. And as long as your relationship progresses, continue to give gifts throughout.

For those of you who have been married or in a long-term relationship for years, it's still important to give gifts to your partner to show that you appreciate him or her. Go beyond the usual Christmas and birthday gift giving and give thoughtful gifts "just because." Try surprising your partner with lunch at a nice restaurant or tickets to a movie he or she's been wanting to see. For some exciting ideas about other ways to keep the spark alive in a long-term relationship, check out Chapter 20, "Does Being Sexy Mean You Must Have Sex?"

Sari Says

If you go on a trip away from your lover, always bring back a little something. It doesn't matter whether it's a silly snow globe that you picked up in the airport or something more personal. The important thing is to bring home a gift to show you've been thinking of your lover.

When it comes to the actual giving of the gift, there are many sexy and fun ways to surprise your lover. Here are some of my favorite ideas:

➤ Put the gift on his or her pillow to be discovered at bedtime.

➤ If you're going away on a trip, leave your lover a little gift, such as a card or handwritten note, to find after you're gone. Spray the card or note lightly with some of your cologne.

➤ If your lover is the one leaving on a trip, hide a small gift or card in his or her suitcase to be discovered later.

➤ Put the gift in the bathroom so it's the first thing your lover sees in the morning.

➤ Put the gift in his or her briefcase.

➤ Hide the gift in the dishwasher with the clean dishes, then ask your lover to unload the dishes.

➤ Put the gift next to his or her place at the dinner table.

➤ Try the old "nesting box" technique. If you're giving a significant gift such as a ring, try putting the jewelry box in a larger box, such as a shoebox, and wrapping that. It will throw your partner off guard, especially if she's been expecting a ring!

With a little imagination, you can make giving the gift as exciting as the gift itself!

Flirt Alert

Don't give gifts to try to influence, control, or manipulate your lover. For example, if you fight all the time, and you are afraid that your lover will leave you, don't give a gift to try to convince him or her to stay. Giving a gift in this case is not sexy; you are trying to make yourself feel better, rather than to show your love. Your lover still may feel good about getting a gift, but it is not a sign of a good relationship and it won't fix the underlying problem.

Great Gift Ideas

Imagine that you are going for a walk with your lover one night. You pick up a stone from the side of the road, hand it to your lover, and say, "This is a gift from me to you, so you'll always remember that our love is the road to true happiness." I am sure that your lover would always cherish that nondescript little stone.

Sometimes it doesn't matter what you give your lover, as long as you are thoughtful enough to give something. But if you are stumped about what you should give, I can help you with a few of my favorite gift ideas.

Deep Quote

"Love is the flower of life, and blossoms unexpectedly and without law, and must be plucked where it is found, and enjoyed for the brief hour of its duration."

—D. H. Lawrence

Flower Power

One of the easiest and most traditional sexy gifts are flowers. From a single red rose to an elaborate arrangement, giving flowers is great on many levels. They are beautiful to look at, they can enhance the sexy surroundings of your lover's home, and they smell great, too. Another great reason to give flowers is that they are often used as a symbol of love. Try some especially fragrant flowers that evoke a particular sexy mood. As I explained in Chapter 13, "Sexiness Begins at Home: Creating a Sexy Environment," you can choose different scents for a different effect:

➤ Lilacs, freesia, pink sweetheart roses for a romantic look and sweet smell

➤ White tulips or daisies for a natural look and smell

➤ Cala lilies, pink carnations, or stargazer lilies for flirty flowers

➤ Red roses, tiger lilies, or bird of paradise for an erotic feel

To make the gift of flowers even more memorable, buy an ornate vase to put the flowers in. That way, the memory of the flowers will live on long after the last bloom dies. Also, your lover will have a beautiful vase ready for the next time you bring home flowers.

Books That Lead to Sexy Looks

Some books make sexy gifts, because they can relay sexy or romantic themes. I've broken them down for you into two categories: romantic gift books and sexy gift books.

Here are some great ideas for romantic books to give your lover:

➤ *The Giving Tree,* by Shel Silverstein (HarperCollins, 1986)

➤ *Griffin and Sabine,* by Nick Bantock (Chronicle Books, 1991)

➤ *Leaves of Grass,* by Walt Whitman (Modern Library, 1993)

➤ *101 Classic Love Poems* (Contemporary, 1996)

➤ *Love Poems,* by Elizabeth Barrett Browning (Contemporary, 1998)

➤ A travel book of a place you want to take your partner

➤ A first edition of your partner's favorite book

➤ A copy of a book that you know your partner loved as a child

Here are some more overtly sexy books you can give. Okay, the last one is a shameless plug, but I promise, this really is a great and sexy book!

➤ *Adonis: Masterpieces of Male Erotic Photography,* by Michelle Olley (Thunders, 1999)

➤ *Erotic by Nature: A Celebration of Life, of Love, and of Our Wonderful Bodies,* by David Steinberg (Down There Press, 1988)

➤ *The Complete Kama Sutra: The First Unabridged Modern Translation of the Classic Indian Text,* by Alain Danielou (Inner Traditions, 1995)

➤ *The Complete Idiot's Guide to Amazing Sex,* by Sari Locker (Alpha Books, 1999)

Sari Says

Write a sexy message in the front of the book, so your lover can read your feelings behind the gift. Then sign it, so your lover will always remember that you gave him or her the book.

Diamonds Are a Girl's Best Friend

If you are giving your lover jewelry, the first step is figuring out how much you want to spend. If you want to buy something inexpensive, go with some silver jewelry. You can get a cool-looking ring, necklace, or bracelet for between $20 and $100.

Photo by The Picture Book.

If you want to spend a little more money, go for the gold. Department stores usually have affordable nice gold jewelry, such as a gold chain necklace with a small diamond for $100 to $200. If you bought the same sort of thing at a fancy jewelry store, it would be closer to $500. The same goes for rings. You can get gold rings set with diamonds and semiprecious stones for a couple of hundred dollars in a less expensive department store, and they will still be good quality. In a jewelry store, the same type of thing would run between $600 and $1,000.

Once you decide how much you can spend, you can choose what to get by considering your lover's personal style. If the gift is for a woman who you have never seen wearing a bracelet, get her a necklace instead. If it's for a man who doesn't wear a watch, go for a money clip instead of jewelry. Consider the person's fashion sense also. For example, if the gift is for a woman who is natural and earthy, silver might be more fitting, with maybe turquoise or amber. If it's for a high-powered go-getter, maybe gold and rubies would work well. For a nice touch, consider getting the jewelry engraved with a loving message.

Lacy, Lovely Lingerie Makes a Thoughtful Gift

As I mentioned in Chapter 11, "Dressing Sexy," lingerie (for women) or sexy underwear (for men) may be the sexiest gift of all. After you give it, you can ask to see it on, and that can lead to only one thing (wink, wink). There are so many different types. Keeping with the categories of sexiness that I have referred to throughout the book, here are a few of your choices.

For men:

➤ For romantic sexiness, buy your guy a great pair of silk boxer shorts.

➤ To be flirty, get him some attractively colored briefs.

➤ To be erotic, get him some snug bikinis or a G-string.

For women:

➤ A romantic gift of lingerie would include a lacy bra and matching panties.

➤ For a more flirtatious style, give her a short silk robe.

➤ More elaborate lingerie, such as a teddy or corset, is erotic, as are a racy garter belt and stockings, or a push-up bra and a thong.

Romantic or flirtatious lingerie is available in any department store. Erotic varieties can be found in adult stores, or specialty lingerie shops. See Appendix C, "Resources," for more information.

Giving a gift of jewelry or lingerie is also sexy because it can be worn over and over, keeping the feeling of love and sexiness alive.

Free Love: No-Cost Gifts

You don't have to spend a lot of money to give a sexy gift to your lover. A gift that you make by hand, or a well-executed creative idea, can be just as thoughtful and exciting as a store-bought gift.

Here are some sexy things you can do for your lover that won't cost you a dime:

➤ Have a radio station play "your" song with your special dedication, and ask him or her to listen.

➤ Present your lover with a handmade "gift certificate" for something like a backrub, a day together in the park, or even a bubble bath for two.

➤ Sing a love song on your lover's answering machine.

➤ Compose a poem or a ballad about your lover. It doesn't have to be ultra-romantic— try a funny poem that incorporates some of his or her likes and dislikes as well as personality quirks.

Deep Quote

"Say you don't need no diamond ring,
And I'll be satisfied.
Tell me that you want the kind of things
That money just can't buy.
I don't care too much for money,
Money can't buy me love."

—The Beatles, "Can't Buy Me Love"

➤ Leave erotic Post-it notes all over his or her house.

➤ Flirt shamelessly with your lover over dinner.

➤ Dance by candlelight in the living room.

➤ Read aloud to your lover before bed (try one of the books I mentioned earlier).

Being a Crafty Lover

Remember how much your parents loved it when you brought home from your elementary school a messy finger painting or a Popsicle-stick house? Now that you're all grown up, giving handmade gifts to your lover can evoke an even more excited response. Of course, you don't have eat a dozen Popsicles to make something for your love. There are tons of "grown-up" things you can make. Sexy handmade gifts are great because they are personal, from the heart, and they don't cost much at all.

Here are some ideas for special gifts that cost under 10 dollars:

➤ Record some of his or her favorite songs on a cassette tape.

➤ Bake cookies and put them in a tin that you decorated with pictures of things your lover likes, including a picture of the two of you. (By the way, you don't have to make cookies from scratch; it's perfectly fine to make the slice-and-bake variety. Remember, it's the thought that counts.)

➤ Bake a heart-shaped cake.

➤ Frame a great picture of the two of you.

➤ Give a few little gifts that symbolize some of the special things you've done together or things you have in common (for example, a CD of a band you heard together, a poster for the first movie that you saw together).

Sari Says

Sexy gifts increase the intimacy in your relationship. They tell your lover that you are always there for each other. Gifts show that you want to make the extra effort to keep the relationship going strong.

Another great inexpensive gift is to make a wonderful card for your lover. You can make it yourself, to make it more personal and meaningful than a store-bought card. Use materials like red construction paper, white doilies, pink tissue paper, glitter, stickers, buttons, and cutout pictures from other cards or magazines. If you want, include a picture of you two together. Write a few lines about why he or she is so special to you, or about the good times that you've shared. Or if you want to go a step further, write an entire love letter.

How to Write a Love Letter

You can write a letter that makes your lover's heart melt with its romantic sentiments, a lighthearted and charming letter that makes him laugh, or an erotic letter that makes her breathe a bit harder. The most important thing is to speak from your heart. Say what you think. It does not have to be flowery or fancy writing. You just want to tell your lover how you really feel: your inner emotions, your deep desires.

Here are some more tips:

➤ Handwrite the letter instead of typing it. Do a practice copy, if necessary, to make sure the finished copy is neat, with no crossed-out words or misspellings.

➤ Think about lines that you've heard in songs that make you think of your relationship.

➤ Seal the letter with a kiss by putting on lipstick, and lightly kissing the envelope.

➤ Lightly spritz the finished letter with your cologne or perfume (make sure the ink is dry first!).

➤ Mail it, even if you live together.

Here's a sample love letter to get you started:

Sari Says

Love letters mean more than just telling someone how you feel. Somehow, seeing the words in print give the person a sense that you mean it, that you stand by what you say, and that you want your love to have a sense of permanence.

Dear Darling,

Every moment of the day you fill my thoughts. I think about how warm and wonderful it feels to hold you close. Your warm breath on my neck, your tender kisses on my face, the feeling of your tongue circling mine. The feeling of your hand on my thigh. I long for you.

Having you in my life is so extraordinary. The little things you do for me, the only-us things we do together, the love you show me every day—that is what makes you the love of my life. Your sexy lips, the way you hold me when we sleep, how good it feels to have you inside me—that is what makes you my sex god! I want you! I need you! I love you!

Love,

Your one and only

Put Some Planning into It

You can think of some other sexy gifts that take a bit of planning. One great idea is to make a video for your lover that shows some highlights of your relationship, like a video scrapbook. Go to all the places that mean something to the two of you, and shoot yourself there talking about your memories. Then just talk into the camera for a few minutes at the end to say how much your lover means to you.

If you don't have a video camera, you can make a real scrapbook instead. It's the same sort of idea. Go to all the places that mean something to you two, take a photo of each place, and include a memento from each one: a menu from the restaurant where you went on your first date; ticket stubs from an event you went to; sand left over in your shoes from your trip to the beach. Buy a nice scrapbook and put it all together with funny, loving, and sexy captions.

Something else you could plan to do for you lover is create a scavenger hunt. Instead of doing this the typical way in which you look for odd objects, give clues for him or her to go to one place, then the next, getting gifts and clues at each stop. All you give to start is the first clue, like "At 5 P.M. you should walk two blocks north from your apartment, then go into the store with the red awning. It will be as fragrant as your morning breath smells to me." When your lover gets there, it is a flower store, and it has flowers waiting for him from you, and the clerk will give him the next clue! You have three places like this; then the final clue is something like "Go to the apartment of the person you love, and the dog will give the next clue." Attached to your dog's collar is the last clue, which is a card from you that invites your lover to a romantic dinner at a nearby restaurant.

"You Look Soooo Sexy!"

Sometimes one of the sexiest gifts you can give someone is a compliment. It costs you nothing, but it can mean so much to your partner. Here are some great things to say to your lover. Say the words often, and make sure you mean them!

➤ "I love you."

➤ "You are so beautiful."

➤ "You're all I've ever wanted."

➤ "You complete me."

➤ "You make me feel safe."

➤ "I love looking at you."

➤ "I love the way you feel."

➤ "You're so much fun to be with."

➤ "You look so sexy."

➤ "I love the way you taste."

➤ "I want to hold you forever."

➤ "I love making love with you."

Tell your lover that you love him or her often. Don't just wait for a special occasion to say these things. Everyone needs to hear how his or her lover really feels. Never assume that he or she just "knows" how you feel. Sure, actions speak louder than words—but words are very important, too.

Flirt Alert

Mean what you say! Don't just say what you think your lover wants to hear. For example, don't tell your partner that you love his or her outfit when you really hate it. Your lover may wear that outfit over and over, thinking that it will turn you on, when you are really turned off each time. (Of course, make sure you use some tact when telling your lover what you really think of the outfit!)

Sex as a Gift

Sometimes, the perfect gift can be a gift of sex. Remember, sex should never be used to manipulate someone, nor should it be used as barter (as in: "I'll have sex with you if you do the dishes tonight"). But, if you want to be fun, sexy, and generous, you can give sexual favors to your lover as gifts. One great way to do this is to write out a "sex coupon" redeemable for whatever sex act you know your lover would enjoy. I include ready-made sex coupons on the tearcard in the front of this book. You can use those, or make up your own. Simply think of the sexy act that you'd like to do, then think of a clever way to say it, for example …

Redeem This Coupon for One Hour of Oral Pleasure

I will taste, lick, and tease you to great heights of ecstasy. You choose the time and place, and I'll be waiting to enjoy you to the fullest

---

If you would rather not give sex as a gift, try a gift of some other sort of physical affection, such as giving a back massage, washing your lover's hair, or holding your lover extra long and close during *afterplay*. Giving pure pleasure and attention can make you and your lover both feel sexy.

Lusty Lingo

Afterplay is the affectionate time that occurs after sex or orgasm, usually consisting of caressing, cuddling, talking, eating, or getting ready to make love again.

The Least You Need to Know

➤ Gifts show your love, and that's sexy. You don't need to spend a lot of money on a gift for your partner; it's the thought that counts.

➤ Sometimes sexy gifts are things that have to do with sex, like lingerie.

➤ Sexy gifts can also evoke sexy feelings, like giving flowers.

➤ Look for fun ways to present your gifts. Surprises can be very sexy!

➤ Telling your lover how you feel toward him or her by writing a sexy love letter is a wonderful gift.

➤ As long as you are not manipulative about it and feel comfortable doing so, it's fine to give sex or other physical affection as a gift to your partner.

Part 4
Sex and Sexiness

Sexiness isn't always about having sex. I think I've made that pretty clear by now. But, come on, when you want to do the deed, sexiness is your best asset. Being sexy is how you express your sexuality—and sometimes what you're saying is, "Hey! You! I want to have sex! Right here! Right now!"

The thing about sex is, if you don't keep it sexy, it can become pretty ho-hum. Now, this is not to say that there's some secret position to cure all that bores you (although I'll tell you about a few ways to add variety and excitement to maintain a sexy sex life).

Sexy sex is about enthusiasm. I'm not talking rah-rah cheerleader enthusiasm, I'm talking about spicing things up: romancing the brain, talking sexy, having sexy fantasies, trying new sexual positions, and creating an imaginative sexy trick or two to leave you both breathless. So, in the wonderful words of Marvin Gaye, "Let's get it on."

Chapter 16

If You Want Me, Just Whistle: Using Sexiness to Initiate Sex

> ### In This Chapter
>
> ➤ Learning to seduce like you mean it
>
> ➤ Flirting, teasing, and tempting your way to sexiness
>
> ➤ Ways to make your body language say what you really want
>
> ➤ Kissing and touching to heat things up to a steamy climax

In seafaring folklore, it's said that the bewitching sweetness of the song sung by the women sirens was so outrageously tempting, sailors abandoned all navigational techniques to steer their ships toward that hypnotic sound and the promise of what lay behind it.

Of course, you don't want your lover to smash into a bunch of rocks, but you do want to be so incredibly tempting that your lover will gladly go anywhere and do anything when he or she feels the lure of your charms. In this chapter, you'll use all the lessons you've learned so far to become the ultimate tempter and keep your lover begging at your bedroom door.

Simply Irresistible

You know when the time comes to get down to business. Maybe you've been dating someone you simply can't resist anymore and with whom you want to feel physically intimate; or maybe it's been a while since you and your significant other have had really great sex, or any sex at all. Or maybe you're just tired of always being the one on the receiving end—maybe *you* want to decide that it's time to do the deed and be the initiator for a change.

Whatever your scenario, it's time to unleash your inner tempter or temptress. He or she is in there, maybe closer to the surface than you realize. You just need a few lessons (or maybe just a refresher course) in the ways of seduction.

Deep Quote

"Eroticism and love are like a dance: one always leads the other."

—Milan Kundera, author of *The Unbearable Lightness of Being*

Like any fine art, the dance of seduction has its own techniques, which can be adapted to your own style once you figure out which you are most comfortable with. There are several ways to go about it. You can choose one, some, or all. Sexual temptation can be broken down into three main components:

1. Intellectual seduction
2. Physical seduction
3. Seduction of the senses

The third component, seduction of the senses, has been thoroughly discussed in Chapter 13, "Sexiness Begins at Home: Creating a Sexy Environment," so in this chapter, I'll concentrate on helping you with the first two: seduction of the mind and of the body.

Sari Says

Movies are more than just entertainment—take a cue from some of these steamier Hollywood flicks to help you plan your own seductive scenes:

➤ *The Postman Always Rings Twice*

➤ *The Unbearable Lightness of Being*

➤ *The Big Easy*

➤ *9½ Weeks*

➤ *La Belle Epoch*

➤ *Risky Business*

➤ *Fatal Attraction*

➤ *Basic Instinct*

➤ *Body Heat*

➤ *Ghost*

➤ *White Palace*

➤ *From Here to Eternity*

Romancing the Brain: Sexy Techniques of the Mind

It all stems from that thing between your ears—if your *brain* isn't turned on, the rest of you will remain sedately indifferent as well. Being sexy is about more than lace panties and hard bodies, it's about having the right frame of mind as well. In order to tempt, lure, titillate, and seduce, you need to stimulate the mind as well as the body of the object of your desire.

Think about when you are watching a movie with a really hot sex scene. *You* aren't having sex, but watching the scene probably gets you all hot and bothered. When trying to seduce someone intellectually, you are using ideas and words to turn up the heat. Whether it be innuendo or out-and-out directness, there are several techniques you can use to make your lover's desire overwhelm you.

Just a Little Flirt

One of the first things we instinctually learn how to do as kids when we begin to discover our sexuality is flirt. Whether it's a boy teasing a girl on the playground at recess, or the shy giving of a heart-shaped card on Valentine's Day, flirting is our first introduction into doing something about mutual attraction.

I've heard both men and women say this same phrase countless times: "I'm a terrible flirt. I just don't know how." I don't believe you don't know how—you've just forgotten. Flirting has even garnered somewhat of a bad reputation: A "flirt" is said to be a tease; someone who isn't serious; someone who needs the attention of everyone to feel attractive. Sure, there are people who flirt to compensate for their own insecurities (see more about that in Chapter 20, "Does Being Sexy Mean You Must Have Sex?"), but on the whole, flirting is simply a coy expression of attraction, of liking, of playfulness.

Flirting is also one of the best ways to lay the groundwork for initiating sex. There are lots of ways to flirt with the object of your desire. In Chapter 12, "Sexy Flirting Techniques," I gave you all the details on how to flirt like a pro. So here, I will sum up the most important points for how to use sexy flirting to initiate sex. Following are some suggestions for techniques that are sure to get you off to a steamy start:

➤ **The art of conversation.** One of the best ways to charm the object of your desire is through your words. You can be having a seemingly innocent conversation, but create an undertow of double entendres that gets you both thinking about things other than the topic at hand. Use spicy descriptions like *sultry, sensual, juicy, hot, tempting, stirring, spicy, heated,* and *sticky.* Drop in verbs like *ache, yearn, long,* and *desire.* For instance, take the following sentence: "Yesterday, I wanted to have a tomato salad, so I went to the store and bought some." Ho-hum. Now, try it this way: "I had the most insatiable, aching appetite for a tomato salad yesterday. I went to the store and bought the juiciest beefsteak I

175

could find. I could barely get my hands around it, it was so plump and firm."
You can see here how simply adding a few more descriptive words turns an ordinary salad into a mini passion play.

➤ **Pay attention.** When you're trying to tempt someone into your bed, the worst thing you can do is be distracted. It sends take-it-or-leave-it signals of disinterest. One of the best ways to subtly flirt is to pay rapt attention to the object of your desire. Make him or her feel like the fascinating center of your universe.

➤ **Do a little dance.** There's nothing more stimulating to the mind than music. Put on something slow and seductive (see the music listings in Chapter 13 for some ideas) and suggest that you take a spin around the floor. The combination of the sultry sounds and physical closeness is an excellent way to get you both thinking about the way your bodies move together—and how they might glide into other activities in the bedroom.

➤ **Feed each other.** Food is often a prelude to sex, especially a romantic dinner. Wherever you're eating—whether it's a candlelight dinner in your living room or the food court at the mall—you can casually offer your lover a bite, then feed him or her. For an even more suggestive move, link arms and feed each other, or get one fork and one dessert and feed each other bites. However you do it, feeding each other can add a sensuality to your meal that can carry over into the bedroom.

Sari Says

If you have kids, you probably find that having sex without interruption is a tricky thing. So plan ahead. This might sound low on the spontaneity scale, but if you know the coast will be clear at 6 P.M. because your parents are taking the wee ones to the latest Disney flick, you can spend all day thinking about all the things you'll do to each other in those blissful hours alone.

Tease to Please

Absence may make the heart grow fonder, but abstinence makes the loins grow molten. I'm not talking about taking cold showers and holding out until the cows come home—that could mess up your sex life! What I mean is seductively teasing your lover all day, then finally letting your lover take you by the end of the day. You can really heat things to the boiling point. This particular technique will take some planning on your end, but it can get you both into such a frenzied state of mind, that the sex that follows is sure to be some of the most passionate you've ever had. To help you set the right mood, use the flirting techniques discussed in the previous section to help you suggest what's to come at the end of the day.

Games People Play

There's a scene in the movie *Stripes* in which Harold Ramos and Sean Young play a childish yet seductive game called "force field." The object of the game is to get as close to each other as possible without touching. The "loser" is the one who breaks the force field. Of course, *Stripes* isn't exactly known as the romantic hit of the century, but that scene is a pretty hot example of how games can "innocently" break the ice and get you from *thinking* about having sex to putting your ideas into *action*. Of course, this doesn't work for everyone, and you should try to feel out your partner to see if he or she is receptive to game playing. If your partner is willing, try one of the following:

➤ "Force field" (as just described).

➤ "Strip" games. It doesn't just have to be poker. Any simple board game can be turned into a contest in which the "loser" bares all. Remember the episode of the TV show *Friends,* in which they played strip *Happy Days* Game?

➤ "Truth or dare." You probably remember this one from school-trip bus rides. Turn it into the R- or X-rated adult version by asking suggestive questions of each other. ("Where have you always wanted to have sex but were too shy to ask?" "What is your most heated sexual fantasy?" And so on.)

Flirt Alert

Slipping a description of your sexual fantasy in your lover's briefcase in the morning, leaving a sexy voice-mail message, or sending your lover a sexy e-mail at work can be a tantalizing way to spice up his or her day. However, do not do this if there is any risk that someone besides your lover could see the message. Bosses can often read employees' e-mail and voice mail, and notes intended only for your lover's eyes can fall into the wrong hands. Use discretion!

All-Day Seduction

You don't have to wait until your date shows up at your home to start seducing him or her; seduction can begin long before the date begins. The afternoon before your evening of lust, call ahead and leave a sexy message in a soft, low voice on his or her voice mail at work; send a sexy e-mail; or, if you're trying to re-seduce your significant other, leave a hot little note in his or her briefcase or day planner describing what's in store for the night ahead. The anticipation will get his or her heart racing all day so that, by the time your date gets to your front door, he or she will already be too hot and bothered to think of anything else.

Live and Direct

Although being coy and using innuendo is an excellent way to set a sexy scene, being direct can be just as effective. Looking straight into someone's eyes and telling that person *exactly* what you'd like to do with him or her is an incredible turnon. Sexy talk can be great if you get into it, and if you know that it turns your lover on. You should find a time to casually ask your lover if this is something that he or she likes. If so, start talking!

If you don't know what to say when you try to talk sexy, here are some tips:

➤ Make a list of all of the slang words you can think of for sexual body parts and acts. Then choose the ones that would sound the sexiest to your lover. Practice saying them, and remember them for when you will want to use them later.

➤ Read pornographic letters in porn magazines, or call phone sex lines and listen to the sexual descriptions. That will give you ideas of scenarios, as well as more thoughts on how to use all those sexy words.

➤ Plan to either describe to your partner a sexual fantasy that you have, or to retell an experience that you two once had. That means that you could start your sexy talk with, "Do you remember how great it felt last Sunday when we made love all morning?" Then go into great detail, using sexy words describing it. Or you could start with, "I've been fantasizing about making love with you. This is exactly what I would love to do with you." Then give the details!

Sari Says

If you like the idea of being direct but are feeling a little shy about it, practice what you want to say ahead of time so that the words come out more naturally. If you're too self-conscious about your words, they'll lose impact. Practice in front of the mirror to gain confidence in talking sexy.

Body and Soul: Sexy Physical Techniques

Using your brain to tempt the body is a great way to set the scene for a night filled with passion. Of course, sex is a physical act, and in addition to using your noggin to get some lovin', you're going to have to use your physical attributes.

Body Language

If a picture is worth a thousand words, body language adds up to the equivalent of an entire library. The way you speak with your gestures and movements helps clue in your partner to just what's going on in that head of yours. I tell you all about it in Chapter 10, "Body Talk: Using Sexy Body Language." Here is just a review of some physical vocabulary to get you speaking the language of lust:

➤ **Make eye contact.** Holding steady eye contact—but not staring—and looking deeply into the limpid pools of another person says, "I want to …." (You can fill in the blank later!) Turning away, looking at your feet, or anywhere except into the eyes of the person you're interested in sends a message of disinterest, or possibly even distaste. You don't want to put out mixed signals. If you do, the other person may be completely shocked by your advances. Eye contact shows someone you're willing go deeper, to be intimate.

➤ **Moisten your lips.** The flick of a tongue around your lips gets the person you want to seduce to focus on your mouth, one of the most sensuous parts of the human body and, of course, gets the person thinking about kissing you. Careful, though, this must be done subtly and not too often. If you do it too much or too obviously, you might look more like you have a bad case of chapped lips than unfulfilled desire!

➤ **Face your partner full on.** Keeping you body unobstructed (no folded arms) and facing toward your partner shows that you are open to

Deep Quote

"She walks in beauty, like the night
Of cloudless climes and starry skies;
And all that's best of dark and bright
Meet in her aspect and her eyes."

—Lord Byron, "She Walks in Beauty"

Flirt Alert

It may seem obvious, but make sure your breath is in kissable condition before engaging in any lip locking. Brush and floss your teeth and swish around a little mouthwash before your love interest shows up.

him or her. It sends the signal that you are completely comfortable with your partner and interested in getting closer.

➤ **Touch your partner.** Touching your partner says, "I want to be near you; I want to have full-on contact with you." Touching a leg, an arm, or even a cheek during conversation is a great way to cue your partner that you want to touch him or her more—and be touched back.

I Just Want Your Extra Time and Your ... Kiss

Some say that kissing is more intimate than sex. If you think about it, that's not too crazy a claim. When you kiss, there's more than just lip locking going on: There's eye contact; physical contact; the feeling of each others' breath as you draw nearer. The kiss is one of the most revered acts of love. Poems and songs have been written about it; statues erected to it; paintings have paid tribute to it. It is the ultimate tool of seduction.

Photo by Ellen Denuto.

Here are some sexy lip tips to show the object of your desire that more is in store:

➤ Make sure your lips are soft, not dry. Wet them a little with your tongue just before making contact if necessary.

➤ Kiss other areas of the face or body before getting to the lips to create anticipation. Kiss his or her ear lobes, neck, forehead, chest, shoulder. Work on these *erogenous* zones a little and then go for mouth-to-mouth contact.

➤ At first, tease a little with slow, soft lip-to-lip kisses. At this teasing point, allow your lips to be *slightly* parted, but don't use your tongue yet.

180

➤ As you feel things getting slightly more intense, open your mouth wider and let your tongue gently flick across your partner's lips. More than likely, your partner will respond by opening his or her lips as well.

➤ Slide your tongue into his or her mouth. This is an incredibly sensual and sexual act, so be careful not to thrust your tongue too aggressively—and no heavy slobbering! Think of your tongue as a gentle instrument of exploration. Allow your tongues to mingle together.

➤ For extra fun kiss each other while you have an ice cube in your mouth, or pass a mint back and forth, or kiss with a mouthful of champagne.

Deep Quote

"A kiss is a lovely trick designed by nature to stop speech when words become superfluous."

—Ingrid Bergman

Once you are horizontal, you can continue using sexy kissing as part of your foreplay. Think of your lover's body as a piece of candy that you want to taste every inch of. There are few things more enticing than the feel of someone's lips against your flesh. Make it your goal to find new erogenous zones that your partner didn't even realized he or she had!

Sari Says

Some fun facts about kissing:

➤ The longest kiss on record lasted 130 hours and 2 minutes from May 1 through May 6, 1978.

➤ On September 15, 1990, a man from New Brighton, Minnesota, kissed 8,001 people in 8 hours—that's over 16 smooches a minute!

➤ In Cork, Ireland, it is said that any person who kisses the Blarney Stone at the fifteenth-century Blarney Castle will from that point forward have the gift of gab.

Stroke Me, Stroke Me

Touching and stroking each other is incredibly erotic. When you touch, you are stimulating each other, physically and mentally. So take some time to linger on your lover's body—the longer you do it, the more heated the sex is going to be. That is, if you even get to the sex. Some people love touching so much, it fulfills them as a complete sexual experience. But, for now, let's say that you want the touching to help you initiate sex. Keep in mind the following:

➤ Let your touch linger. Keep it smooth and tender. Avoid jerky, quick movements.

➤ Don't go straight for the obvious. Wait to touch his or her genitals. First, arouse your partner by caressing everywhere that is not an obvious erogenous zone, such as the arms, feet, neck. Then sensually stroke the areas near the hot spots, such as the inner thighs and lower stomach. Finally, touch the more obvious places.

➤ Remember that the genital and nipple areas tend to be very sensitive. Unless you know your partner likes the rough stuff, be gentle, while still administering a firm enough touch to make it felt.

➤ Use your mouth—it's not just for kissing other lips. Kiss near and around the obvious to prime your partner for the ultimate in pleasure.

➤ Try a sensual massage. Massage is a great way to simultaneously relax and tantalize your partner. Use slow, rubbing movements (don't pinch or press so hard that it hurts your partner). Try a little aromatic massage oil to help your hands glide more easily over your partner's body.

Deep Quote

"Sometimes he'd say he'd like to caress me because he knew I longed for it, and he'd like to watch me as the pleasure came. So he did ...."

—Marguerite Duras, *The Lover*

Getting to the bedroom isn't that difficult a task, but when you use sexy words and deeds to initiate sex, it just makes the end result that much more pleasurable for you and your lover. Release your inner seducer or seductress—I know you've got it in you!

The Least You Need to Know

➤ There's more to sex than just the deed—leading up to it with sexy techniques makes the lovemaking that much steamier.

➤ Erogenous zones aren't for the body only—use your brain to stimulate your partner's sexual imagination. Flirt, tease, and tempt, and you're guaranteed a hot night of great sex.

➤ Sometimes taking the direct approach is just as sexy as alluding to it. Try taking control.

➤ Pay attention to your body language—send an open message and you'll get an open response.

➤ Kissing and stroking are the ultimate in foreplay. Pay close attention to all those ignored spots—you just might find a new erogenous zone on your lover's body.

Chapter 17

How to Have Sexier Sex

In This Chapter

➤ Using condoms and birth control to stay safe and prevent unwanted pregnancy

➤ How to rub a woman the right way for more orgasms

➤ Making sex last longer by delaying ejaculation

➤ Getting in shape with sexy exercises

➤ Sexual positions that can spice up your sex life

Up to this point, I've been telling you that sexiness is not just about sex. And that's right. It's not just about sex. But part of it is! This chapter will help you and your partner put more fun, excitement, and, well, *sexiness* in your sex life!

Have you ever heard the joke that sex is like pizza; you can never have bad pizza or bad sex? Well, let me tell you, I've had some bad pizza in my life, and that makes me sure that people can have bad sex. One of the biggest complaints I hear people have about sex is that their sex life is not sexy enough. Sex should be sexy to keep it hot, and this chapter will tell you how!

Sexy Sex with Condoms and Birth Control

Before I get into explaining all the sexy ways to have sex, I want to make sure you know that you need to protect yourself against unwanted pregnancy and sexually transmitted diseases.

You have surely heard that you must use condoms every time you have sex in order to avoid getting a sexually transmitted disease like HIV, the virus that causes AIDS. Some people complain that condoms decrease sensitivity. Yes, wearing a condom does not feel like going *au naturel*. However, the small amount of difference in the physical sensation is nothing compared with the tremendous amount of peace of mind that you get from protecting yourself. Also, there are ways to make condoms part of the foreplay, so that you actually enjoy using them.

For sexy sex with condoms, use condoms that will add some excitement. Try colored or scented condoms, like Durex Colors and Scents. They come in orange, banana, and strawberry flavors. Yum! Or try polyurethane (plastic) condoms, instead of latex condoms, like the condoms called Avanti. Many people say that these feel more natural.

Flirt Alert

Some people say that lambskin condoms feel more comfortable than latex or polyurethane condoms. However, do not use lambskin condoms if you want to protect yourself from sexually transmitted diseases. They are not effective against sexually transmitted diseases, including HIV.

When it comes to birth control, making it sexier means finding a method that works best for you, and interferes the least with your sexual spontaneity. Birth control pills usually rank the highest in this category, since the woman is protected against pregnancy all the time, with few or no side effects. Norplant implants or depo provera shots also work well for some women but tend to have more side effects. Other women prefer to use another method such as a diaphragm, or foam and condoms. To find the best method for you, talk with your health care provider or Planned Parenthood (see Appendix C, "Resources," for contact information). Now that we've covered the condom and birth control issues, let me share with you some ways to make your sex life sizzle.

Improving Your Sexual Fundamentals

Before you get into the really wild things that you can do to jazz up your sex life, you need to improve the fundamental issues in your sex life. Issues such being in a sexual rut, having more orgasms, and controlling ejaculation are the basics you need to improve on before you can make things sexier. Let's take a closer look at these issues.

Get Out of That Rut!

Sexual ruts aren't fun. Period. You may think things are going along swimmingly with the same sexual routine that you've been using for years on end, but variety is always appreciated. Try to take note of a few things next time you start your usual love serenade:

➤ Does your partner appear unenthusiastic, or less enthusiastic than he or she used to be?

➤ Does your female partner climax? (Are you sure?)

➤ Does your partner seem distracted during sex?

➤ Has he or she stopped trying to seduce you?

Any or all of these could be warning signs that your routine is becoming just that—routine. Never fear, though, you can get yourself out of this rut. Instead of rolling over at the same time on the same nights with the same moves, surprise your partner with a little variety.

If you always begin foreplay with a few cursory kisses on the mouth, start exploring, Columbus! Travel your partner's body like it's a new land you've never been to. Kiss him or her in places you haven't gone near in awhile: ears, toes, behind the knee, on the inner thighs. Get your lover all steamed up. Try a different sexual position. Use a little dirty talk if you think he or she will go for it. Remember, if the sex is great for your partner, chances are you'll be having fun, too.

Flirt Alert

Don't be lazy about hygiene. Take a quick survey of the way you smell and look. If you realize you could be a little more pleasing to the senses, take a quick shower, splash on a light cologne, brush your teeth, and change your clothes—or just take them off!

Photo by The Special Photographers.

If you aren't enthusiastic, you're making it harder for your partner to be excited, too. Many people fall into a pattern of letting the other person do all the work during intercourse. Not only is that bor-r-r-r-ing, it's not fair. Don't be just the receiver: Try to find new places on your partner's body that get his heart racing. Also, have fun being the initiator. Take control. Suggest a new position that you haven't used in a long time or at all. Women, don't give up so easily on your own orgasm for fear he's going to get impatient. He can have fun with you while you both find the "spot" and the right combination of movements.

How Women Can Have More Orgasms

Guys, if you want to keep the sex in your loving relationship going strong, one of the best ways is to keep the woman coming back for more. Finding out how she has the best orgasms the most easily during sex can make sex sexier.

There are many women who do not have orgasms from intercourse. You see, if you have intercourse by focusing on the motion that a man needs to have an orgasm (the back-and-forth motion of the penis thrusting in the vagina), then a woman's clitoris may not be getting enough stimulation. In order for a woman to orgasm, she needs contact on her clitoris. Her clitoris would need to be rubbed similar to the way she would rub it during masturbation, often with direct contact in a circular motion. If you're a guy and you want your woman partner to have more orgasms during sex, try some of the following techniques:

Sari Says

If a woman has trouble having orgasms, she may want to use a vibrator—even during sex. As long as she feels good it is sexy.

Sari Says

Most men last longer the second time they have sex, if they do it more than once in a night. This means that you can have a quickie (or he can masturbate) just to get the first time out of the way. Then the second time, he may be able to last longer.

➤ **Get your pelvis closer to hers during intercourse.** When you are thrusting, stay close, so that you are rubbing her clitoris and pelvis area against your pelvis or pubic bone. Let her "grind" her clitoris against you.

➤ **Have her get on top.** Being on top during sex puts her clitoris in more direct contact with your pubic bone, so she can "rub herself off" on your body.

➤ **Let her use her hand on her clitoris.** While your penis is in her vagina, allow her to slip her hand between your bodies so she can stimulate her clitoris to orgasm.

➤ **Use your hand on her clitoris.** While your penis is in her vagina, sneak your hand down to her clitoris and stimulate it so that she can have an orgasm (as if you were masturbating her).

How Guys Can Last Longer

To keep your sex life sexy, you'll want sex to last for more than a few minutes. One way to do this is for the guy to hold off longer before he ejaculates. Here's one way you can play around with having the man you love last longer.

To control ejaculation, a man must be able to recognize the feeling *before* the point of no return, and reduce his sexual arousal just enough that he does not reach the point of no return until he is ready. Guys can learn how to pinpoint their level of sexual excitement, and keep it at a level that will give their partners pleasure, without coming.

Your sexual excitement increases as you get closer to orgasm. Think of it as being on a scale from 0 to 10. Zero means you don't feel any arousal. Ten is what you feel during orgasm. Try to get your body and mind to stay at an even level of excitement during sex (around level 7 or 8) without getting to the point of no return, also called ejaculatory inevitability, which would be around level 9.

Try practicing this technique while you're masturbating:

➤ When you feel yourself getting close to orgasm, label that feeling in your mind with an appropriate number.

➤ When you feel like you're getting close to level 8 of arousal, try to take it down a notch, remaining at 7 so you don't lose control and reach level 9, which would put you on the brink of orgasm.

➤ The best way to do this is to stop masturbating when you reach about level 8; then start again when your excitement gets down to about 5 or 6. You should practice this daily or at least several times each week, so that you eventually can masturbate for about 30 minutes without ejaculating until you're ready.

Once you've mastered these counting skills, you can try the same sort of thing during intercourse.

A Workout with Extra Benefits

Besides having great orgasms and lasting longer, great sex is about moving your bodies in all sorts of sexy ways. When it comes right down to it, sex is a physical act, and you need to be physically fit for it. Now, don't panic. I'm not talking jumping jacks and squat thrusts (hmmm, maybe that last one could be sort of fun). Here are several simple exercises you can do to get the most important muscles for sexual enhancement in tiptop shape.

Deep Quote

"I think that making love is the best form of exercise."

—Cary Grant

Kegel-Mania

It's time for all you women to do your Kegel exercises. I'm talking about working on your *pubococcygeal muscles* (PCs). These are the muscles that run from the back to the front of your pubic bone and encircle the vaginal area. By working these muscles, a woman's vagina will feel tighter, especially to the man whose penis is inside her. Just like working out any muscle in your body, the better shape your PCs are in, the better your erotically aimed activities will be. The Kegel exercise is one of the best ways to develop these muscles.

To learn how to do Kegels, first you need to isolate the PC muscle. While you are urinating, concentrate on stopping the flow of urine. It will feel like you are clamping down inside your vaginal area. You may notice the feeling of the walls of your vagina moving in toward each other. That's the PC muscle flexing. Do not flex your anus, thighs, or abs—just your PC. Once you can feel it and isolate it, get off the toilet, because it's time to begin your workout.

I'll explain three types of Kegel exercises that you can alternate for variety. For maximum benefit, perform Kegels every day, doing a total of about 200 per day. Sounds like a lot, doesn't it? But it's not strenuous. It's a simple flexing of a small muscle. If you're ready, you can try it along with me right now. To start, get in a relaxed position, sitting, standing, or lying down. You can do Kegel exercises in one of three ways:

➤ Tighten and relax the PC muscle 10 times in a row. Do this for 10 sets per session, twice a day.

➤ Tighten and hold for three to seven seconds. Do this for 10 sets per session, up to twice a day.

➤ Tighten the muscle slowly, in increments—tightening and relaxing. It might help to think about it as a pulsing, or as stopping, like an elevator stopping on every floor. Do this for 10 sets per session, up to twice a day.

Lusty Lingo

Pubococcygeal muscles, or **PCs** for short, are a triple set of muscles that run from the back to the front of your pubic bone and surround the openings of your vagina and rectum. Kegel exercises help you to develop these muscles by contracting and relaxing them.

One of the greatest things about Kegels is that no one can tell if you're doing them, because the action is entirely inside your vagina. Your body won't move. You won't even break a sweat! That means that you can do them anytime, anywhere—sitting at your desk at work, while you are watching TV, standing in line at the post office, lying in bed at night, whether you are alone or not. So get started, and in as soon as two weeks you will be enjoying the results!

The Added Benefit of Abs

Do you like the way toned abs look with a cropped shirt or in a bathing suit? Well, there's more benefit to a tight tummy than just the outer appearance. No matter how much fat you have on your stomach, exercising your abs can help make you stronger and look more fit. Besides being good for your back, toned abs, as well as strong lower back muscles, also can help increase your sexual pleasure by allowing you to better control the position of your pelvis.

The two things you need to do to achieve good muscle control here is stretch and tone. For stretching, try this exercise:

1. Lie on your back, arms stretched wide, in line with your shoulders and flat on the floor, palms down.

2. Lift your right knee to a bending position with your foot flat on the floor.

3. Gently bring your right knee over to your left side, twisting from the waist, as far as you can.

4. Return your leg back to its original position flat on the floor.

5. Repeat three to five times for each side.

When you do this, you will feel the stretch from your waist to your buttocks, and up your spine.

The second exercise you can do to get ab and back control is abdominal lifts. This is a simple exercise that you can easily fit into your busy schedule, because it doesn't take more than five to 10 minutes, depending on how many crunches you work up to:

1. Lie on your back with knees bent, feet flat on the floor.

2. Place your hands behind your head.

3. Lift your head and upper body off floor 8 to 12 inches.

4. Simultaneously, tilt your pelvis toward the ceiling slightly.

5. Hold for two to three beats and return to your original position.

6. Repeat 10 times, eventually working up to 30 to 50 crunches.

Hot Quads

For amazing on-top action, get those *quadriceps* (front thigh muscles) in tiptop shape. It will give you added vigor and endurance. Take a tip from the dance world when trying to tone the quadriceps—a ballet stretch known as the *plié* is one of the best exercises for this:

1. Stand beside a chair (or steady piece of waist-high furniture) and place your hand on the chair to keep yourself steady.

2. Stand with your feet slightly more than shoulder-length apart, toes pointing out to each side.

3. With your back straight and head up, bend from the knees and lower yourself as low as you comfortably can.

Lusty Lingo

Quadriceps are the extensor muscles in the front of the thigh that are divided into four parts. A **plié** is a French word meaning "to bend." In ballet, it is an exercise that involves standing with feet slightly more than shoulder length apart and bending the knees.

191

4. Hold for two to three seconds, and return to an upright position.

5. Repeat 10 times, working up to 30 to 40 dips.

You have some basics about how to have sexier sex, and you are fit and ready to go for it. Here's what you've been waiting for: Let's have a look at some of the most erotic sexual positions you and your partner can get into.

Ready for Sexier Sex?

There are many types of sex play that are sexy. You and your partner can experiment to find your favorites. One type of sex that is very erotic is eye-to-eye sex, which makes you and your partner feel totally connected. You see, when sex is about genital-to-genital contact instead of *person-to-person* contact, that's not too sexy. To really feel the connection with your partner, look deeply into each other's eyes.

There's another type of sex that is the opposite of eye-to-eye sex. It's hot, it's hurried, it's sweaty: It's the "quickie." Unlike eye-to-eye sex, with the quickie you hardly even have time to focus. But it's another sure-fire way to make sex more fun. You and your partner can have a quickie before leaving for work. You can have one during your lunch hour. You can have one with your clothes still on, or you can rip each other's clothes off in the heat of passion. You can have one while you're in the kitchen with guests waiting for you in the living room. Or have one in a public bathroom. So many ways, so little time!

Photo by Barnaby Hall.

The Newest, Sexiest Sex Positions

Are you bored with the basic sex positions: man on top, woman on top, doggy style, sitting, and standing? Do you want to try some wild new sexy positions? If you do, then you've come to the right part of the book. Check these out!

The Snuggle

This loving position is a variation of the "spoons" position. The woman and man lay on their sides. The man enters the woman's vagina from behind. He can stimulate her breasts or clitoris by reaching around. She can touch his back or butt by reaching back. They thrust by pushing against each other.

Moving very gently in the snuggle position can be very sexy. It can be almost as if you were just snuggling, maybe even falling asleep, when you decide to naturally drift into having sex instead.

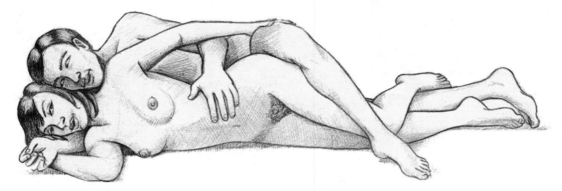

Illustration by Jessica Wolk-Stanley.

The Leap Frog

To get into this sexual position, the man sits on his knees with his legs under him. The woman crouches directly in front of him, looking in the same direction that he's looking in, so he is looking at the back of her head. He puts his penis into her vagina from behind. By pushing up and down on her bent legs, she can lower and raise herself to meet his thrusts. It looks like a game of leap frog!

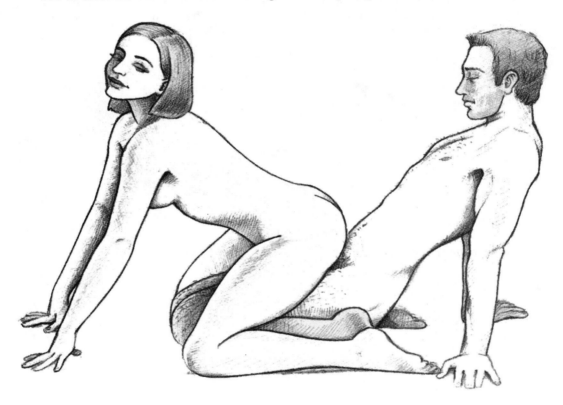

Illustration by Jessica Wolk-Stanley.

The Erotic Edge

The woman sits on the edge of a low sofa or ottoman. Her legs are at a 90-degree angle to her body, with her feet flat on the floor. The man kneels between her legs, facing her. Her legs are on either side of his thighs. His penis enters her vagina in this position. She can either have her arms around his waist, or lean back on her arms and use them to push up to thrust. He can thrust by rocking back and forth.

Illustration by Jessica Wolk-Stanley.

195

All In

In this position, you can have several types of stimulation at once. The man lays flat on the floor, facing up, with his legs stretched straight out. The woman lays face down on top of him, but she positions her head near his feet, so her feet are near his head. Then he puts his penis in her vagina. She and he each can suck on each other's toes. The woman can reach her clitoris to stimulate it. The man can reach her anus if she likes him to stimulate that. They are "all in" each other.

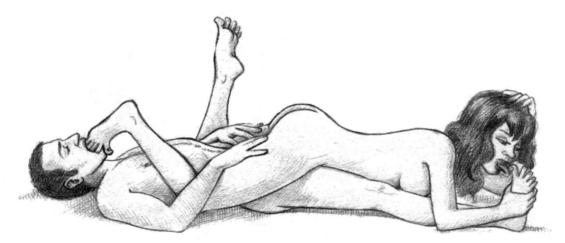

Illustration by Jessica Wolk-Stanley.

Carried Away

For this sexy position, the man has to be rather strong, and the woman lithe and limber. He stands up, picks her up, and penetrates her, while she has her legs wrapped around his waist. She can thrust by raising and lowering her self, which he can assist with by moving her with his arms. He can walk around, carrying her while they have sex.

Illustration by Jessica Wolk-Stanley.

The Least You Need to Know

➤ Using condoms or another form of birth control protects you against un-wanted pregnancy and sexually transmitted diseases. Being smart about sex is very sexy.

➤ Improving your grasp on the fundamentals—such as a woman having more orgasms and a man lasting longer—can make sex sexier.

➤ Getting fit by doing sexy exercises can help heat things up.

➤ Try some new exotic sexual positions to spice up your sex life.

Chapter 18

Super Sexy Sex

In This Chapter

➤ Enhancing trust for sexy sex

➤ Playing some fun sex games

➤ The turnon of talking sexy

➤ Having sexy oral sex

➤ Having sexy adventures in exotic locations

➤ Making your sex life sexier by role-playing

➤ How Tantric sex and S/M may enhance your sex life

You know from the last chapter that sexier sex means being able to express what you want sexually, being in good shape for sex, and integrating lots of variety into your sex life.

So what is *super* sexy sex? Well, it takes your connection with your partner to a higher level, and it brings your sexual adventures up another step. The sexiest sex takes place when you are so close to your partner that you can do anything you want. When you feel comfortable experimenting, you can live out your creative ideas and sexual fantasies. Sound good? Then let's get started!

In Us We Trust

The sexiest sex is possible only when you and your partner trust each other enough to be able to express your deepest sexual desires. Here are some ways to do that:

➤ **Listen without judging.** When your partner talks about his or her sexual desires, if they sound good to you, discuss your interest in them. But if they don't sound appealing to you, just say that's not something you're into, without judging your partner.

➤ **Tell each other three things about your sex life that you have rarely shared with anyone.** The more you learn about each other's sexuality, the better you will be able to understand each other.

➤ **Tell the truth about what you like and don't like.** If you let your partner do things to you sexually that you don't really care for, you won't have sexy sex. Be honest about what feels good to you.

Once you and your partner feel comfortable opening up to each other about sex, and you can trust each other, you can then talk in more detail about your sexual desires and fantasies.

Sex Games

There are a lot of sex games you can play with your partner to make things sexier. I'm not talking naked Monopoly, although that could be fun. All I mean by "games" are simple ways to find adventure in your sex life. Let's start with the light switch.

Lights On or Off?

Sometimes feeling each other's bodies during sex when the room is pitch black can be a great sexy turnon. Other times, seeing your partner's body with all the lights on can be very hot. To have sexy fun, vary the ways that you use lighting during sex.

Play with Your Food

Playing with food during sex certainly can be sexy. Try these ideas:

➤ Use a spray can of whipped cream to decorate your partner, then lick it off.

➤ Use flavored jams to add a fruity taste to sex.

➤ Try a chocolate treat by drizzling chocolate syrup all over each other.

➤ On a hot day, use ice cubes to tease your partner all over, especially those sensitive nipples.

➤ Dangle grapes above your lover, feeding them to him or her one at a time.

Using Sex Toys

Dildos and vibrators are two sex toys that you may want to play around with during sex. You can look for sex toys that resemble penises and have a very sexy look. Or if you want the sensations but you don't care about looking sexy, then you can get a dildo that looks like a plain cylinder, or a vibrator that looks like a shoulder massager. Go to a store that sells sex toys to check out the variety, then see what works best for you.

Talking Sexy During Sex

Moaning and groaning during sex can be a sexy turnon. Talking during sex can be even sexier to some people. First, find out if this is something your lover would like you do to make your sex life sexier. If it is, start practicing.

When you are talking sexy, try the following:

➤ Explaining what you're doing to yourself.

➤ Explaining what the other person is doing to you.

➤ Explaining what you want to be doing.

➤ Explaining what you want done to you.

Sari Says

The best-selling vibrator, called the Hitachi Magic Wand, actually doesn't look sexy at all, since it resembles a shoulder massager. But if you like the electronic buzz, it's the sexiest way to go, because it's powerful and great at helping women have intense orgasms!

Most importantly, let yourself go during sex. Don't be afraid of what sounds and words might come out of your mouth. Remember, you want to be sexy! So let yourself be sexy.

Lick It Good: Oral Sexiness

Having oral sex is one of the sexiest ways to fully experience your partner's sensuality. As I explained in Chapter 7, "Getting Over Inhibitions About Sex," if people have inhibitions about oral sex, they can learn to get over them, in order to find more fulfillment and diversity in their sex lives.

Performing oral sex on a woman, or *cunnilingus,* allows you to see, smell, and taste her while you stimulate her. You can even experience her orgasms close up.

When you perform oral sex on a woman, try some sexy variations:

➤ Flick the tip of your tongue.

➤ Lick long licks with the flat part of your tongue.

Lusty Lingo

Performing oral sex on a woman is also called **cunnilingus,** which comes from the Latin, *cunnus* meaning "vulva," and *lingere,* meaning "to lick." Performing oral sex on a man is called **fellatio,** which is derived from the Latin word *fellare,* meaning "to suck."

201

➤ Use the edge of your tongue back and forth.

➤ Lick from her vagina to the top of her clitoris.

➤ Stroke her inner labia (vaginal lips) with your fingers as you lick her clitoris.

➤ Carefully separate each part of her genitals with your tongue. Do the same with your fingers.

➤ Put a finger or two inside her vagina and slowly move them in and out.

➤ Use your tongue to penetrate her vagina, and move it in and out.

➤ If she enjoys anal stimulation, touch gently around her anus, or slowly slide a lubricated finger inside her anus.

➤ Ask her where she likes to be licked. To give her an orgasm, focus in on the place that responds best to your tongue. If you keep up a rhythm in that area, it should put her over the top.

Oral sex on a man, *fellatio*, can be sexier if you try some of these variations:

➤ Lick the entire length of his penis up and down with the flat part of your tongue.

➤ When his penis and your mouth are very wet, slide the whole penis down your throat as far as you can. (It helps to breathe through your nose to keep the gag reflex from kicking in.)

Flirt Alert

Vaginal secretions and semen can carry sexually transmitted diseases, including HIV, the virus that causes AIDS. To protect yourself from disease transmission, use a condom when you have oral sex on a man, and use a dental dam or plastic wrap when you have oral sex on a woman.

➤ Run the tip of your tongue up from the base to the head of his penis, then in the same motion, circle under the coronal ridge (under the glans on the head of the penis).

➤ Flick the tip of your tongue back and forth on his frenulum (the tiny indentation under the coronal ridge of the glans).

➤ While your mouth is focusing on licking and sucking the head, move your hand up and down the shaft of his penis for a combo hand job/blow job. Keep up a steady rhythm to bring him to orgasm.

➤ Hold or massage his testicles in your hand, or take your mouth off of his penis and gently lick his testicles, and put them in your mouth.

➤ If he likes anal stimulation, touch gently around his anus, or slowly slide a lubricated finger inside his anus.

Having oral sex on each other at the same time is deeply gratifying and highly erotic for some people. This position, also called sixty-nine, allows a couple to get turned on by giving and receiving oral sex at the same time. Try it for sexy fun during oral sex.

Deep Quote

"Won't you go down where it's warm inside? Where I cannot hide? Where all life begins? That's where my love is. Now, what could be better than a home-cooked meal? How you want to eat it depends on how you feel. You can eat all you want and you won't get fat, now, where else can you go for a meal like that? It's not fair to be selfish or stingy, every girl should experience eating out."

—Madonna, "Where Life Begins"

You're My Fantasy!

One of the best ways to add excitement to your sex life is by using sexual fantasy. Almost everyone has fantasies about sex—they are natural, normal, and healthy. Whether it's sex in an exotic location or having a threesome, you and your partner can discuss your fantasies and think about whether you'd like to act them out together. If you and your partner agree on some fantasies that you both like, then acting them out is another way to add more excitement to your sex life.

If You Can Imagine It, Should You Do It?

You can imagine anything about sex, but should you do everything you imagine? No, of course not. There are some sexual fantasies that should never be acted out, such as anything that is not consensual. For example, if your fantasy is that you want to force someone to have sex with you, you can never act it out! That's rape, and is a horrendous crime against another human being.

Sari Says

Having a rape fantasy is not abnormal, and it is not unhealthy. However, if taking someone by force is your all-encompassing fantasy and you feel overwhelmingly preoccupied with this idea to the extent that you actually think you could do it, please seek professional help from a therapist!

203

However, if you talk about your fantasy with your partner, and your partner is comfortable with it and agrees to let you *pretend* that you are forcing him or her, you can act out that fantasy. That's role-playing, which I will explain soon. First, let's take a look at some common fantasies.

Sexy Fantasies You Can Act Out

People fantasize about all sorts of things. If you and your partner agree on any of these fantasies, then maybe you can act out the fantasies together.

As I mentioned, there are some fantasies that should never be acted out. There are other fantasies that you may want to act out, but you may never have the chance to, like sex with a movie star. Also, there are fantasies that may not be smart for you to do, like sex with your boss. But within the realm of sexual fantasies, there are plenty that you could act out if you have a partner who is interested in exploring sexy sex.

Sari Says

Never act out a sexual fantasy with your partner unless you both agree that you definitely want to try it. You must have full consent, and you must agree to stop if either of you begins to feel uncomfortable.

Deep Quote

"Nothing risqué, nothing gained."
—Alexander Woollcott, American essayist

Here are some fantasies you and your partner might try acting out:

➤ **Threesome or group sex.** Some people would never want to act out a fantasy of group sex, because they want to keep sex between just the two of them. But for other people, inviting someone else into their bed could be a big thrill. Imagine the feeling of six hands, three tongues, six nipples, and three sets of genitals!

➤ **Sex in public.** Can you imagine that you're having sex while under a blanket on a crowded beach, in the back seat of your car in a movie theater parking lot, or in the back corner of packed dark nightclub? If you can image it, maybe you'd want to try it. Part of the thrill is the fear that you may get caught. But you should not get caught! If you are sure that you can get away with it, and still have the excitement, then maybe it can work for you. Do be discreet, though—not everybody wants to watch you and your partner having sex, and if it's too public a display, you could even be charged with indecent exposure or lewd behavior.

➤ **Sex while someone is watching.** You unbutton your shirt slowly and seductively, but you feel a certain thrill, because you know that you are really showing off as you are being watched by your partner. Being an *exhibitionist* can be very exciting for some people. If being watched does not embarrass you, then you can show off for your lover. Or both of you can have sex while others watch. That is, if you can find some willing *voyeurs*.

➤ **Sex in an exotic location.** If you want to spice up your sex life, varying where you do it can be wonderful! There are so many places you can go to make you sex life even sexier, from the mountains to the woods to the ocean ... let your imagination roam!

Where, Oh Where, Should We Do It?

Here is a list of some exotic locations that can sex up your sex life:

➤ **On a beach.** You can do it under a beach blanket, in the water, or on the open sand, if no one is around. Some people find the sand abrasive to their genitals, but for others, it's worth the clean up.

➤ **On an airplane.** Sure, the flight attendant will suspect you two when you come out of the tiny bathroom together. But it's the only way to join the *mile-high club!*

➤ **In the backyard.** Who said you had to travel to have sex in an exotic location?

➤ **In the woods.** Remember to wear your bug repellent, and go for it under the trees on a soft blanket of pine needles.

➤ **In the car.** I don't advise you to have sex while the car is in motion, but there's nothing wrong with parking!

➤ **In a hot tub.** Bubbles, water, heat ... sounds like sexy sex!

➤ **In an elevator.** Press the stop button and you're good to go. If the elevator has a mirror on the ceiling, it can be really hot. Just make sure there's no security camera in the elevator!

➤ **In a swimming pool.** Jump in, the water's fine. Just be sure to choose the private pool in your back yard, rather than the pool at the Y.

Lusty Lingo

Exhibitionists are people who get a sexual thrill out of having others watch them being sexual or nude. **Voyeurs** are people who get erotic pleasure from watching others engage in sexual acts or nudity.

Lusty Lingo

The **mile-high club** is an expression used to mean someone who has had sex while in flight in an airplane. (It's just an expression, not a real club.)

➤ **In a public bathroom.** It's not the most romantic place, but for a quickie, sometimes it can be sexy. Make sure you lock the door!

For a super sexy time, why not commit to making love in a different location every week!

*Photo by Richard
Seagraves.*

Sari Says

In addition to the suggestions I've mentioned here, try to notice what scenes turn you on in movies and television. If there's a particular scene that really gets you or your partner going, act it out.

Me Tarzan, You Jane: Role-Playing

Without having to find a new location, you can let your imagination transport you to new places. Role-playing can also be a really fun way to spice up your sex life. In fact, role-playing can be one of the best ways to begin changing the same old routine into a steamy romp.

Think of scenarios that you could both easily slip into. If the pressure to come up with something on your own is leaving you stumped, go for the most basic ideas, no matter how silly they seem:

➤ Teacher and bad pupil who has to stay after school
➤ Police officer or warden and prisoner

➤ Repair person and repairee

➤ Pizza delivery boy and hungry housewife

➤ Hotel room maid and hotel guest

➤ Burglar and resident

➤ Celebrity and groupie

These make-believe roles all sound really silly, it's true, but the fun of stepping into someone else's shoes for a little while can not only be tons of fun, but also very, very hot.

Mystical Connection: Tantric Sex

As I discussed earlier in this book, sexy does not mean only erotic sexiness. There is a way to make your sex life super sexy by integrating a more natural, peaceful, loving, spiritual aspect of sex. Tantra is a spiritual form of sexual expression. It is said to heighten and prolong the connection that exists between partners during sex. It originated from Taoist and Buddhist philosophies.

Tantric sex teaches that sexuality is part of your whole being—a mental, physical, and spiritual union. People who practice Tantra say that they feel such a strong bond that when they orgasm, their energy combines and lifts them up to the heavens and they become one with the universe. Pretty cool, huh?

Tantra can help make your sex life sexier, by teaching you to be in the moment during sex and find more meaning from sex. One of the basic Taoist philosophies is that sex—like life—is not about the destination, it's about the journey. So, in other words, when it comes to sex, it's not about the big "O." The concept of "achieving" an orgasm, and the notion that an orgasm is the "climax" of sex, goes against Tantric principles. The most important point of Tantra is to feel an allover sensation of connection to your partner.

Lusty Lingo

Tantric sex is a spiritual type of sex that is based in Eastern philosophies of Taoism and Buddhism. It is said to help couples reach a deeper, more loving sexual connection.

Deep Quote

"Tantra says deep inside you are already free; you are already un-blocked; you are already radiant; you are the beginning and the ending; you are the source; you are the earth; you are the sun and the moon; you are the universe."

—David and Ellen Ramsdale, authors of *Sexual Energy Ecstasy*

Incorporating the spirituality of Tantra into your sex life can be sexy. Here are some exercises you can try.

Breathing in Harmony

Tantric couples practice breathing in sync to help themselves feel close and achieve harmony in their relationship. If you want to learn to breath in harmony, lay down with your partner in the "spoon" position with both of you on your left sides, facing in the same direction. You and your partner should close your eyes and relax. Inhale slowly, holding it for a few seconds. Then exhale slowly. Really concentrate on the in and out of your breathing. Your partner should be doing the same.

Focus on your partner's breathing. When you feel comfortable with the rhythm of your own breathing, pay attention to the in and out of your partner's breathing. Try to get your breathing in sync with your partner's. Breathe in and breathe out at the same time.

Continue this synchronized breathing for five full minutes. It might seem like a lot at the beginning, but soon you will not be thinking about the time, and you will be feeling only the sexy closeness.

Prolonging the Tantric Sex Act

As I mentioned earlier, one of the sexy things about Tantra is that it is not just about an orgasm that originates from the clitoris or penis. It is about sex that lasts, and a full body orgasm that lasts. Some describe it as "riding the wave" of sexual energy.

Sari Says

Even if you do not want to get in to Tantric sex in its most literal and complete sense, you can still incorporate some elements of it into your sex life. For example, simply looking into each other's eyes during sex can make your sex life sexier.

The following steps can help you achieve this:

1. Have the man insert his erect penis in the woman's vagina, but not thrust; just rest it there and feel what you each feel like together.

2. Have the man withdraw his penis from her vagina and use it to gently massage her clitoris and vaginal opening.

3. Then have him slide his erect penis back inside her vagina again.

4. Repeat this cycle several times. Most of the time, you should each feel as if you're hovering on the brink of orgasm.

5. When you finally decide to release into orgasm, the penis should remain inside the vagina, thrusting gently until climax. The man can also use his penis to massage the woman's clitoris until orgasm.

During all of these steps, breathe together the way you did in the first exercise. Keep breathing and focusing during orgasm. This may give you the sensation of a "full-body orgasm" in which you feel a radiating sensation all over your body, not just in your genitals.

Also, keep your eyes open during sex. Many people who practice Tantra say that they feel a deep, even more intense love when they are staring into their partner's eyes during orgasm. This can all provide for some super sexy sex!

S/M: An Exchange of Power

When some people hear the term *S/M* (sadism and masochism), they think of pain and whips and chains, and they are completely turned off. For others, S/M seems intriguing, and even something that can make their sex life super sexy.

S/M involves the exchange of power, and may or may not involve pain. It is about one partner giving up control, totally letting go, and allowing the other partner to make the sexual choices. Those choices may involve things like teasing, spanking, or tying up. The sadist is the partner who dominates; the person being dominated is the masochist.

If you want to see if S/M could make your sex life sexier, try a gentle bondage session. Bondage refers to tying up a lover for the sexual pleasure of taking control over him or her. Use a soft silk or cotton scarf to tie your partner's wrists, or have your partner tie your wrists, loosely (of course).

When your partner is tied up you can also have your way with him or her sexually. Of course, you must have gotten consent for whatever you want to do—before you tie up your partner. Talk about it, script it out, decide the details beforehand. Then when you are doing the tying (or you are tied up), you will have an idea of what could go on. Remember, S/M is about consensual power play!

You can also try blindfolding each other a la that hot scene in *9½ Weeks*. You can use props (ice cubes, fruit, honey, body paints, or feathers, for

Lusty Lingo

S/M means sadism and masochism. The sadist is the partner who dominates the masochist. The term S/M is applied to a number of activities that typically involve the exchange of power and sometimes pain between consenting partners.

Flirt Alert

Never tie knots that are too tight to untie. And never tie anything around your partner's neck, or your own neck.

Flirt Alert

Of course, bondage, like any S/M behavior, must be completely consensual. Never "surprise" a partner by tying him or her up. That *is* abuse, not sex. If either partner becomes uncomfortable, the other must stop immediately.

example) to titillate your partner, or you can just explore your captive's body, using the element of gentle surprise to turn your partner on.

Whatever you try, make sure that you and your partner first agree on a "safe" word: a word other than "stop" that you can say if you want to stop. The reason for this is that many people who do S/M like to say "stop" and not mean it. Find a neutral word, like "red" that means "stop" to both of you. That way if you are all tied up, and your partner starts running ice cubes on your body, but it's too cold and not sexy, you can get him or her to stop. S/M is sexy only when it's safe.

Whether it is S/M, Tantra, or role-playing, variety is the spice of sex and the path to super sexy sex. So have fun with the wide world of sex!

The Least You Need to Know

➤ If you trust your partner, you will have sexier sex.

➤ There are lots of sex games that can add sexiness to your sex life.

➤ Oral sex can make your sex life sizzle.

➤ Having sex in exotic locations can be very sexy.

➤ Fantasy and role-playing can add spice to your sex life.

➤ Tantric sex and S/M may add to your super sexy sex life.

➤ All sex acts, including sex games, role plays, and S/M, must always be consensual and agreed on ahead of time by both partners.

Chapter 19

Keeping the Sexy Spark in Your Love Life

In This Chapter

➤ How being in love is sexy

➤ What men and women can do to break out of the same old routine

➤ Finding time for sex

➤ Using all five senses to put the sizzle back in sex

How many times have you heard someone proclaim the following: "After you get in a long-term relationship/move in together/get married, the sex goes right down the drain"? Pretty often, I'd bet. I'm going to fill you in on a little-known piece of info—it's a terrible lie.

Sure, some couples fall in love and subsequently fall into the taking-each-other-for-granted habit. But that doesn't have to be the case. In fact, that shouldn't be the case! There are plenty of couples out there who know the greatest secret of all: Being in love means you're free to be as sexy as you dare and, as a result, have mind-blowing sex. It also means that you have the time and trust to work on your sex life, if it needs some jazzing up. In this chapter, I'm going to show you how being in love is the basis for some of the sexiest sex you've ever experienced. So grab the one you love and let's get down to business.

Take the "L" Out of Lover and It's Over?

Having sex with someone for the first time is, because of sheer excitement alone, nearly always great. The newness of discovering each other's bodies gives you that in-credible shock wave that, if it could be bottled, would outsell Viagra. The rush is truly like a drug. Unless, however, you plan on living your life with a string of one-nighters, you are eventually going to fall prey to the "L" word (love), which, inevitably, leads to the "R" word (relationship).

A relationship should never be the death knell to great sex. Yes, it takes effort on both your parts to keep the heat, but it is well worth it. Sex in a mutually loving relationship is great for many reasons:

➤ You get to know each other's likes and dislikes.

➤ You learn to trust each other implicitly.

➤ You are free to try out new things without the risk of your partner thinking you're totally strange.

➤ There is more room for the element of surprise.

➤ You know the other person is going to be there when you wake up in the morning.

➤ You respect each other.

➤ You aren't self-conscious.

➤ There's less risk of contracting a sexually transmitted disease (if you are both faithful).

➤ It brings you closer together.

For all these reasons, sexual relations between two people who love each other can be the hottest you've ever had. Love is sexy.

Many of us make the mistake of thinking that the familiar is boring. There is nothing further from the truth. Familiar just means that you are comfortable enough with someone to be able to express yourself in different ways. Feeling familiar, emotionally linked, and safe with your lover is big part of why sex with someone you care for is so pleasurable.

New may be titillating and exciting for the short term, but don't forget that new also is a sea of unknown. When a relationship between two people is in the early stage, both people are enmeshed in a guessing game of self-consciousness about the way they look, sound, and act. On the other hand, familiarity and comfort allow you to take your partner by the hand and lead him or her into erotic realms without the guessing game. Familiarity opens you both to a world of sensual exploration.

Deep Quote

"Only the united beat of sex and heart together can create ecstasy."

—Anaïs Nin

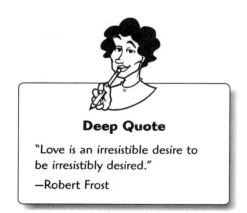

Deep Quote

"Love is an irresistible desire to be irresistibly desired."

—Robert Frost

One of the best ways to keep love alive is to keep sexiness alive, too. This chapter will go on to show you that, while love is sexy, sex with someone you're in love with may take some spicing up to keep it sexy.

Making Time for Sex

Being a loving couple also may mean that you are a married couple, or a couple who's living together. With the added joy of being around each other all the time, you may also have the added stress of finances, kids, in-laws, your jobs … and less time to do what you love doing, including having sex.

Finding the time for sex can be tricky. Try to find out-of-the-ordinary times for sex. This can add variety, and sexiness. Here are some suggestions:

➤ Try weekends, after work (but before dinner), or long before bedtime.

➤ Make love all day long on a rainy Sunday.

➤ Make "sex dates" and stick to them.

➤ Leave work a half-hour early just to have sex.

➤ Meet on your lunch break for a sexy rendezvous.

➤ Wake up an hour earlier, and do it at dawn.

➤ Turn off the television at night—have sex instead of watching *Nightline*.

➤ Use food as a sex toy, and eat dinner in bed.

➤ Make love in the shower.

Even finding the extra few minutes for a quickie will bring the two of you closer together. Finding time for sex will remind you about a sexy way of being with someone you love: having sex!

Sari Says

The Kama Sutra, the ancient tome of sexual pleasure, was written with married couples in mind. It was thought that the ability of couples to please each other sexually was key to a strong union and, thus, a strong-er society.

Pillow Talk

One of the many benefits of sex with someone you love is it's pretty hard to shock each other. The chances are pretty good that you won't say something that will end the relationship. However, when it's time to create a sexy mood, you do need to set some ground rules so that you don't engage in talk that is a turnoff. Some likely fire extinguishers of the flames of passion include the following:

➤ Complaining about your job.

➤ Worrying about the bills.

➤ Stressing about your children.

213

Flirt Alert

Make sure you find out if there's something your partner doesn't like or is offended by. You don't want to discover your significant other's distaste for certain terms or role-playing mid romp.

➤ Talking about your ex.

➤ Whining about your parents.

If you or your partner start talking about turnoff topics, gently remind him or her that there is a time and place for everything, and now is the time for pillow talk.

Make pillow talk part of your sex play. Make it into a little foreplay game called "I Like." Each of you takes turns saying what you like best to hear when you're in bed. You might even surprise each other with secret fantasies you haven't expressed yet. To spice up "I Like" even more, turn down the lights, light some candles, and whisper what you most desire in each other's ears. Soon you'll find yourself doing what you like.

Sari Says

Get the fires stoked early on by calling your partner during the day and giving him or her a little hint about what's to come that evening. Simply saying "You know what I want you to do to me later?" is enough to heat the waters to a rolling boil before you're even in the bedroom. Make sure you speak in a low, gentle voice to really clinch the mood.

The Big Five

Sight, smell, hearing, touch, taste—the five senses are your pathway to sensual exploration. Don't ignore them! More detail on the senses is included in Chapter 13, "Sexiness Begins at Home: Creating a Sexy Environment," but just to recap, seduction truly does begin with the senses. What follows are more suggestions for heating up your loving cup—guaranteed it will runneth over!

Sight

Instead of closing your eyes during sex, try looking into each other's eyes. Also, vary the look of your surroundings to make sex even sexier.

➤ Use soft lighting.

➤ Light candles.

➤ Put on something alluring.

➤ Watch a porn movie together.

Smell

Scents can enhance sexual pleasure—whether it's your natural body aroma or the fragrance you use. For added olfactory stimulation, vary the smells.

➤ Sweat, get dirty, then sniff each other during sex.

➤ Light incense.

➤ Enjoy the smell of your favorite foods cooking.

➤ Put on your spouse's favorite cologne or perfume.

➤ Have sex outdoors, and drink in the fresh air.

Deep Quote

"Blake said that the body was the soul's prison unless the five senses are fully developed and open. He considered the senses the "windows of the soul." When sex involves all the senses intensely, it can be like a mystical experience."

—Jim Morrison

Hearing

To make sex sexier, play with your sense of sound. Sex does not have to be silent.

➤ Put on soft, sexy music (maybe something you both used to get down to when you were first together!).

➤ Play hard, pounding music with a great beat.

➤ Make sounds during sex.

➤ Whisper sweet nothings.

➤ Say sexy things.

Touch

When you think of touch during sex, you may think that it just means touching each other's bodies in the usual way. But that's the problem. After years together, the usual way gets to be too usual. To make touch sexier you can do many things.

➤ Use a softer touch than usual.

➤ Run a feather up and down your partner's body.

➤ Scratch each other's backs.

➤ Try a rough touch such as a love slap (if your partner agrees).

➤ Make love in the shower. Feel the rushing water as you rub your slippery bodies against each other and lather each other up.

Taste

When sex always tastes like Crest toothpaste you know you could use some sexiness. Vary your tastes.

➤ Taste each other's morning breath.

➤ Use food and sex, any way you can think of.

➤ Taste alcohol on each other's breath.

➤ Drink in the taste of your lover's love juices.

Now, it's your turn. With these lists as a guide, sit down with your partner and come up with at least five more ways for each sense that you can make your sex life sexier. No matter how you vary the senses, try to be as creative as possible. The devil is in the details.

Sari Says

Bath time can be lots of fun if you share it with your partner! Take a long, luxurious bubble bath with your spouse. Or, if you want to go solo, put up a see-through shower curtain so you can tantalize your lover with some peekaboo action. Hold a towel open for your partner when he or she steps out of the shower to show your love.

Our Love Is Here to Stay (So Let's Play)

Being in a long-term, healthy, loving relationship doesn't have to be boring or lose its heat as the years go by. You need to remember that the trust you have built up with your partner is not only the foundation of a solid, good marriage or partnership, but it's also the secret ingredient to really hot sexy sex. When you love and trust each other, you are free to do, say, and act upon sexual fantasies and impulses that you wouldn't dream of trying with someone new. (If you need a refresher course on some of the things you and your partner can do to fire up your sex life, review Chapter 18, "Super Sexy Sex.")

Deep Quote

"I like my body when it is with your body."

—e. e. cummings

Improving the level of intimacy you have with your partner does more than just enhance sex. It brings you closer as a couple. Try going on dates together. Read Chapter 14, "Sexy Dates," for some great ideas for fun, offbeat dates. Also, try learning new things together. You could learn how to Rollerblade—buy the skates together, then go out to a park together to practice. Take classes in ballroom dancing, so when you go to a formal event, you'll be ready to cut the rug together. Or take a weekly scuba-diving class together, and after you get certified, go away on a Caribbean vacation to try out your new skill. The more you learn, the more you can expand your horizons, and the more you learn together, the more you will have in common.

Photo by Wayne Calabrese.

In the day-to-day rush of life, it's easy to get bogged down with work, bills, kids, family obligations, and a host of other responsibilities. But remember, you came together in the beginning because you were attracted to each other—not because you can fix a flat tire, make a great spaghetti sauce, have the whitest whites in town, or can balance a mean checkbook. It takes a little more work to remember not to take each other for granted—but it's well worth the long-term benefits.

The Least You Need to Know

➤ Sustaining a loving, trusting relationship leaves you free to be as sexy as you please.

➤ Make time for sex, and enjoy sexual variation.

➤ Talk about what you like to do sexually.

➤ Use all five senses to spice up your sex life.

➤ Create sexy dates or learn new things together to keep your relationship exciting.

Chapter 20

Does Being Sexy Mean You Must Have Sex?

In This Chapter

➤ Reviewing the rules of sexiness

➤ How to be sexy without being a tease

➤ How to avoid using sexy behavior in the wrong way

➤ Knowing how and when to tone down your sexiness

➤ When it's okay to be sexy in your relationships—and when it's not

As I hope you've learned by now, looking great and being sexual is only part of the whole sexy package. Being sexy is about having a good self-image and a positive attitude, including tons of confidence. Being sexy is being an attractive person, inside and out. But can someone ever be *too* sexy? That's what we'll explore in this chapter.

Remember the two rules I outlined for you back in Chapter 4, "The Sexy Advantage"? In case you forgot, they are: *Sexy does not equal immoral, distasteful behavior* and *being sexy does not necessarily involve the act of sex.*

Keeping these rules in mind, I'll help you figure out how you can be sexy without being a tease. When should you tone down your sexy aura? How do you manage levels of sexiness in relationships?

Take Off the "Y" and You've Got ... Sex?

Using sexiness to initiate sex is exciting, as you learned in Chapter 16, "If You Want Me, Just Whistle: Using Sexiness to Initiate Sex." Not only does it help you to establish a particular mood and pace, it makes you ultimately desirable and can set the stage for great sex. But does being sexy always translate into having sex?

The answer is, of course not. All humans are sexual beings: sexuality is just a part of our personality, part of the way we are. It's important to accept our sexuality as part of our innate nature without judging it. Being sexy is certainly part of our sexuality; however, it isn't a train out of control. Being sexy is a multifaceted expression of who we are and how we want to be perceived—whether it be physically, emotionally, intellectually, or spiritually.

Stimulating the brain is just as important as tantalizing the eyes. Being sexy is a way to do both—but not necessarily at the same time. You have the power to gauge your sexiness. Consider what you want your result to be:

➤ Are you looking to attract others socially?

➤ Do you want to make your presence known in a particular situation?

➤ Do you want to entice someone into bed?

Each of these requires a different level and direction of sexiness—and all are within your power to create.

Just a Little Tease

Remember that one girl or guy back in high school who had a "reputation"? Every school had at least one, and around that person swirled a hundred trashy stories about his or her supposed sexual prowess. Most of the time, the stories weren't even a little bit true. These people gained their reputations by simply being sexy. As far as guys were concerned, this made them "studs"; their female counterparts weren't as lucky. They were, more often than not, labeled "easy" or a "tease."

Of course, this was back in high school and I would hope by now that you have learned a little more about people, but just in case you skipped out on Grownups 101, here are a few more rules to live by:

Sexy people are not necessarily having tons of sex.

I have a friend who is absolutely one of the sexiest people I have ever seen. Not only is she drop-dead gorgeous, but it's almost as if she has the ability to hypnotize people. Men trip all over themselves when they see her on the street. However, she can count the sexual partners she has on one hand and still have fingers left over. She chooses to limit her number of sexual partners, and she respects herself for her choices. Case in point: Don't judge other people, especially when it comes to sexuality. You may well be dead wrong about them.

> *Sexy does not always equal having sex all the time.*

Just because you like chocolate cake, that doesn't mean you want to eat it every day, all the time, right? Well, if you are a sexy person, that does not translate into wanting to have sex all of the time. There's a big difference between being a tease and being sexy (more on that in a bit).

> *You need to be a good sexy receiver, as well as sexy transmitter.*

Throughout this book, you've learned lots of ways to be sexy for many different occasions, but you also need to learn how to read sexiness in others. There is always the chance that someone is misdirecting his or her sexiness; however, keep in mind this simple rule of thumb: As you do not want to be judged, don't judge others.

Even with all that said, you still may be wondering: "Where is the line drawn between being a tease and simply being sexy?"

Not the Teasing Kind

In order to manage your sexiness, you can control the signals you send. While there may be some who will misread you and your intentions, you aren't at fault if you are cognizant of what kind of sexiness you call attention to. You are not necessarily being a tease if you are the following:

➤ **Flirtatious.** Flirting, like a sexy smile, or being flattering in conversation, is a way of getting to know someone and creating a friendly atmosphere. If you are in a situation where you are using flirty behavior to break the ice and not being overtly sexual in your flirtation, you are not being a tease. On the other hand,

Flirt Alert

Some people use their sexiness to attract many, many sex partners. The need for attention and sex is more important to them than a sense of pleasure or fulfillment. These people usually have issues such as insecurity and low self-esteem. Seeing a therapist can help.

Flirt Alert

You need to be responsible in the way you use sexy behavior. Because being sexy does not necessarily mean you want to have sex, be careful about what kind of signals you are sending to others. Save the come-hither looks and suggestive body language for when you truly want to have sex. Otherwise, if you are merely trying to attract others, you *will* be perceived as a tease.

it's possible to go too far with the flirting. If you run your foot up someone's leg or make a suggestive remark and have no intention of following through by having sex with the person, you will be considered a tease.

➤ **Engaging.** Paying undivided attention to someone does not mean you are promising to make this person the center of your universe, sexual or otherwise. Engaging someone and paying attention when that person speaks is polite and draws the person in. It is not considered teasing behavior. However, if in the course of your engaging, you don't give some signals (or statements) that you're not interested, the other person could get the wrong idea and think that your undivided attention equals sexual attention.

➤ **Dressed in flattering clothing.** Ever heard that horrible phrase, "She was asking for it"? It's just wrong. You are not necessarily being a tease because of the clothes you wear. If you are walking around in a G-string and five-inch stiletto heels, okay. Yes. You are putting out a very clear message. However, a skirt above the knee or a formfitting top that shows cleavage does not automatically indicate an invitation for sex. But if you are wearing something that's provocative, you need to be careful that you're not sending out sexual signals that could bring unwanted attention.

Sari Says

Being a tease really only means you promise to have sex with someone, fool around heavily with that person, and then change your mind. Of course, anyone has the right to change his or her mind about wanting to have sex—even at the last moment. However, you run the risk that the other person may believe you were a tease—in some way insincere about going as far as you did.

Remember, being sexy does not always mean you are acting the siren or Herculean God. Sexy behavior invites people in, engages them, and makes them notice you. It does not mean you are a tease.

See Jane Tease

Just as important as knowing when being sexy is okay, you should also know when you are crossing the line. If you *want* to tease and it is part of your lure to build up the heat for steamy sex later, great. That's fine. But don't make promises you can't keep. Most people like attention, and there's nothing wrong with that. But some people crave it so intensely, they engage in behavior that solicits a sexual response from those around them. This is when teasing is *not* okay. Not only is it false advertising, it can also get you into trouble.

Maybe you're not sure your behavior is always on the up and up. Or maybe you're a big tease and you don't even realize it. To find out, answer the following questions as honestly as you can to help determine if you are misdirecting your sexy signals:

1. Have you ever flirted overtly with a friend's spouse or significant other?

    Yes ____ No ____

2. Have you ever used sexy behavior to win an advantage over your colleagues when the competition is tight?

    Yes ____ No ____

3. Have you ever used sexy behavior to get something (for example, drinks, gifts, a promotion, money, favors) from someone in whom you weren't interested?

    Yes ____ No ____

4. When you are at a social occasion, do you have a hard time relating to others unless it is through sexual innuendoes and flirting?

    Yes ____ No ____

5. When concerned about whether or not others like you, do you turn on your sexuality full steam to ensure that you have their undivided attention?

    Yes ____ No ____

If you answered yes to even one of these, you might want to re-examine your behavior and motivations for it. It could be that you use your sexuality to get attention, no matter what kind it is, and lots of it.

Everyone gets insecure at times, but if you find your insecurities are like a bottomless well that you endlessly try to fill up by any means necessary, especially by using your sex appeal, it's time to check that behavior. You are being a tease. Period. Not only does being a tease eventually render you powerless as far as being sexy goes—as if you are sexually crying wolf—it also make you more lonely in the end. There is nothing wrong with being sexy, but nobody likes a tease full of empty promises.

When in doubt, keep it subtle. If you are in a situation where you are concerned that maybe you might be sending the wrong signals, take it down a notch.

Toning Down Your Sexiness

There are many shades of sexy. Sometimes, however, it can be difficult to know when and how to tone down your own sexy quotient. The following are some rules of thumb to help guide you when you are in situations where you are unsure.

Sex and the Workplace

In the workplace, it is absolutely fine to be a dynamic, sexy person. However, you *never* want to bring sex into the office. It is absolutely not appropriate under any circumstances. Even with the raised consciousness on the issue, it is too easy to encounter sexual harassment on the job. You don't want to be on the receiving end of sexual harassment, and you don't want to invite it, either. I know you must be thinking that there is no way some one could "invite it." You may think that's like saying a woman "asked for it" by the way she dressed. But the fact is the workplace is another world. You need to keep your sexy signals limited to the ones discussed in Chapter 5, "Different Types of Sexiness"—those that imply self-confidence, not sex. Acceptable sexy characteristics at work include any or all of the following:

➤ The ability to get people to listen

➤ Being trustworthy

➤ Being determined and dynamic

➤ Being uninhibited and not shy

➤ Not being hindered by outside opinion

➤ The ability to seize opportunities

➤ The ability to turn a negative situation into a positive one

➤ Being intelligent

➤ Having charisma

➤ Being a leader

Sexy Stats

Not surprisingly, the majority of sexual harassment cases show women as the victims. According to the *National Men's Resource Calendar*, 50 to 67 percent of sexual harassment is committed by men toward women; 15 to 30 percent are cases of women committing sexual harassment toward men.

To make sure that you don't come across as inappropriately sexy at work, keep these things in mind:

➤ Don't make physical sexy gestures, such as lip-licking or gazing deep into someone else's eyes.

➤ Refrain from touching or hugging people at work.

➤ Don't dress suggestively. Keep your appearance professional.

Avoid problems at work by toning down your sex appeal if necessary. Remember, there's a time and a place for everything.

A Friend in Need

If you notice that most of your friendships with those of the opposite sex frequently seem to end up in a conflict of "Why can't we be more than friends?" you may want to take stock of how you are acting around your friends. If your cravings for attention find you turning on the charm a little too strongly around your pals, you could be sending them the wrong messages.

Pay attention to the way you act with friends of the opposite sex: Are you very flirtatious? Do you try to get a sexual reaction from them by using sexual behavior? If so, tone it down. It is misleading. Also, it makes those near and dear to you feel that you don't really value their friendship, but only the reflection of yourself that you see in their eyes. Eventually, this vanity routine gets old and will leave you with fewer and fewer friends. Does this mean you can't flirt with your friends? No, but you need to make sure that your motivations aren't of a selfish nature. Flirting in fun with your friends is fine—but flirting with them because you crave attention is a negative way to use your sexuality.

Flirt Alert

Is it true that friends make the best lovers? Well, you certainly need to respect and care deeply for the person with whom you choose to be in a sexual relationship. But tread carefully when trying to take a friendship to the next level—make sure that you're both ready to go this route; otherwise, not only do you lose out on a possible love interest, but you also lose a good friend.

Just the Two of Us

Showing your full-on sexy self in a love relationship is always appropriate, right? Well, not so fast. There are times in every relationship where you need to turn down the heat a little.

Sexual relationships are, of course, the one area where you can show the sexy side of yourself more often than in any other area of your life. However, there are times when being sexy just isn't appropriate:

➤ When your partner needs to discuss something serious with you.

➤ When you need to discuss something serious with your partner.

➤ When you are around your partner's family (of course, affection is great, but nothing sexual).

➤ When you are around your partner's friends.

➤ When you are around your partner's co-workers and higher-ups (such as at the office Christmas party).

In each of these instances, if you turn on the super-sexy charm, your partner may well perceive that you are not taking him or her seriously or, worse, that you don't respect your partner. Just as your significant other values your sexy nature when you turn it on just for him or her, your partner also will value the fact that you know to turn it off at the appropriate times.

This might make being sexy seem like something you switch on and off like a light. That's not exactly so. There are many sides of sexiness—intelligence, charm, strength, and trust, to name a few. If you save the super steamy stuff for when you're both behind closed doors, your partner will see that you respect him or her. When you have respect between the two of you, you create the solid groundwork for being more free with each other than you could ever have dreamed. And just wait until you see how sexy that is!

The Least You Need to Know

➤ Being sexy does *not* mean you always want to have sex.

➤ Sexiness is multifaceted—it is every wonderful part of your personality. You can choose what parts of it you want to show at the appropriate moments.

➤ Teasing is okay in sex, but not when you use it just for the sake of getting attention. Make sure your motives are pure before turning on the charm.

➤ Save the steamy stuff for when you and your lover are at the right time and place.

Part 5

Sexy Superstars

You're sitting in the dark of a movie theater. The initial credits begin to roll, the music trickles from the speakers, the camera lens zooms around the setting, flitting here and there, until, finally, it settles upon … the icon of glory you've come to see: the sexy superstar.

Sexy superstars are part of a fantasy-scape that entices the brain like the ultimate sexy drug. Whether they are the stars of large or small screen, representatives of film, video, audio, stage, sports, or other types of public figures, we can learn something from the way they seduce us. Whether it's Madonna or Julia Roberts, JFK Jr. or Jim Morrison, each star exudes his or her own, special sexy quality that we can learn from.

This part reveals the secrets of the femmes fatales and macho men we've all grown to know and lust over throughout the years. They are the ultimate teachers—let's see if we can pick up a tip or two from their glitter and glam.

Chapter 21

Sexy Women We Can Learn From

In This Chapter

➤ Taking a cue for what's sexy from some female superstars

➤ How sexy sirens like Marilyn Monroe and Madonna show us how to flaunt our sexuality

➤ How Jane Fonda, Tina Turner, and Sophia Loren show that women can be sexy at any age

➤ How naturally sexy women like Julia Roberts, Meg Ryan, and Halle Berry make looking sexy look easy

Women celebrities have been defining styles of beauty and sexiness for decades. Many men enjoy seeing sexy images of women in movies, magazines, music, and TV. For women, however, it's not just about enjoying their looks. Women can learn from the sexiness of stars, and they can choose if they'd like any to become their own sexy role models.

Of course, there are many types of sexiness and many different types of women. In this chapter I chose women as sexy role models who represent several different styles: erotic sexiness, sexiness that lasts over decades, and natural sexiness. You may see these women as our society's ideals of sexiness, but keep in mind that everyone has different tastes as to what is attractive. While you might not find all these women meet your criteria for what's sexy, I'm sure that you can glean a few sexy qualities from each of them.

Sexy Sirens

Overt sexiness has been best portrayed by classic sex symbols, who, along with flashing their skin, reveal an attitude of erotic power. Marilyn Monroe and Madonna are two stars who are quintessential sex symbols. Read on to see if you agree, and if you do, find out what you can learn from each of them so you can be a sexy siren, too!

Madonna

Some say it's Madonna's world and we just live in it. Since the early 1980s, no woman has created more controversy, caused more media speculation, or spawned more impersonators than Madonna—and few have enjoyed as many hit records and awards. Her long and thriving career is due to not only her talent and willingness to take chances, but also to her business savvy.

Born in 1958 near Detroit, Madonna Ciccone is the eldest of eight children. She has said that vying for attention in the large family gave her performing skills very early on. Her mother's death from cancer when she was six shaped her early life. She threw herself into artistic outlets such as school plays, cheerleading, piano lessons, and ballet. Madonna's dancing skills took her to college on scholarship, then to New York. After working odd jobs to get by, and then getting involved with prestigious dance troupes, such as Martha Graham and Alvin Ailey, she found her way into the club scene and pop music world.

Little did we know that the same woman who burst onto the scene in the early 1980s with bubblegum pop such as "Holiday" and "Lucky Star" and who sang such provocative songs as "Like a Virgin" or "Erotica" would eventually turn inward and produce a body of work such as "Ray of Light," which shows a more spiritual introspective side. Of course, that's what Madonna is best known for: transforming her image with each phase of her life. She even succeeded in her film work with *Evita,* for which she won a Golden Globe. Madonna has had phenomenal success with her albums and her stunning live shows. But Madonna has always been about more than just her music and movies. She has used her fame to raise money to fight AIDS and intolerance before it was fashionable. As a strong woman with an immense amount of ambition, she has shown that compassion is a quality that we all can have. And she has shown us that once you hit your 40s, you can become a mom and enter a new phase of life.

Sari Says

Legend has it that Madonna arrived in New York with only a few dollars in her pocket. She asked a taxi driver to "drop her in the center of it all," and was let off in Times Square.

Madonna.

(Photo by Archive Photos)

Learning about being sexy from Madonna doesn't mean you have to be photographed hitchhiking in the nude, as she was in her book, *Sex*. Consider the following:

➤ Don't be afraid to change your look. Experimenting with new hairstyles, hair color, or clothing styles can spice things up and help you to create an exciting new image.

➤ Being successful doesn't mean losing your compassion. Volunteer time and/or money whenever possible to causes you hold dear.

➤ Be dedicated. While the rest of us are still in bed, Madonna has already worked out, read scripts, and written a few songs. Go the extra mile for things that are important to you.

➤ Enjoy sex, but don't take it too seriously. Always remember that sex can and should be fun and not something to hide.

➤ Know how to handle attention. Madonna has remained levelheaded even with her immense fame. Don't become overwhelmed by attention that you get.

Deep Quote

"I want to rule the world. Every time I reach a new peak, I see a new one and want to climb. It's like I can't stop. Maybe I should rest and admire the view, but I can't. I've got to keep on pushing. Why? I don't know. I don't know what motivates me. I just know I've got to do it."

—Madonna

Sexy Stats

Marilyn may not have been quite as stick-thin as today's actresses, but she did manage to keep a great figure much of the time. While there are some accounts that she occasionally wore a size 14 or weighed around 135 pounds, most records report her measurements as 35-22-35, her height at around 5'5", and her weight at around 118 pounds. That certainly is slim and shapely.

Deep Quote

"It was wonderful to be around her, she was simply overwhelming. She had so much promise. It seemed to me that she could really be a great kind of phenomenon, a terrific artist. She was endlessly fascinating, full of original observations ... there wasn't a conventional bone in her body."

—Arthur Miller

➤ Don't be afraid to take on new challenges. Madonna has taken on many roles over the years, as a singer, dancer, author, producer, executive, actress, and mom.

Marilyn Monroe

Marilyn Monroe's image may be one of the most recognizable of all times. Her career spanned 16 years, yet since her tragic death nearly four decades ago she has remained an immortal icon. Born Norma Jeane Mortenson in 1926, she never knew her father, and she lived with her mother only briefly off and on, because her mother was mentally ill. She spent most of her childhood in a foster home. Because of this instability as a child, she often escaped into her own little fantasy world, and she dreamed of being an actress. She married young to get away from her troubled home life. Even though she was working in a factory, not trying to "get discovered," her beautiful looks and magical presence were noticed. In 1944, she was photographed by the Army as a promotion to show women on the assembly line contributing to the war effort. One of the photographers asked to take more pictures of her. By spring of 1945, she had appeared on 33 covers of national magazines.

In 1946 she divorced her husband, and signed a contract with 20th Century Fox Studios. She had minor film roles at first; she then appeared in a number of films that established her as a solid star, including *Gentlemen Prefer Blondes, How to Marry a Millionaire, Some Like It Hot,* and *The Misfits.* Her sexy blonde bombshell image was a huge success by this time.

She married baseball great Joe DiMaggio; however, the marriage lasted only two years. Perhaps the breaking point came when he reportedly became upset during the filming of the famous skirt-blowing scene of *The Seven Year Itch.* One year later, she married playwright Arthur Miller, whom she admired for his great intellectualism; that marriage was short-lived as well. It was widely reported that she had an affair with President John F. Kennedy, so it was quite shocking when she sang her infamous breathy version of "Happy Birthday" wearing a sheer, tight gown at the President's gala birthday celebration in Madison Square Garden on May 19, 1962.

Tragically, Marilyn Monroe was found dead from a drug overdose in 1962. Much has been speculated about the events surrounding her death. To this day, while it is most often stated that her death was suicide, many believe this may not have been the case. However sad the circumstances of her death, no one will ever forget her beautiful looks and her personal magnetism.

Marilyn Monroe.

(Photo by 20th Century Fox)

Here are a few things we can learn about sexiness from Marilyn:

➤ Don't worry about where you came from; concentrate on where you're going! If you develop confidence, you can be sexy and even famous.

➤ It's okay to sound a little ditsy, but don't *be* ditsy. Marilyn's "dumb blonde" routine helped catapult her to fame, but she was really very sharp.

➤ Depending on the occasion, don't be afraid to dress provocatively. Marilyn's costumes were some of the sexiest—and most memorable.

➤ Practice a sexy walk. Watch the scene in *Some Like It Hot* in which she sashays past the train. To get a lot of wiggle she'd walk in high heels, placing one foot directly in front of the other.

➤ Do some flirting. Marilyn's breathy "boop-boop-be-do" while singing "I Wanna Be Loved by You" is classic flirtation.

Ageless Beauty: Still Sexy over 60

Sexiness lasts a lifetime if you know how to keep up your sexy attitude and appearance. This section focuses on women who are great role models for sexiness at any age. They all became famous when they were sexy in their 20s. But age and all that life brought them has only made them sexier over the years!

Jane Fonda

Daughter of the legendary actor Henry Fonda, sister to Peter Fonda, and aunt to Bridget Fonda, Jane was destined to become a star. She attended Vassar College, and then she began her career as a model, while studying acting at the Actors Studio. Her screen debut in *Tall Story* marked the beginning of a highly respected acting career. In her earlier films, such as *Barbarella,* she had a blatantly erotic sexy image. Yet, she also had a natural sexy look in movies such as *Barefoot in the Park,* in which she starred opposite Robert Redford.

Jane underwent a controversial period in which she got involved with anti-establishment causes and anti-war activities during the Vietnam War. Her visit to North Vietnam at the height of the conflict earned her the nickname "Hanoi Jane." Her film work that followed was more thoughtful than her previous work, highlighted by two Academy Awards for her performances in *Klute* and *Coming Home* and five Oscar nominations for Best Actress, including for *They Shoot Horses, Don't They?, Julia,* and *On Golden Pond,* which she made with her father.

In the 1980s Jane shifted her focus to fitness. She started the aerobic exercise craze with the publication of the best-selling *Jane Fonda's Workout Book* and exercise videos. Jane Fonda has had a varied career, as well as a varied love life. She has been married to and divorced from three powerful men: Roger Vadim, a French filmmaker; Tom Hayden, a California senator; and Ted Turner, a media mogul. As a woman who is over 60, she is still fit, gorgeous, and open to new challenges. Today, Jane leads the Georgia Campaign for Adolescent Pregnancy and Prevention to help teen girls cope with sexuality issues and improve their futures.

Jane Fonda.

(Photo by Archive Photos)

We can pick up a few pointers from Jane on what's sexy:

➤ Don't be afraid to change with the times. Jane's sexy images evolved with each decade.

➤ Stay fit and healthy. You don't have to star in your own exercise video, but you should stay fit.

➤ Express your individuality. Even though she followed in her family's footsteps, Jane is her own person.

➤ Wear contemporary but classic styles, at any age. Jane always dresses fashionably and tastefully.

➤ Speak your mind. Jane expressed her opinions about everything from fitness to the Vietnam War. An opinionated woman is sexy!

Deep Quote

"Women are not forgiven for aging. Robert Redford's 'lines of distinction' are my old-age wrinkles."

—Jane Fonda

Tina Turner

Sexy, over 60, and wearing the shortest mini skirts around, Tina Turner is still vibrant and going strong. She is one of the most amazing female rock stars, with her powerful voice, her unforgettable story, and her remarkable trademark legs. Born Anna Mae Bullock in 1938 in Tennessee, she and her family picked cotton. At age 18, she met and soon married Ike Turner, a bandleader who started her singing career. The partnership, which produced hits like "Proud Mary," was marked by physical and emotional abuse.

With little money but a lot of bravery and determination, Tina finally walked out on Ike. She climbed her way back to the top of the pop charts in 1984, when she released her comeback album "Private Dancer," which won four Grammies and spawned the number-one hit "What's Love Got to Do with It?" Tina has also appeared in the movies *Tommy* and *Mad Max: Beyond Thunder Dome,* and has done advertisements for a hosiery company, spotlighting her still-spectacular legs.

Another medium she conquered was writing, with her autobiography, *I Tina.* Despite the scars from her earlier marriage, Tina has been in a love relationship with the same man for many years. She

Deep Quote

"Sometimes you've got to let everything go. If you are unhappy with anything, whatever is bringing you down, get rid of it. Because you'll find that when you're free, your true creativity, your true self comes out."

—Tina Turner

still goes on stage reaching millions of fans worldwide with her incredibly energetic performances. Tina remains "simply the best."

Tina Turner.

(Photo by Gary Merrin)

With her guts and perseverance, Tina can teach us plenty about what's sexy:

➤ Never give up. No matter how much adversity one goes through, your dreams can come true if you keep going after them!

➤ Get away from people who hurt you. Tina's strength became apparent and her sexiness could only really shine once she got out of her abusive relationship.

➤ Show off your best feature. Micro-minis made Tina a hit. Can you imagine how her life would have been altered if she had been self-conscious about her legs?

➤ Dance. Moving your body the way Tina does is not only sexy, it helps keep you fit. Check out a video of her stage performances to see more.

➤ Write down your thoughts. You needn't write a book to tell your story. Keeping a journal of your private thoughts can be just as empowering.

Sophia Loren

Sophia Loren was one of the first foreign stars to attain a level of international success comparable to America's domestic talents. When she received an honorary Academy Award in 1991, the presenter summed up her value, saying she is "one of the genuine treasures of world cinema."

Born in 1934, Sophia was raised solely by her mother where they lived in poverty in the war-torn town of Pozzuoli, Italy. While in her early teens, Sophia worked as a model. She became involved in acting in films under the encouragement of producer Carlo Ponti. She had bit parts in a number of small Italian films, including a part in Federico Fellini's *Variety Lights*. In 1953, she landed a leading role in *Africa Under the Sea* and the title role in the film adaptation of the Verdi opera *Aida*. In 1957, Loren appeared in her first English-speaking part in the action-romance *Boy on a Dolphin*. Later that year, she was cast as the object of Cary Grant's affection in the World War II epic *The Pride and the Passion*.

Sophia Loren arrived in Hollywood in 1958. She was heralded as an international sex symbol because of her performances in *Desire Under the Elms, Houseboat, The Black Orchid*, and *It Started in Naples*. She also acted in more serious roles, such as a widowed mother in the Italian wartime drama *Two Women*, for which she won an Academy Award for Best Actress. She starred in *El Cid* with Charlton Heston, and a series of Italian films alongside Marcello Mastroianni, including *Yesterday, Today and Tomorrow* and *Marriage Italian Style*.

In 1975, she published her autobiography, *Sophia Loren: Living and Loving*, which was made into a movie for TV in which she played both herself and her mother. She has continued to star in movies, including making a revival of sorts among younger audiences in the 1990s as the sex symbol in the comedy *Grumpier Old Men*, opposite Walter Matthau and Jack Lemmon. In recent years, she has also written a cookbook, *Sophia Loren's Recipes and Memories,* which features her favorite Italian recipes and stories from her childhood. For more than 30 years, she has been married to Carlo Ponti, the producer who first encouraged her to act. Theirs is one of the longest-running love stories.

Sophia Loren.

(Photo by Archive Photos)

Deep Quote

"There is a fountain of youth: It is your mind, your talents, the creativity you bring to your life, and the lives of the people you love. When you learn to tap this source, you will truly have defeated age."

—Sophia Loren

If you want to seem like an international sexy star, try some of the following:

➤ Maintain devotion to your family. Sophia has been with the same man for decades, and she says that the most important people in her life are her children.

➤ Dress sexy without looking trashy. Sophia often shows her cleavage, but always looks tasteful.

➤ Be a classic. Sophia is not trendy. Her sex appeal is due to her timeless beauty.

➤ Don't be afraid to take on new challenges as you get older. Sophia was known for her Italian romantic and dramatic roles, but found as she got older that she could be a hit in comedies, too.

➤ Travel to gain a worldly sexiness. Italy (and much of Europe) is quite romantic, and even as a visitor, you can learn about the European sensibility of sexiness.

Naturally Sexy

Have you ever seen photos of celebrities without makeup, fancy hairdos, or a smashing wardrobe? If you have, then you know that some of them may look amazing in the movies, but in real life, they're not so hot. That is, except for few amazingly sexy natural women. They not only look sexy naturally, they all possess a style of casual elegance that is packed with sex appeal.

Julia Roberts

A 10-thousand-watt smile, jubilant laugh, gorgeous hair, glowing confidence, and a tall graceful body: These are the traits that most people think of when they think of Julia Roberts. She was born in 1967 in Smyrna, Georgia. Her parents ran an acting school. When she joined her brother Eric in New York, he was already a well-known actor.

Julia's first major roles were in 1988 when she appeared in *Mystic Pizza* and *Satisfaction.* The following year she took on a more serious role in *Steel Magnolias,* alongside veteran actresses Sally Field and Shirley MacLaine. Her breakthrough performance was in *Pretty Woman,* with Richard Gere, in which she played a prostitute with a big heart who falls in love. This mega-hit movie made Julia one of the most famous women in Hollywood, making her name synonymous with "pretty woman."

Julia has gone on to star in many movies, but romantic comedies remain her forte, such as *My Best Friend's Wedding.* Today she is one of the most highly regarded actresses in Hollywood, continuing to show her acting skills in films such as *Erin Brockovich.*

But money and fame aren't everything. Julia has become a goodwill ambassador with UNICEF, making visits to disadvantaged communities in Haiti and India. She has also gone through some ups and downs in her personal life, but has found love and happiness with actor Benjamin Bratt.

Take a few cues from Julia on being sexy:

➤ Laugh. Julia is almost always photographed wearing her trademark wide smile.

➤ Focus on happy, light, positive topics in conversation. Keep complaints about your private life to yourself.

➤ Look sure of yourself. Julia always looks proud, confident, and mature.

➤ Fall in love. Sure, I know, everyone wants to be in love. But the fact is, when you are, you may just glow the way Julia does when she is in love.

Deep Quote

"I don't get angry very often. I lose my temper rarely. And when I do, there's always a legitimate cause. Normally I have a great lightness of being. I take things in a very happy, amused way."

—Julia Roberts

Julia Roberts.

(Photo by Archive Photos)

Meg Ryan

Meg Ryan was born Margaret Mary Emily Anne Hyra in Fairfield, Connecticut. By the time she was a teen, her sex appeal was apparent, and she was voted "cutest" by her high school class. She studied journalism in New York, then began pursing a career as an actress. Her onscreen debut was as Candice Bergen's daughter in *Rich and Famous*. She was also featured on the soap opera *As the World Turns* for two years. Meg was in the cast of a short-lived TV series and had some small film roles before her career began taking off when she landed a supporting role in the blockbuster *Top Gun*, with Tom Cruise. It was in the hit *When Harry Met Sally* that she established herself as a star. She became known for her naturally sexy styles in other romantic comedies with Tom Hanks, such as *Sleepless in Seattle* and *You've Got Mail*. Her wholesome sexiness gives her widespread appeal, and she remains a popular actress.

Meg's style has been described by *The Washington Post* as "wild-pony beauty." She appears most often with tousled hair and casual clothes. She looks like the impish girl next door, cracking jokes and just shooting the breeze. But there's something about her that's very sexy, too. Forever to be known for the scene in which she demonstrated her orgasm-faking skills in *When Harry Met Sally,* she has shown that the natural, casual girl always gets the guy, and certainly knows all about sex.

Deep Quote

"Things that are authentic are what's beautiful to me. I find people's exuberance or mystery or their simplicity beautiful, as opposed to just the way their eyes and face are."

—Meg Ryan

Meg Ryan.

(Photo by Max Miller)

This blonde, blue-eyed natural woman can help us learn how to be sexy, if we pay attention to the following suggestions:

➤ Try the "right out of bed" look. Tousle your hair and keep your style casual to capture the Meg Ryan look.

➤ Allow yourself to let go during orgasm. Being free and even loud during sex can be sexy, and it's something your partner might find sexy, too. (But don't fake an orgasm, if you want to honestly enjoy sex.)

➤ Relax and let it all hang out. Don't be afraid to really be yourself.

➤ Dress casually. You don't have to dress up in a fancy gown to look sexy; khakis and a white T-shirt can be just as appealing.

Halle Berry

Her incredible charm, charisma, and glow have won legions of fans for this enchanting actress. Born in 1966 to a white mother and a black father in Cleveland, Ohio, cruel taunts about her being biracial shaped Halle into a shy child, who nurtured a dream of becoming an actress. By age 17, she realized that skin color was not at all a detriment, as her looks propelled her to the top of beauty pageants, including Miss Teen All-American, Miss USA, and Miss World. This doe-eyed beauty gave up a successful modeling career to become an actress in the late 1980s. She got her first break starring, appropriately enough, as a teenage model on the 1989 TV series *Living Dolls*, and then went on to her first feature film, Spike Lee's *Jungle Fever*. She proved she was not just another model-turned-actress when she landed her starring roles as *femmes fatales* in the romantic comedy *Strictly Business* and the action comedy *The Last Boy Scout*. She stretched her acting muscles in roles such movies as *Losing Isaiah*, *Bulworth*, and *Introducing Dorothy Dandridge*, for which she won a Golden Globe.

One of Halle's greatest strengths is her style. She has an elegant fashion sense, wearing sleek, sexy designer outfits that are sensual and formfitting, while being romantic, delicate, and refined. But it takes more than beauty to be sexy. Halle earned a reputation for tenacity. She has won roles that would otherwise go to white actresses, by convincing executives that she is best for the job. She can also be tough, bouncing back from a difficult divorce from baseball player David Justice. In addition, since she was diagnosed with diabetes, Halle has become a volunteer for the Juvenile Diabetes Association. Halle is also a model for Revlon's Most

Deep Quote

"I could relate to Dorothy [Dandridge] and her struggle. There's still no spot carved out for a black leading lady. I'm still banging on those doors."

—Halle Berry

Unforgettable Women advertising campaign, and although she has never posed nude, *Playboy* named her among the 100 sexiest women of the century. She has a romantic sexy look because of her beauty, but her mind and her style let it come shining through.

Halle Berry.

(Photo by Rose Prouser)

Here's what you can learn about being sexy from Halle Berry:

➤ Sexiness can be subtle. Simplicity and elegance reign supreme for Halle. She always chooses amazing designer gowns, but they simply flatter her already gorgeous looks.

➤ Look confident and show your strength. Support and defend yourself—whether that means winning roles or working to find a good relationship.

➤ Believe in yourself, and help others open their minds. Halle never let childhood taunts about race discourage her. Instead she knew she could help others understand these issues by using her talents to communicate important messages about race.

➤ Supporting a cause is sexy. Get involved with a cause that you have a personal connection to.

Being a sexy woman is not just about how you dress or pose for the camera. It's about presenting your best qualities and creating a life that you are proud of. You can pick up tons of ideas from celebrity women about what to wear or how to carry yourself, but take note also of how they took control of their lives in order to achieve their dreams.

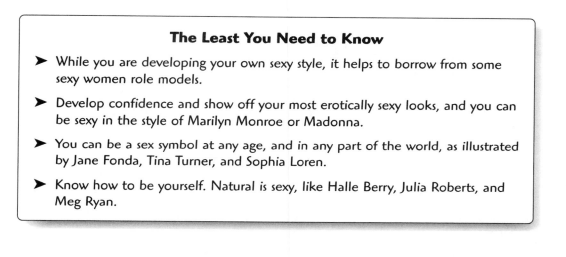

The Least You Need to Know

➤ While you are developing your own sexy style, it helps to borrow from some sexy women role models.

➤ Develop confidence and show off your most erotically sexy looks, and you can be sexy in the style of Marilyn Monroe or Madonna.

➤ You can be a sex symbol at any age, and in any part of the world, as illustrated by Jane Fonda, Tina Turner, and Sophia Loren.

➤ Know how to be yourself. Natural is sexy, like Halle Berry, Julia Roberts, and Meg Ryan.

Chapter 22

Sexy Men We Can Learn From

In This Chapter

➤ Taking a cue for what's sexy from some male superstars

➤ How legends like John F. Kennedy Jr., Elvis, and James Dean can show us how to make our sexy style memorable

➤ How hunks like Brad Pitt, Denzel Washington, and Cary Grant can teach us how suave can be sexy

➤ How naturally sexy men like Jim Morrison, Tiger Woods, and Harrison Ford can show us how to exude sexiness without even trying

Have you ever caught yourself staring at a celebrity's photo in a magazine to see how he gets his look? Or watching a performer on TV or in a movie, and studying his every move, trying to remember how you can replicate his sexy style? Role models are helpful in many ways. When it comes to sexiness, it can certainly be educational to examine some of the sexiest role models we have: sexy male stars.

Because there's not just one type of sexiness, there's not just one type of sexy male role model. Men we admire come in different styles: natural, rugged, sweet, playful, and even shocking. As you'll see in this chapter, some of the things they have in common are that they all seem to be confident, energetic, focused, creative, giving, and pretty darn hot.

While these men might not all fit with your idea of what's sexy, you can take note of their sexy qualities. Noticing what other people think of as attractive can give you a lot to go on if you want to become sexier.

Sexy Legends

This section depicts men who we have known and loved, those who have defined sexiness to several generations. They are our sexy "royalty": the Prince of Camelot, the King of Rock 'n' Roll, and a movie star we'll never forget. Even after their deaths, they remain in our hearts as some of the sexiest men who have ever lived.

John F. Kennedy Jr.

As the son of America's thirty-fifth President, John F. Kennedy Jr. faced the spotlight with dignity, intelligence, and charm from the moment he was born. He inherited not only striking good looks from his parents, but also their moral and ethical values, and their ability to enthrall a nation with their every move.

After graduating from Brown University in 1983 and then New York University Law School in 1989, John Jr. could have done anything he wanted. He chose public service by becoming an Assistant District Attorney for the City of New York. Politics was in his blood, yet John Jr. refused any offers to run for political office. Instead, in 1995 he founded *George* magazine as an outlet for his political interests. However, the magazine covered more than just politics. He also illustrated his knowledge of how celebrity and sexuality sells—each issue featured a sexy celebrity posing as a political figure, such as Cindy Crawford dressed as George Washington, sporting a bra top, white wig, and tight pants; and Drew Barrymore posing as Marilyn Monroe when she sang the famous "Happy Birthday, Mr. President" to his father.

Over the years, the 6'1", 190-pound muscular hunk dated celebrities such as Daryl Hannah and Madonna, becoming a fixture on the gossip pages. In 1988 he was chosen *People* magazine's Sexiest Man. When he married in 1996, many women seemed broken-hearted that their fantasy man was no longer single. In a small, secret ceremony, he married Carolyn Bessette, a stunning blonde who had worked as a publicist for Calvin Klein. Tragically, in 1999, Kennedy was a victim of the "Kennedy curse" when he, his wife, and her sister died in a plane crash off Martha's Vineyard. We all mourned the death of a captivating man in his prime, who had also brought millions to tears 35 years earlier when the nation watched John Jr. saluting his father's coffin.

Deep Quote

"It's hard for me to talk about a legacy or a mystique. It's my family. It's my mother. It's my sister. It's my father. We're a family like any other. We look out for one another. The fact that there have been difficulties and hardships, or obstacles, makes us closer."

—John F. Kennedy Jr.

John F. Kennedy Jr.

(Photo by Victor Malafronte)

Being born to a legendary President and First Lady gave John Jr. huge advantages in life, but there is still much we can learn from how he lived his life:

➤ Think before you speak. John Jr. was admired for what he said and also for what he didn't say. He rarely spoke to the press, but when he did speak in public, he did so with poise and confidence.

➤ Don't always strive to be the center of attention. It was often said of John Jr. that he blended in with people wherever he went; that he was just a "regular guy" who didn't put on airs.

➤ Try to show some modesty. Always be grateful for advantages that have been handed to you.

➤ Stay fit and active. John Jr. was athletic and known for Rollerblading and biking to get around.

➤ Get a good education. It's sexy when someone makes a commitment to becoming educated and reaching a goal.

➤ Do what makes you happy. Don't worry about what others expect you to do, as long as you determine how you can use your talents to achieve your personal goals.

➤ Always remember the importance of your family. John Jr. kept up his family name and image, and spent a great deal of time with the extended family he loved so dearly.

Elvis Presley

Known the world over simply by his first name, Elvis Presley is considered by millions to be the greatest performer who ever lived, the King of Rock 'n' Roll. As a child in Memphis, he began singing in church and was greatly influenced by gospel music as well as by country and blues. He cultivated an outsider image, with styled hair, long sideburns, and ostentatious clothes. In the mid-1950s Elvis began his recording career and instantly became an international sensation, with songs like "Love Me Tender," "Blue Suede Shoes," and "Hound Dog."

Sari Says

If you want to learn to move like Elvis, watch some of his old movies. Play his records, and see if you can dance the way he did. If you still feel inhibited about dancing, take some dance lessons.

He excited young crowds with his voice and his electrifying performances on stage. His hip-swiveling routine, in which he gyrated across the stage and plunged to his knees at dramatic moments in a song, was unprecedented and prompted fan mania. When he performed on television, "Elvis the Pelvis," as he was dubbed, could not be shown below his waist, because in those sexually conservative times he would ruffle the censors.

Elvis also became a movie star, with films like *Love Me Tender, Loving You,* and *Jailhouse Rock.* In 1957 Elvis was drafted into the Army, which gave him another level of sex appeal: a man in uniform serving his country. Even in the latter part of his career he remained wildly popular, performing in front of sold-out shows.

Elvis Presley.

(Photo by Frank Driggs)

Elvis's dependency on drugs increased and his health declined throughout the 1970s until he died on August 16, 1977. Many of his millions of fans still hate to believe that this rock legend is dead—they insist that Elvis is still alive, regularly reporting "Elvis sightings" to the tabloids.

Elvis is considered a sexy role model for millions who like his style. Here's what you can learn from the King about being sexy:

➤ Use your body. Know how to move and dance to turn people on.

➤ Use your voice. A sexy tone of voice can get you far.

➤ Be original. Pick a style that's really "you"! Elvis's style captured people's attention.

➤ Don't be afraid to shock some people; that will thrill others.

➤ Alter your image from time to time. Whether in an army uniform, a jailhouse costume, or a glittery jumpsuit, Elvis knew how to surprise his fans.

Deep Quote

"Some people tap their feet, some people snap their fingers, and some people sway back and forth. I just sorta do 'em all together, I guess."

—Elvis Presley

James Dean

James Dean was born in 1931 and grew up on a farm in Indiana. In his early 20s, he became a legend for disaffected teens worldwide. In his brief career, Dean starred in just three films: *East of Eden, Rebel Without a Cause,* and *Giant.* However, what he may have lacked in quantity, he made up for in unadulterated attitude and charisma. James Dean will always be universally known as the symbol of adolescent angst and rebellion. He personified reckless youth, and his image demanded respect and admiration. In his faded jeans and leather jacket with a cigarette dangling from his mouth, his image is timeless and classic. James Dean died in 1955, leaving a legacy that remains strong decades after the car crash that took his young life.

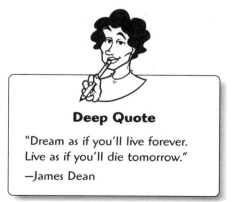

Deep Quote

"Dream as if you'll live forever. Live as if you'll die tomorrow."

—James Dean

Although developing James Dean's persona full-time might not be a wise move, you can certainly have some fun and make quite an impression by trying the following:

James Dean.

(Photo by Hulton-Archive)

➤ Dress the part. Put on faded jeans and a leather jacket, and see if you can channel James Dean's spirit for a few hours.

➤ Act young and spirited. It wasn't that long ago that you were young, carefree, and rebellious. Try to recapture that feeling.

➤ Drive a sexy car for a day. Even if you could never afford one, you can rent a Porsche or some other great car. Maybe for a big date? (But please, be a bit more careful than he was when you're driving!)

Handsome Hunks

Stars of yesterday and today have shown us many sexy looks. From the rough and tumble to the smooth and suave, we love their sexy images. Women drool over them, while guys sit back and watch with fascination. Maybe we could be a little sexier if we took notice of their style.

Brad Pitt

Raised in a small town in Missouri, Brad Pitt with his blond locks and washboard abs came to define the word "hunk" in the 1990s. Many people discovered him when he had a small role seducing (and then robbing) Geena Davis in *Thelma and Louise,* and wondered: Who is that incredibly sexy guy, and why isn't he in more films? Since that time, Brad Pitt has starred in a wide range of films, including *Interview with the Vampire, A River Runs Through It, Seven,* and *12 Monkeys,* for which he received an Oscar nomination. He also received the coveted *People* magazine title of "Sexiest Man Alive" twice. Not satisfied with just being a pretty face (and a pretty body), he has taken roles that challenge him and allow him to continue to evolve as one of the few true A-list actors working today. Millions of adoring female fans watched as he almost settled down with actress Gwenyth Paltrow, and sighed when he married another actress, Jennifer Aniston, in July 2000.

Brad Pitt.

(Photo by Frank Edwards)

We can all take a few lessons on being sexy from Brad Pitt:

➤ Do your crunches! Nobody has abs like Brad Pitt, but maybe you want to try. Although having an amazing physique shouldn't be the most important thing about being sexy, it certainly doesn't hurt to do what you can to stay in shape.

➤ Go blond. If you don't have blond hair like Brad Pitt, see your stylist and consider having your color highlighted for a new look.

➤ Don't rely solely on your looks. Being a pretty face or body isn't enough; make sure you are appreciated for the qualities that you hold within.

➤ Don't forget your roots. Part of Brad Pitt's appeal comes from his wholesome, Midwestern charm.

Deep Quote

"They hand me a script. I act. I'm here for entertainment, basically, when you whittle everything away. I'm a grown man who puts on makeup."

—Brad Pitt

Sari Says

Ever notice that when Gwenyth Paltrow was engaged to Brad Pitt, she started to look a little like him? Both cut off their long locks and dressed in a similar style. Jennifer Aniston, Brad's wife, looks like him, too. She let her hair get long and straight, the same as Brad's, and got more buff, lean, and tan, like Brad. In fact, it's not uncommon for men and women who've been together a while to begin to resemble one another.

Denzel Washington

Denzel Washington has a powerful sexual and romantic presence. And it's not just a few people who think he's a hunk. In a *Newsweek* magazine cover story about the biological basis of the perception of beauty, he was used as a key example in a scientific explanation of why he is considered an extremely handsome man.

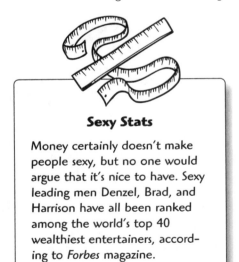

Sexy Stats

Money certainly doesn't make people sexy, but no one would argue that it's nice to have. Sexy leading men Denzel, Brad, and Harrison have all been ranked among the world's top 40 wealthiest entertainers, according to *Forbes* magazine.

Now in his 40s, Denzel has been a major star for well over a decade. He first became a star in NBC's hit medical series *St. Elsewhere* in the early 1980s. He went on to win worldwide acclaim and a Best Supporting Actor Oscar as a runaway slave who became a Civil War soldier in *Glory*. He has chosen several roles in which he has played noble or historical figures, such as his unforgettable portrayal of the title role in *Malcolm X,* as an attorney who defended an AIDS patient in *Philadelphia,* and as wrongly convicted boxer Rubin Carter in *The Hurricane*. Throughout the 1990s he also radiated his good looks and positive spirit playing macho men in big-budget productions such as *Pelican Brief, Crimson Tide,* and *Courage Under Fire.* Denzel credits his marriage of over 10 years and his involvement in raising his four children for much of the reason why he stays grounded.

Denzel Washington.

(Photo by Deidre Davidson)

Here are some things you can learn about sexiness from Denzel Washington:

➤ Look well-groomed. Denzel always looks clean, neat, and fit.

➤ Follow your faith. He never lets fame or money cloud his belief, or get in the way of his being virtuous.

➤ Don't allow work to come before family. A star is not sexy if he enjoys the love he gets from fans over the love that he receives from his family.

➤ Understand history. In choosing historically important roles to play, Denzel has shown an intelligent side to being sexy.

Deep Quote

"Life is family. You know, rushing to get home because my son's got a football game, and I'm going to be there. We drive to the game and watch him and discuss it afterward. That's life. Acting is not life to me. It's making a living."

—Denzel Washington

Cary Grant

Born Archibald Leach in England in 1904, Cary Grant was raised in a poor family, yet he successfully overcame his humble beginnings to become one of our favorite classic movie stars. His debonair and witty on-screen persona, along with his classic good looks, made him one of the sexiest actors of all time. He starred in films for over 30 years, appearing in such classics as *North by Northwest, The Philadelphia Story, To Catch a Thief, Houseboat, An Affair to Remember,* and *Arsenic and Old Lace.*

Cary Grant became the man who women wanted to marry and who men wanted to be like. For many, he represented all the ideals of masculinity rolled into one—at times appearing virile and commanding, and at other times appearing charming with a delightful *joie de vivre*. He combined chiseled dark good looks with brilliant comic timing and a smile that melted hearts from afar. In 1970, he received a special Oscar for lifetime achievement from the Motion Picture Academy of Arts and Sciences. Cary Grant died in 1986.

Cary Grant.

(Photo by Archive Photos)

Cary Grant is a sexy role model, one whose image still inspires copycats and intense admiration. You, too, can emulate the image of Cary Grant by following these tips:

Deep Quote

"I pretended to be somebody I wanted to be until finally I became that person. Or he became me."

—Cary Grant

➤ Be inspired by classic styles. Try not to jump onto every silly trend; the classic looks will always prevail.

➤ Don't take yourself too seriously. Being serious and thoughtful is wonderful, but don't be afraid to show off your playful side as well.

➤ Try to be charming and understanding. Treating people with respect and compassion is something that will make you feel better and will make the people around you respect you in turn.

➤ Age gracefully. Getting older doesn't have to mean losing your appeal. Many think Cary Grant became more and more attractive as he got older.

Naturally Sexy

Appearing to not even try, these sexy celebrities have made such an impression on us. They strut, without trying. Make bedroom eyes, when they are just minding their own business. And their smiles light up a million hearts. Naturally sexy men show us that sexiness is a quality that you exude if you have it—and maybe if you don't, you can learn a bit from their examples.

Jim Morrison

No one can compare to Jim Morrison. As lead singer of the 1960s rock group The Doors, he was an innovator, inspiration, and to many, a genius. His inspired lyrics and passionate yet shocking performances made him a legend in rock, with such songs as "Light My Fire," and "L.A. Woman."

He certainly didn't live the life of the boy next door, and instead, at his peak, he shocked many with his blatant glorification of drugs, alcohol, and simple raw sexuality. But you couldn't deny the astounding and lasting appeal of Jim Morrison who made other rock stars appear tame and boring by comparison. Everywhere he went, Jim Morrison was immersed in adoration and controversy, and his performances attracted much attention from local law enforcement agencies. In March 1969, he was even arrested and charged with "lewd and lascivious behavior" after exposing himself to an audience during a concert.

Because of the stress of repeated police harassment, Morrison and his wife moved to Paris, where he wrote poetry. Unfortunately, Paris did not prove to be a more sedate life for him. Twenty-seven-year-old Morrison was found dead in his bathtub on July 3, 1971, the victim of an apparent heart attack related to his use of drugs and alcohol. He was buried at the famous Pere Lachaise Cemetery in Paris, among notables such as Balzac, Molière, Oscar Wilde, and Chopin. Today, thousands of visitors (including immense busloads of tour groups) from all around the world crowd around his headstone, which is protected against vandalism by security guards.

Deep Quote

"I am interested in anything about revolt, disorder, chaos—especially activity that seems to have no meaning. It seems to me to be the road toward freedom .... Rather than starting inside, I start outside and reach the mental through the physical."

—Jim Morrison

Flirt Alert

Drug and alcohol addiction has ended the lives of many of the world's sexiest men and women. If you have a problem with drugs or alcohol, please get help immediately from a group like Alcoholics Anonymous (AA). Your local phone book is a good place to start.

Jim Morrison.

(Photo by Andrew Maclear)

You can have some fun and take lessons on being sexy from Jim Morrison without exposing yourself and getting arrested:

➤ Get into leather. Morrison's trademark tight leather pants always gave him a sexy look.

➤ Glance with an intense look and no smile. Jim Morrison was a pro at flashing a sexy look at the camera. For variety, try it once in a while.

➤ Be unconventional. Let your inhibitions go and become a little wild.

➤ Listen to some old Doors albums. Absorb Jim Morrison's intensity and see where it takes you.

➤ Try writing or reading some inspired poetry. Much of Jim Morrison's appeal stemmed from the intense lyrics he crafted.

Tiger Woods

Tiger Woods was not out of the crib before he took an interest in golf, at age six months, by imitating his father's golf swing. By the time he was two, he appeared on the *Mike Douglas Show,* making putts with Bob Hope. Tiger Woods went on to break many records as an amateur golfer as he grew up. Since becoming a professional golfer in 1996, when he was only 21 years old, he has accomplished tasks once thought to be impossible—revolutionizing golfing by breaking record upon record, as well as smashing the race barrier, and with his popularity, even turning millions of nongolfers on to the sport.

Tiger leads with the most the victories in a career among active players on the PGA Tour. He has won at least 30 major tournaments, including the 1997 Masters Tournament, 1999 and 2000 PGA Championships, 2000 U.S. Open Championship, and 2000 British Open Championship. He was the youngest person ever to win the Masters, at age 21. Yet his accomplishments go far beyond the mere millions he has made by winning championships and obtaining lucrative endorsement deals.

As a charming man with a fascinating diverse heritage (half African-American and half Thai), he defied our conceptions of what a golf pro is "supposed" to look like, and became one of the most successful sports figures of our time. At 6'2" and 180 pounds, Tiger's fit physique and dashing good looks have helped his sexy image. Yet it's not just his winning smile that makes him so handsome—his close relationship with his family has made Tiger Woods an inspiration to many.

Deep Quote

"It doesn't matter whether they're white, black, brown, or green. All that matters is I touch kids the way I can through these clinics and they benefit from them. I have this talent. I might as well use it to benefit somebody."

—Tiger Woods

Tiger Woods.

(Photo by Gary Hershorn)

Tiger Woods has shown that being sexy doesn't have to mean starring in a Hollywood feature. There are several simple lessons we can learn from his appeal:

➤ Don't hide the affection you have for those close to you. Tiger's closeness to his family is well publicized and one of the things we all love about him.

➤ Set a goal, and go for it. Tiger had a single vision. He plays his heart out because he's always aiming for a new record or a personal goal.

➤ Inspire others. Mentoring children or being a role model is an enormous responsibility, and helps demonstrate the importance of helping others develop and grow.

➤ Find a clothing color that works and make it your own. Tiger and that red shirt go hand in hand. See if there's a color or style that works as well for you, and adopt it as your trademark.

➤ Smile a lot. Looking happy and enthusiastic is always sexy, and it doesn't take much effort on your part!

Harrison Ford

Sometimes, being sexy means not trying too hard. Harrison Ford is arguably the most successful actor in history when measured by the billions of dollars brought in by films he has starred in. Born in 1942, Ford grew up in suburban Des Plaines, Illinois. In 1972, he was offered a role in George Lucas's *American Graffiti,* and the combination of Lucas and Ford became movie history. Most prominently, he starred in the *Star Wars* trilogy and was the lead the *Indiana Jones* films.

Harrison Ford is at his best when he portrays the average man faced with extraordinary circumstances. In an era when explicit sex and violence are the norm, Harrison has starred in box office hits that were for the most part ones we could share with our children. He could charm audiences and Princess Leia as the "scoundrel" Han Solo, and just a few years later, portray the United States President as an action hero in *Air Force One.*

Harrison Ford. Harrison mastered the art of appealing to women as the hard-working, honest man next door and captivating men as the conflicted action hero they all want to become.

(Photo by Hulton-Archive)

Try injecting a little bit of Harrison Ford's sexiness into your personality by doing the following:

➤ Be comfortable with who you are. To be naturally sexy, you need to be confident in your own skin.

➤ Find an accessory that defines who you are and stick with it. Indiana Jones would never have gotten out of that snake pit without his trusty hat.

➤ Use your sense of humor, even in trying circumstances. A little bit of subtle humor is often essential to making a good impression or getting through a tense or awkward moment.

➤ Casual is great; try not to overdress. Throw on the tux if you're going to the opera, but otherwise, always remember that by dressing casually, you can put yourself and others at ease.

➤ Be a rock in stressful situations. People are attracted to those who are able to stay calm under pressure.

For some people, being sexy does come naturally, yet it also helps to take some cues from those who are seen as sexy by our society. Now that you have a better idea of why some of these celebrity men are sexy, you can think about how you can find that sexiness within yourself. Take a look at these men, not as people to copy, but rather, as styles that may already exist in yourself, which you can highlight when you want to be sexy.

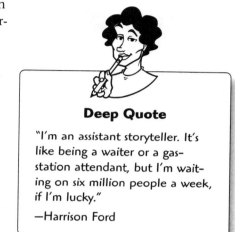

Deep Quote

"I'm an assistant storyteller. It's like being a waiter or a gas-station attendant, but I'm waiting on six million people a week, if I'm lucky."

—Harrison Ford

The Least You Need to Know

➤ We can all learn a few things about sexiness by looking at male celebrities.

➤ Watching how stars dress can give some cues about what can be sexy, whether it is having a flashy style, like Elvis, or "branding" yourself with a notable item of clothing, like Indiana Jones's hat.

➤ It's sexy when a man is close to his family, such as JFK Jr. and Tiger Woods.

➤ Good looks are always sexy, like Brad Pitt's and Denzel Washington's.

➤ Sometimes sexiness can be a little wild, as in the style of Jim Morrison or James Dean.

➤ When a man is sexy, he lives on as a legend, like Cary Grant.

Sexy Self-Evaluation

If you were asked the question, "How sexy are you?" how do you think you'd answer? Would you sit up a little straighter in your chair and, with the confidence of 100 movie stars, say, "I'm drop-dead sexy!"? Or would you look down at your feet, blush brighter than a summer tomato, and say, "Oh, I'm not that sexy. Maybe I'm a little bit cute, but I'm not really the sexy type."

Pish-posh. Anyone can be sexy—in fact, anyone can be *very* sexy! By using your physical appearance, attitude, intelligence, flirtatiousness, body language, or a combination of any or all of those things, you can be sexy. For many of people, though, it may be difficult to see how they can be sexy.

What follows is a quiz I've designed to help you pinpoint how sexy you are and, depending on your answers, direct you to specific chapter references that can help you enhance your particular kind of sexiness. Just circle the answer that best describes you.

Quiz: How Sexy Are You?

1. Which one of these items would you most prefer to have next to your skin?

   a. Fine cashmere.

   b. Leather.

   c. Cotton.

   d. Shetland wool.

2. What do you prefer to sleep in?

   a. Silk anything.

   b. Nothing.

   c. A T-shirt.

   d. Flannel PJs.

3. Which food item do you find most enticing and enjoyable to eat?

   a. Strawberries with champagne.

   b. Hot fudge.

   c. Cold grapes.

   d. A grilled cheese sandwich.

4. Which activity do you feel most attracted to?

   a. A nice, hot, scented bubble bath by candlelight.

   b. Skinny dipping at midnight.

   c. Sunday on the couch talking with a good friend.

   d. Catching up on all the things you didn't get to do around the house during the week.

5. Which recording artist best fits your musical taste?

   a. Nina Simone.

   b. Prince.

   c. Dave Matthews.

   d. John Tesh.

6. When you are attracted to someone, you prefer …

   a. A flirty game of cat and mouse—there's nothing like a little sexual tension.

   b. The direct approach—you know what you want and you know how to get it.

   c. Subtle clues like touching the other person's arm or leg during conversation.

   d. To wait for the person to approach you.

7. When you read a book, you like to …

   a. Languish in the whole experience of being transported to another, fictitious world. Sometimes you find you even dream about the characters.

   b. Read the last page before you start—you like knowing what's going to happen and then piece it all together as you go along.

   c. Find someone else who's read what you just read and talk about the different nuances of the book.

   d. Read nonfiction, if you read at all. Fiction is really impractical.

8. What kind of movies do you prefer?

   a. Romantic epic where the ending isn't obvious or easy to predict.

   b. Thrillers with a sexy twist.

   c. Romantic comedies.

   d. Movies usually are not very good, so they seem like a waste of time.

9. What would be the best way to receive a gift from a lover?

   a. A treasure hunt full of clues you have to figure out in order to get to the goods!

   b. You don't care, as long as you can rip open the package. Opening it is half the fun.

   c. Over a nice dinner for two alone at home.

   d. Money in an envelope. It's just easier to pick things out yourself.

10. What was your favorite game as a kid?

    a. Dress up. You loved pretending you were someone else and then looking the part.

    b. Marco Polo—it's hide and seek with a twist!

    c. Go Fish.

    d. Monopoly.

11. If you had to give a speech in front of a group, you would ...

    a. Relish it—you love being the center of attention.

    b. Be a little nervous initially, but then really enjoy the rush once you're up there.

    c. Resign yourself to the inevitable and start preparing—maybe even find some props to distract the audience from looking at you the whole time!

    d. Desperately search for someone else to do it for you.

12a. For the women only: Would you ask a man out for a date?

    a. Absolutely—if he says no, he's losing out.

    b. Sure, but you'd probably have to think about it for a few days to work up the nerve.

    c. Maybe. If you felt he was more shy than you were, you might seize the moment.

    d. No way. The rejection would be horrifying.

263

12b. For the men only: You are in a bar with some friends and the best looking woman you've ever seen (in real life, anyway) walks in with a friend or two. You …

    a. Approach her without reservations and strike up a conversation. Hey, you want to get to her first—she's gorgeous!

    b. Wait a little while to get the courage, and then approach her, but bring a friend along so you don't seem like you're coming on too strong.

    c. Eventually buy her a drink and have the bartender give it to her. If she likes you, she'll probably come over and say something.

    d. Sigh and think, "A woman like that doesn't even know I'm alive."

13. You are going to a party. You have a shirt in each of the following colors. Which color do you wear?

    a. Red.

    b. Blue.

    c. White.

    d. Beige.

14. If you could be an animal, which animal would you be?

    a. Horse.

    b. Dog.

    c. Cat.

    d. Turtle.

15. It's Saturday night and you really want to try that new Latin dance club you've been hearing so much about. You …

    a. Try calling a few friends to see if anyone is up for it. Everyone is busy, but you go anyway. It's easy to meet people at a dance club.

    b. Call friends until you find someone who can go with you.

    c. Can't find anyone to go, so you stay in. You can go another time.

    d. Don't ask anyone. Everyone's probably already got plans.

16. When you look in the mirror, what is your general reaction?

    a. You think you look great—you know you'll never be in *Vogue* or *GQ*, but that's all fantasy, anyway. You think you're very attractive.

    b. You think you look pretty good. Sure, you have your moments of doubt, but you try not to let them get the best of you. You know what your assets are.

    c. You feel dissatisfied at times. There are certain areas of your body that plague you and make you feel self-conscious.

    d. You feel horrible and unattractive. If you had the money to have plastic surgery, you'd seriously consider it.

17. Complete the sentence: If the lights are on when my lover and I begin foreplay before sex, I …

    a. Wouldn't care at all. Part of the experience for me is seeing my lover and my lover seeing me. It's a real turn on.

    b. Would leave them on if it's inconvenient to turn them off. I feel a little self-conscious with them on, but I usually get over it pretty fast!

    c. Would find a way to turn them off if I could. I worry about what he/she will think of me without clothes on.

    d. Wouldn't let things get going until the lights are off and we're under the covers. If not, I'd feel way too exposed.

18. What sentence best describes how you feel about your body?

    a. I look fabulous. I wouldn't change a thing.

    b. I think, for the most part, I look good. There always seems to be one area or another that I'm trying to work on, but I'm healthy, and that's what really counts.

    c. I feel like I've spent my entire adult life trying to drop 20 pounds. If I could, I really think I would look great.

    d. Is there such a thing as a full-body transplant?

19. How many areas of your body do you want to change?

    a. 0.

    b. 1–2.

    c. 3–4.

    d. 5 or more.

20a. For the women: When you go to the beach, what do you wear?

    a. As little as legally possible. Thong is your middle name from June to August.

    b. You've been known to put on a bikini sometimes.

    c. A one-piece.

    d. A baggy T-shirt and shorts.

20b. For the men: When you play your favorite sport, how do you feel about taking off your shirt?

    a. Take it off? It's off before you hit the court/field!

    b. You don't think much about it. If it's hot, it's hot, and usually you don't mind peeling off a layer or two as the game heats up.

    c. You wear a tank top to avoid the situation. That way, you can keep cool without feeling too self-conscious about your body.

    d. You don't play sports because you feel awkward and out of shape.

21. If your lover wants to try something new during sex, you …

    a. Welcome it. Variety is the spice of life.

    b. Usually welcome it—there are some things that aren't your style, but you're pretty open to trying most new things.

    c. Can't switch gears that fast. You need advance notice—you don't like being surprised in the bedroom and want time to consider change.

    d. Refuse. You don't feel comfortable with anything except the standard, missionary position in the dark.

22. You would be most likely to initiate something new during sex …

    a. Always!

    b. Sometimes.

    c. Rarely.

    d. Never!

23. When are you most likely to have sex?

    a. Any time!

    b. Most times—if the mood is right, you're there.

    c. You prefer nighttime and the dark. You just feel more comfortable that way. If the mood is right, though, you can be talked into some afternoon delight.

    d. In the dark, at night, before bed. Period.

24. Have you ever, or would you consider, using sex toys, dirty talk, or other sexual variations during foreplay and intercourse?

    a. Are you kidding? You invented them!

    b. Sure, you've experimented with some sex variations, although not much. You're open to them, however.

    c. Maybe. You've definitely never used a "gadget," but you've dabbled in dirty talk. You feel a little shy about it.

    d. Absolutely, positively no way.

25. Which words best describes you in bed:

    a. Insatiable, erotic, experimental.

    b. Open, steamy, sensual.

    c. Inhibited, shy, distracted.

    d. Practical, systematic, straight-laced.

Rate Your Answers

You'll notice that the quiz questions were grouped into certain aspects of sexiness—sensuality, mystery and spontaneity, confidence, body image, and sexual openness.

Of course, it's impossible to discover the full spectrum of someone's personality simply by giving a quiz and looking at the answers. Human beings are complex and can't be reduced to simple a, b, c, or d responses. However, you should be able to get a general idea of where you stand on each of the categories and possibly show you where your sexy quotient could use a little boost. Here's the key to your answers.

Questions 1–5: Sensuality

If you answered mostly a's, you are very in tune with the sensual world. You respond to touch, smell, taste, and sound and know that using your senses is an important part of interacting with a love interest.

If you answered mostly b's, you, too, are in touch with the sensual world, but you tend to favor the more overtly sexual. You send a very clear message to those in whom you are interested. Depending on the kind of person you are trying to attract, though, you may want to read up on the softer side of sensual pleasures—for more on this, check out Chapter 11, "Dressing Sexy"; Chapter 13, "Sexiness Begins at Home: Creating a Sexy Environment"; Chapter 14, "Sexy Dates"; Chapter 15, "Sexy Gifts for the One You Love"; and Chapter 19, "Keeping the Sexy Spark in Your Love Life."

If you answered mostly c's, you enjoy sensual pleasures, but you tend to like clean scents, plain, light colors, and anything cotton. You have a wonderful, natural, sensual nature. If this is you, you may want to try experimenting—add a new scent, try some new music, maybe even a splash of color. You can also benefit from taking a look at the tips in Chapters 11, 13, 14, and 15.

If you answered mostly d's, the first thing you should do is turn to Chapter 3, "Attitudes That Define Sexiness," and then to Chapter 8, "Developing a Sexy Attitude." Some of your hesitation at diving into sensual pleasures could benefit from boosting your confidence. Next, dive into the sensual world of Chapters 11 through 16.

Questions 6–10: Mystery and Spontaneity

If you answered mostly a's, you love the element of gentle surprise and find that a little mystery and spontaneity goes a long way to creating a sexy aura.

If you answered mostly b's, you like to take control of situations. You are spontaneous, yet direct. This is, of course, incredibly sexy. However, you might want to try adding a little mystery into the mix. This is not to say you should change your personality. I suggest this only because you might find that mystery heats things up to a roiling boil that can only add to your sexy quotient. Read Chapter 8 to find out how to bring out more mystery. Then take a look at Chapter 10, "Body Talk: Using Sexy Body Language"; Chapter 12, "Sexy Flirting Techniques"; Chapter 15 about sexy gifts; Chapter 16, "If You Want Me, Just Whistle: Using Sexiness to Initiate Sex"; and Chapter 19 about keeping sexiness alive in a long-term relationship.

If you answered mostly c's, you enjoy a little mystery in your love life, but spontaneity is probably not your forte. Read Chapter 8 about how to develop your sexy attitudes, Chapter 12 about flirting, Chapter 15 about sexy gifts, and Chapter 16 about initiating sex.

If you answered mostly d's, you have a wonderful, practical nature and your diversified portfolio is probably the envy of your friends. Mystery and spontaneity, however, are all but lost on you. Listen, practical is great and you certainly shouldn't change this about yourself. Practical and sexy, however, are the oil and water of romance. It's my guess that you bought this book looking to add some spice into your life. Check out Chapter 1, "Defining What Is 'Sexy'"; Chapter 3 on defining sexy attitudes; Chapter 4, "The Sexy Advantage"; Chapter 5, "Different Types of Sexiness"; and Chapter 8 for the basics of sexy attitudes. If you want to graduate into some serious sexy techniques, go on to Chapters 10, 12, 14, and 15.

Questions 11–15: Confidence

If you've answered mostly a's here, we've got to find a way to bottle what you've got going on. You've got confidence to spare!

If you answered mostly b's, you have a healthy confidence that suffers from the occasional nervous jitters. There's no need for you to review the basics, but you might want to read Chapters 8, 10, and 4 to remind you of why confidence is the ultimate love potion.

If you answered mostly c's, your confidence could use some work. Read Chapters 3, 4, 8, and 10.

If you answered mostly d's, you are more than likely painfully shy and are hoping for some help here. Don't worry, you've come to the right place. Read Chapters 3, 4, 8, 10, 11, and 12.

Questions 16–20: Body Image

The a's have it—you are confident about your body and feel great in your own skin.

Did you choose mostly b's? You're doing great. You have a healthy body image and generally feel pretty good about the way you look. Still, you might want to take a look at Chapter 6, "Getting Over Inhibitions About Your Body," for a body-image tune-up every now and again.

If you answered mostly c's, you are probably in the majority. Unfortunately, many, many people don't feel as confident about their physical attributes as they should. You need some work, but you *can* learn to become confident about your body. Chapter 6 is for you!

If you answered mostly d's, you need a serious body-image makeover. Start with Chapter 2, "Your Sexy Body," and then move on to Chapter 6 (and do the exercises there—they're important for you!).

Questions 21–25: Sex

If you answered a's most of the time, nothing shocks you. I wouldn't be surprised if you had a trapeze and a mirrored ceiling above your bed. You live for sex. Experimenting is a way of life. All I will say to you is, don't overlook the tenderness and sensuality of a loving sex when you look deeply into each other's eyes. Also, you may feel as if you're open to everything, but you might tend to pooh-pooh the good, old, stand-by missionary position. It's a classic for good reason!

If you found b's were the dominant letter of choice, you have a healthy, open attitude about sex. You don't shy away from experimenting if you're comfortable, and you even initiate new ideas if there's something you really want to try. Check out Chapter 17, "How to Have Sexier Sex," for some new things to try; and Chapter 18, "Super Sexy Sex," if you're looking for something more exotic.

Were there many c's in your results? If so, you tend to be shy and probably worry too much about "doing it right," and therefore are more likely to stick with missionary, in-the-dark, sex rather than trying something new (although you can be talked into it by someone who you really trust). Read Chapter 7, "Getting Over Inhibitions About Sex"; Chapter 16 about initiating sex; and Chapter 19 about keeping the sexiness alive in your love life. When you start to feel a little more comfortable with the notion of experimenting, check out Chapters 17 and 18.

If you've got mostly d's on your list, you're missing out. There's nothing wrong with knowing what you want and what you like, but you may be needlessly closing yourself off to new experiences. Give some thought to your behavior and read over Chapter 7. This is really the place to start for you. Good luck! I know you can be sexy!

Glossary

adult store   A euphemism for a store that sells sexually explicit books, magazines, videos, or sex toys.

afterplay   Affection that occurs after intercourse or orgasm, usually consisting of caressing and cuddling, talking, or getting ready to make love again.

anal sex   Sexual contact with the anus. Usually this term specifically refers to a penis penetrating an anus in anal intercourse; yet some people may consider any sexual contact with the anus, such as digital or oral contact, to be a part of anal sex.

anorexia   A potentially life-threatening eating disorder in which people (mostly girls) have a distorted view of their bodies so they starve themselves to get thinner.

aphrodisiac   A substance that is alleged to stimulate or increase sexual desire, although in actuality it may not have a physical affect on the person.

arousal   Stimulation of sexual interest.

ben wa balls   Small solid metal balls that are inserted into the vagina to supposedly increase sexual arousal by rubbing together.

birth control   Prevention of pregnancy by using a device such as the birth control pill, IUD, diaphragm, Norplant, or condoms.

body image   A person's self-image, or mental picture, of his or her own body, and the attitudes and feelings he or she has toward his or her appearance. Body image determines how attractive a person thinks he or she is.

body language   Nonverbal communication using facial expressions, gestures, and posture.

bondage   Tying up a lover for the sexual pleasure of taking control over him or her. Bondage should always be completely consensual.

bulimia   Eating disorder that affects primarily young women, who vomit after eating to try to lose weight.

charisma   A special magnetic charm or appeal.

choreography   The composition and arrangement of movement, especially dance.

clitoris   A small organ located on the vulva that contains a bundle of nerve endings and has the sole function of giving sexual pleasure and orgasm to the woman.

compatibility   The condition of being well-matched with a partner for a sexual or nonsexual relationship.

conceited   Overly confident and self-assured to the point of flaunting it obnoxiously.

crush   An intense feeling of affection for someone you hardly know. Characterized by lustful feelings, worries that feelings will not be reciprocated, and sometimes, feelings of jealousy. Also know as infatuation.

cunnilingus   Oral stimulation of a woman's vulva, clitoris, and/or vagina. (From Latin *cunnus,* meaning "vulva," and *lingere,* meaning to "lick.") Some people refer to it in slang as "going down on a woman" or "eating her out."

date rape   A sexual assault, or forced sex, perpetrated by someone the victim was on a date with at the time.

deep throat   A form of oral sex in which the penis is voluntarily penetrated deeply into the recipient's throat.

depression   A feeling of deep sadness usually marked by inactivity and a sense of dejection.

desire   Refers to a strong interest in sex.

dildos   Cylinders of plastic, rubber, or latex that are used for insertion during sex (either vaginally or anally). They may be shaped like a penis, or just be smooth and oblong, or even look like an animal.

ectomorph   A person whose body shape has very little fat, small bones, and little muscle (your basic supermodel).

ego   One of three divisions of the psyche in psychoanalytic theory that mediates between you and your reality, by helping you understand the world around you, and adapt you to fit into it.

ejaculation   The expulsion of semen from the penis. Semen most often spurts out in conjunction with orgasmic contractions.

ejaculatory inevitability   The point at which a man has reached ejaculation and can no longer control the fact that he is about to ejaculate. Also known as "the point of no return."

endomorph A person whose body shape has a medium bone frame and a medium amount of fat. Thought of as "average" body type.

engaging Paying undivided attention to someone.

erection Enlargement of the penis due to blood flowing to the area which causes it to become engorged.

erogenous zones Areas of the body that respond to sexual stimulation.

erotic Derived from "Eros," who is the Greek god of sexual love. All things erotic are said to encompass the life-preserving instinct to reproduce.

erotica Literary or artistic work having sexual qualities or a sexual theme, such as photographs, drawings, and films that arouse sexual interest or may be used to enhance a sexual experience.

exhibitionists People who get a sexual thrill out of having others watch them being sexual or nude.

facial symmetry Defines a person's face when their features appear even, equal, balanced, and virtually identical on both sides of their face, as if a line were dividing the face down the center.

fantasy Creation of the imagination, which may be expressed or merely conceived.

fellatio Oral sexual stimulation of the penis. Derived from the Latin word *fellare,* meaning "to suck." It is most commonly called a "blow job," even though blowing is not part of oral sex. In slang, it is also called "going down on a man" or "sucking him off."

feminine Displaying characteristics that are considered typical of a female.

feng shui The ancient Chinese art of arranging one's surrounds so they are in harmony with one's spirit.

flirting Playfully gaining the attention and admiration of others, often someone whom a person is attracted to.

foreplay Sexual stimulation that occurs prior to intercourse. This includes kissing, caressing, and sometimes oral sex.

French kiss A kiss during which both partners' mouths are open and their tongues are in contact.

frenulum An indentation or tiny fold of skin located in the ridge under the glans of the penis, which has many nerve endings.

full-figured Usually refers to a body size that is larger than a size 14. See also **Rubenesque.**

fun-house mirror effect Seeing your body not as it is, but with a warped, distorted, negative view that results in insecurity and low self-esteem.

gag reflex   The biological reflex that causes you to gag when the back of your throat is stimulated.

glans   The head of a penis.

group sex   Sexual interaction involving three or more people at the same time.

G spot   An area located on the front of the inner upper wall of the vagina that may be highly erogenous in some women. First described by Ernst Gräfenburg, a German obstetrician and gynecologist.

hand job   Giving manual stimulation to a man. It can also be called "masturbating him" or "jerking him off."

HIV   Human Immunodeficiency Virus, the virus that causes AIDS.

hormones   Chemical substances that are secreted into the bloodstream by glands in the body. Many hormones have a bearing on sex.

impotence   A man's inability to achieve or maintain an erection of sufficient firmness for penetration during intercourse. It is also called erectile dysfunction.

inhibition   Something that holds you back, controls, discourages, or impedes you from being free or spontaneous.

innuendo   An allusion or hint at something other than the most obvious meaning.

intimate space   The space of six inches to two feet that two people automatically keep between their bodies during an intimate conversation.

Kegel exercises   Repeated contractions and release of the pubococcygeal muscles to strengthen them and increase sexual sensitivity. Developed by Dr. Alfred Kegel.

kinesics   The scientific study of body language.

love   A strong kinship, bond, devotion, admiration, or attraction.

lust   An intense desire for sexual contact.

masculine   Displaying characteristics that are considered typical of a male.

massage   A soothing technique of rubbing the body (often the back), which incorporates gliding and kneading strokes that improve circulation and relax muscles.

ménage à trois   Sexual contact among three people at the same time. Also known as a threesome. Translated from French as "household of three."

menopause   The cessation of menstruation in women and the natural decline in female sex hormones, which usually occurs for most women during a two-year period starting as early as age 35 or as late as age 60.

mesomorph   A person whose body shape has a large frame and big strong muscles, such as a professional wrestler.

mile-high club   An expression used to mean someone who has had sex while in flight on an airplane. It's just an expression, not a real club.

missionary position   The sexual position in which the man lies on top of the woman, and both are facing each other during intercourse.

mitzvah   The Hebrew word for a meritous or charitable act.

monogamy   A sexually exclusive relationship, usually as part of a committed relationship.

mutual masturbation   Sexual contact in which you manually stimulate your partner's genitals at the same time as he or she stimulates yours.

mystique   An air or attitude of mystery and reverence surrounding something or someone.

natural   In accordance with or determined by nature; being true to one's original self.

oral sex   Sexual stimulation of genitals using the mouth.

orgasm   Sexual climax, marked by blood flow to the genitals, psychological tension, and erotic pleasure. In slang, this is referred to as "coming."

personal space   The area that immediately surrounds a person, two to four feet.

pheromones   Chemical sex attractants that are detected by smell, but usually have such a mild scent, that they are not consciously noticeable.

plié   The French word meaning to bend. In ballet, it is an exercise that involves standing with the feet slightly more than shoulder-length apart and bending the knees.

pornography   Written, spoken, or visual material that stimulates sexual feelings in the observer, listener, or reader. The term "pornography" comes from the Greek word *porneia,* which means "the writings of and about prostitutes." Also known as porn or porno.

power   Control over your own life; or control, authority, or influence over others. Ability to produce an effect.

premature ejaculation   Ejaculation before the man wants it to occur. It could mean that he ejaculates only seconds after his penis goes into the vagina, or he could even ejaculate just prior to penetration, when he is really excited.

proxemics   The scientific study of how the amount of space around people affects them by making them relaxed or anxious, and why people allow others into their personal space.

pubococcygeal (PC) muscles   Pelvic muscles that extend from the pubic bone in the front, around both sides of the sex organs, and back to the tailbone. Control over the PC muscles can enhance sexual response in women and men.

quadriceps Large extensor muscles in the front of the thigh that are divided into four parts.

quickie A brief sexual encounter that is often accompanied by spontaneity and some degree of risk.

risque Verging on impropriety or indecency; off-color.

role-playing Acting out different roles, often for variety in sexual play.

romantic Having an inclination toward romance, that is, an emotional appeal of what is heroic, adventurous, mysterious, or idealized. An expression that is usually marked by love or affection.

Rubenesque Suggestive of the female bodies in the painter Rubens' works; plump or rounded usually in a pleasing or attractive way. See also **full-figured.**

sadism and masochism (S/M) The term applied to a number of activities typically involving exchange of power or pain between consenting partners, often during role-playing, or referring to the tools and methods for restraining and exerting physical tension and/or erotic pain. The sadist is the partner who dominates the masochist.

safe word A word or words used as a signal between partners to halt a sexual activity during an S/M scene.

seduction The act of enticing someone into feelings of sexual desire.

self-confidence Confidence in oneself and in one's powers and abilities. The power to be independent and proud of your abilities.

self-depricating Critical, belittling, or judgmental of one's self; often taking the form of making negative jokes about one's self, as in self-depricating humor.

self-empowerment Having the self-actualization or influence over yourself that you feel as if you're in control of your life.

self-esteem Confidence and satisfaction in oneself; self-respect.

sensory Relating to sensation that conveys nerve impulses from the sense organs to the nerve centers.

sensuality Relating to or providing pleasure through gratification of the senses.

sex education Formal or informal lessons that teach you about sex. Informal sex education includes what you learn about sex from friends, parents, siblings, television, movies, magazines, newspapers, music, and the culture all around us. Formal sex education may include classes provided in a school or in a religious setting. Sex education, formal and informal, may include information about biology, psychology, social issues, cultural issues, moral issues, and ethical issues.

sexiness A component of sexual desire, which is transmitted through behavior, look, gesture, or innuendo.

sexual fantasy An image or sexual scenario that you create with your imagination and may or may not act out.

sexual harassment Uninvited and unwelcome verbal or physical conduct.

sexuality The quality or state of being sexual; the expression of sexual receptivity or interest. All aspects of your personality and behaviors that are affected by your being male or female.

sexy Suggestive, attractive, interesting, appealing, stimulating, or erotic. Defined by many different styles, such as flirtation, romance, eroticism, and naturalness.

sixty-nine Mutual oral sex, so named because the couple participating resembles the numbers 6 and 9 when they are in this sexual position.

sleazy Erotic sexiness that goes so far that it is said to be marked by low character or low quality, and often connotes something that is illegal or unethical.

social space The space of four to 10 feet that people automatically leave between their bodies during conversation when they are in a social setting.

tantric sex A spiritual type of sex that is rooted in the Eastern philosophies of Taoism and Buddhism. It is said to help couples reach a deeper, more loving sexual connection.

tease To tantalize, especially by arousing sexual desire or curiosity without intending to satisfy it.

threesome A sexual interaction involving three people.

vibrator A battery-operated or electric vibrating device that is usually intended for sexual stimulation, but can also be used to massage the shoulders, neck, back, buttocks, belly, hands, and feet.

vomeronasal organ (VNO) A small nasal cavity that detects the scent of pheromones.

voyeur A person who gets erotic pleasure from watching others engage in sexual acts or nudity.

vulva The collective term that refers to all of the external female sexual structures; includes the clitoris and the vagina, and all other part of the genitals.

Resources

Listed here are the phone numbers and Web sites for organizations that can give you more information and referrals to help you in your quest for sexiness.

Additional Information

About Sari Locker

You can read more about Sari Locker, her books, lectures, monthly live Web chats, and television projects at www.sarilocker.com.

Sexuality Information and Education

Sexuality Information and Education Council of the United States
212-819-9770
www.siecus.org

Sexual Health, Birth Control, and Pregnancy Options

Planned Parenthood
1-800-230-PLAN
www.plannedparenthood.org

Aging

American Association of Retired Persons (AARP)
1-800-424-3410
www.aarp.com

Referrals

Sex Therapists

American Association of Sex Educators, Counselors, and Therapists
319-895-8407
www.aasect.org

Marriage and Relationship Therapists

American Association of Marriage and Family Therapists
202-452-0109
www.aamft.org

Support, Counseling, and Referrals for Abuse and Rape

Child Help USA
1-800-4-A-CHILD
www.childhelpusa.org

National Domestic Violence Hotline
1-800-799-SAFE
www.ndvh.org

Rape, Abuse, Incest National Network
1-800-656-HOPE
www.rainn.org

Sexually Transmitted Disease Information, Counseling, and Referrals

National AIDS Hotline
1-800-342-AIDS
www.ashastd.org

National Herpes Hotline
919-361-8488
www.ashastd.org

National STD Hotline
1-800-227-8922
www.ashastd.org

Drug and Alcohol Abuse

Drug and Alcohol Abuse Referral Hotline
1-800-821-4357
www.macad.org

Eating Disorders and Body Image Problems

American Anorexia and Bulimia Association
212-575-6200
www.aabainc.org

Teen Counseling

Teen Counseling Help Line
1-800-621-4000
www.nrscrisisline.org

S/M Information

The Eulenspiegel Society
212-388-7022
www.tes.org

Tantric Sex Information

Tantra.com
707-823-3063
www.tantra.com

Lingerie Stores

Fredericks of Hollywood
1-800-323-9525
www.fredericks.com

Victoria's Secret
1-800-888-8200
www.victoriassecret.com

Sex Toys, Videos, and Condoms

Adam and Eve
1-800-765-ADAM
www.adameve.com

Condomania
1-800-9-CONDOM
www.condomania.com

Durex Condoms
www.durex.com

Good Vibrations
1-800-289-8423
www.goodvibes.com

Index

C

X-Z

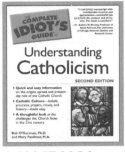

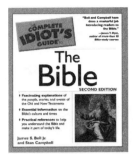

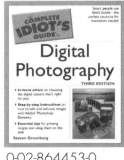
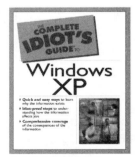